Family and Succession Law in Poland

Family and Succession Law in Poland

Fourth Edition

Stanislawa Kalus
Magdalena Habdas

This book was originally published as a monograph in the International Encyclopaedia of Laws/Family and Succession Law.

Founding Editor: Roger Blanpain
General Editor: Frank Hendrickx
Volume Editor: Walter Pintens

Wolters Kluwer

Published by:
Kluwer Law International B.V.
PO Box 316
2400 AH Alphen aan den Rijn
The Netherlands
E-mail: international-sales@wolterskluwer.com
Website: lrus.wolterskluwer.com

Sold and distributed by:
Wolters Kluwer Legal & Regulatory U.S.
7201 McKinney Circle
Frederick, MD 21704
United States of America
E-mail: customer.service@wolterskluwer.com

ISBN 978-94-035-3851-8

e-Book: ISBN 978-94-035-3853-2
web-PDF: ISBN 978-94-035-3852-5

The Authors

Prof. Dr hab. Stanislawa Kalus (born in 1943 in Mielec, Poland) is an emeritus full Professor of the Faculty of Law and Administration, Department of Civil and Private International Law, the University of Silesia in Katowice and a retired judge in the Court of Appeals in Katowice, where in 1990–2008, she tried private law cases, including ones concerning family law.

She has an LLM from Jagiellonian University (1965), LLD from the University of Silesia (1975), Habilitation from the University of Silesia (1989), and has cleared the State Judges' Exam (1967). She has been a full-time professor (2004) and active judge in the Court of Appeals in Katowice (1990–2008). For the past twenty years, she has been the expert of Sejm (the lower house of the Polish Parliament), working on drafts of many statutes. She is a member of such organizations as the Katowice Branch of the Polish Academy of Sciences and the World Society of Mixed Jurisdiction Jurists. She is a member of the Family Law Codification Committee established by the Ombudsman for Children's Rights in 2012, a participant in the succession law working group of the Polish Commission for the Codification of Civil Law, and an active participant in the Common Core of European Private Law project.

Her publications (extract) include the following: *Ochrona prawna obrotu gospodarczego (Legal Protection of Commercial Trade)*, editor, Warszawa: Lexis Nexis, 2011; *Ustawa o gospodarce nieruchomościami. Komentarz* (*The Management of Real Estate Act. Commentary*), together with G. Bieniek (ed.), Z. Marmaj, E. Mzyk, Warszawa: Lexis Nexis 2005 (4th edn, 2011); *Kodeks Rodzinny i Opiekuńczy. Komentarz* (*Family and Guardianship Code. Commentary*), together with H. Ciepla, et al. (ed.), M. Sychowicz, Warszawa: Lexis Nexis, 2000 (4th edn, 2009); *Pozycja prawna uczestników rynku nieruchomości* (*The Legal Position of Participants in the Real Estate Market*), Warszawa: Lexis Nexis, 2009; *Opieka nad osobą całkowicie ubezwłasnowolnioną* (*Guardianship over a Fully Incapacitated Person*), Katowice: Wydawnictwo Uniwersytetu Śląskiego, 1989; 'Liability for Medical Damages', in *Tort Law in Poland, Germany and Europe*, edited by B. Heiderhoff & G. İmij (München: Sellier, 2009), 47–75; 'Mediacja w postępowaniu w sprawach rodzinnych (Mediation in Family Law Proceedings)', in *Ewolucja polskiego postępowania cywilnego wobec przemian politycznych, społecznych i gospodarczych* (*Evolution of Polish Civil Procedure in the Context of Political,*

Social and Economic Changes), edited by H. Dolecki & K. Flaga-Gieruszyńska (Warszawa, 2008), 25–33; 'Konstytucyjne źródla zasad polskiego prawa rodzinnego (The Constitutional Sources of Polish Family Law Principles)', in *Prawo a wartości, Księga jubileuszowa Profesora Józefa Nowackiego* (*Law and Values. Essays in Honour of Professor Józef Nowacki*), edited by I. Bogucka & Z. Tobor (Kraków: Zakamycze 2003), 101–114; 'Ewolucja polskiego prawa rodzinnego w świetle integracji europejskiej (The Evolution of Polish Family Law in the Context of European Integration)', in *Materiały z Konferencji: 25 lecie Powszechnego Sądownictwa Rodzinnego w Polsce* (*Materials from the Conference: 25th Anniversary of Courts of General Jurisdiction in Family Law Matters in Poland*) (Zakopane, 2004), 21–24; 'The Notion of Real Estate and Rights Pertaining to It, in Selected Legal Systems', together with Magdalena Habdas, in *Modern Studies in Property Law, vol. III* (Oxford, Portland, Oregon: Hart Publishing, 2005), 251–270; 'Perspektywy stworzenia europejskiego prawa rzeczowego (The Prospects for Creating a European Property Law)', in *Rozprawy Prawnicze – Księga Pamiątkowa Profesora Maksymiliana Pazdana (Legal Essays in Honour of Professor Maksymilian Pazdan)*, (Kraków: Zakamycze, 2005), 625–635; 'Z problematyki cywilnoprawnej nowoczesnych porodów (Civil Law Problems Concerning Modern Methods of Childbirth)', in *Materiały z VII Sympozjum Sekcji Psychosomatycznej Polskiego Towarzystwa Ginekologicznego* (*Materials from VII Symposium of the Psychosomatic Section of the Polish Gynecology Association*) (Tychy, 2002), 2–6.

Associate Professor (Dr hab. Prof. UŚ) Magdalena Habdas (born in 1973 in Katowice, Poland) is a faculty member at the Faculty of Law and Administration, Institute of Legal Studies, the University of Silesia in Katowice.

She has an MA in English from the University of Silesia (1996), LLM from the University of Silesia (1997), MSc in Property Valuation and Management from Sheffield Hallam University (1998), LLD from the University of Silesia (2002) and Habilitation from the University of Silesia (2013). She is a Certified Real Estate Valuer (state examination 1999) and certified attorney (since 2013). She is the Head translator of the *International Valuation Standards* issued by the International Valuation Standards Committee (8th edn) and of *European Valuation Standards* issued by TEGoVA (6th edition). She has been the General Editor (2004–2007) of *Real Estate* – the quarterly published by the Silesian Association of Valuers. She was a participant in the succession law working group of the Polish Commission for the Codification of Civil Law, is an active participant in the Common Core of European Private Law project, a member of the National Qualifications Committee responsible for examining prospective real estate valuers. In 2015, she was awarded a National Education Committee Medal by the Polish Minister of National Education.

Her publications (extract) include *Property and Trust Law in Poland*. International Encyclopaedia of Laws, eds A. Verbeke, V. Sagaert & Alphen aan den Rijn, NL: Wolters Kluwer, 2018; *Publiczna własność nieruchomości (Public Ownership of Immovables), Warsaw: Lexis Nexis 2012, Przedsiębiorstwo jako przedmiot stosunków prawnorzeczowych (The Enterprise as An Object of Rights in Rem)*, Katowice: Wydawnictwo Uniwersytetu Śląskiego 2007; 'The Evolution of Joint Parenting in Poland – The

Legal Perspective on Lessons Learned and Still to Be Learned', *International Journal of the Law, Policy, and the Family* vol. 33 (2019), doi: 10.1093/lawfam/ebz010; 'Implementing the Mortgage Credit Directive 2014/17 in Poland. Challenges and Dilemmas,' in The *Impact of the Mortgage Credit Directive in Europe. Contrasting Views from Member States*, edited by M. Anderson & E.A. Amayuelas (Europa Law Publishing, 2018), 384–423; 'Balancing the Rights of Tenants and Landlords in the Context of Rent Regulation – Polish Experiences in the Light of ECtHR Case-Law', in *Tenancy Law and Housing Policy in Europe. Towards Regulatory Equilibrium*, edited by Ch. U. Schmid (Cheltenham, UK; Northampton, MA: Edward Elgar Publishing, 2018), 199–238 (co-author: G. Panek); 'The Tenant's Home and the Landlord's Property – The Polish Struggle to Achieve a Balance of Rights', in *Law and the Precarious Home. Socio Legal Perspectives on the Home in Insecure Times*, edited by H. Carr, B. Edgeworth & C. Hunter (Oxford, London, New York, New Delhi, Sydney: Hart Publishing, 2018), 109–135; 'Quasi-Public Property: Public Spaces in Private Hands', in *European and International Cross-Border Private and Economic Relationships, and Individual Rights*, edited by B. Heiderhoff & I. Queirolo, *Scritti di diritto Privato Europeo ed internazionale* (Arricia: Aracne, 2016), 63–111; Polish Report in *European Condominium Law. The Common Core of European Private Law*, edited by C.G. van der Merwe (Cambridge: Cambridge University Press, 2015); 'Expropriation Law in Poland', in *Expropriation Law in Europe*, edited by J. Sluysmans, S. Verbist & E. Waring (Deventer: Wolters Kluwer, 2015), 407–432; 'The Community of Owners' Regulation of Common Property in Polish Condominium Schemes', Modern Studies in Property Law, vol. VII, edited by N. Hopkins (Oxford – Portland, Oregon: Hart Publishing, 2013), 127–149; 'Kontrowersje wokół dziedziczenia ustawowego małżonka spadkodawcy (Controversies concerning intestate succession of the surviving spouse)', in *Rozprawy z prawa Prywatnego. Księga pamiątkowa dedykowana Profesorowi Aleksandrowi Oleszce*, edited by A. Dańko-Roesler, J. Jacyszyn, M. Pazdan & W. Popiołek (Warsaw: Stowarzyszenie Notariuszy RP, 2012), 172–192; 'Building on Someone Else's Land – The Legal Consequences of Encroachment in Polish Law', in *Festschrift fur Prof. Stanislawa Kalus. Ius est ars Boni et aequi*, edited by M. Habdas & A. Wudarski (Frankfurt am Main: Peter Lang Verlag, 2010), 201–226; 'Public Real Estate – Private Law Reality or Fiction?', in *Property & Security: Selected Essays*, edited by B. Edgeworth & L. Bennett-Moses (Sydney: Thomson Reuters, 2010), 33–48; 'Bank Loan Contracts in Polish Law – The Legal Position of the Borrower', in *Unconscionability in European Private Financial Transactions. Protecting the Vulnerable*, edited by M. Kenny, J. Devenney & L. Fox O'Mahony (Cambridge: Cambridge University Press, 2010), 289–307 (co-author S. Kalus); 'My Home Is My Castle – But Is My Castle Truly Mine? Polish Historical Immovables as Objects of Ownership', *Opinio Juris in Comparatione* 2, no. 5 (2010): 1–19; 'Tortious Liability in Polish Law for Damage Caused by Minors', in *Tort Law in Poland, Germany and Europe*, edited by B. Heiderhoff & G. İmij (Munich: Sellier, 2009), 103–120; 'Pozycja prawna małżonka spadkodawcy na tle prawno porównawczym (The Legal Position of the Surviving Spouse in a Comparative Context)', *Rejent* no. 2 (2006): 58–82; 'Polish Apartment Ownership Compared with South African Sectional Titles', *Stellenbosh Law Review* no. 1 (2006) 165–189 (co-author C.G. van der Merwe).

The Authors

Table of Contents

Table of Contents

List of Abbreviations

Common Terms

Art.	article in a statute
cf.	compare with
ed.	Editor
e.g.	for example
etc.	et cetera
ibid.	*Ibidem*
i.e.	id est
no.	Number
s.	Section
vol.	Volume

Statutes and Legislation

ABGB	Austrian Civil Code
BGB	German Civil Code
CREA	Central Register of Economic Activity
CRP	Constitution of the Republic of Poland
CSRL	Civil Status Registration Law
FGC	Family and Guardianship Code
LNA	Law on Notaries Act
LRM	Land Registers and Mortgages Act
PCC	Polish Civil Code
PCPC	Polish Civil Procedure Code
PIL	Private International Law
PPC	Polish Penal Code

Authorities/Offices

BMDRO	Births, Marriages, Deaths Registration Office

List of Abbreviations

ECtHR	European Court of Human Rights
PCCCL	Polish Commission for the Codification of Civil Law

Commonly Cited Supreme Court Case Reports

OSNC	Orzecznictwo Sadu Najwyższego – Izba Cywilna
OSP	Orzecznictwo Sądów Polskich
OSNPG	Orzecznictwo Sądu Najwyższego – Izba Pracy i Gospodarcza
OSPiKA	Orzecznictwo Sądów Polskich i Komisji Arbitrażowych

General Introduction

§1. General Information about the Country (Demographic Data)

1. Polish territory covers 322,575 km^2. This area is inhabited by approximately 38,000,000 people, although the population number is decreasing as a result of such phenomena as a decrease in birth rate accompanied by a generally stable death rate, low fertility and natural growth rates,[1] as well as considerable post EU accession migration abroad, especially to European Union (EU) Member States. The number of emigrants fluctuates, some of them return, but on the whole, over 2,000,000 people left Poland as a result of migration.[2]

2. In the context of Polish family law, there is demographic data that reflects the annual number of marriages formed, including church marriages entered into after the 1998 amendment of the Family and Guardianship Code (FGC)[3] which produce civil law effects, as well as marriages entered into before the Registrar of Births, Marriages and Deaths Registration Office (BMDRO), or before a Polish consul abroad. At the turn of the 1980s and 1990s, around 250,000 matrimonies were concluded annually. Since that time, the number of concluded marriages has been decreasing, however with a notable high of 258,000 in 2008.[4] Nevertheless the number of concluded marriages continues to decline and amounted to 228,300 in 2010; 188,000 in 2015; 192,400 in 2018, and 183,400 in 2019.[5] Data shows that almost 80% of children are born to married couples, with just over 20% of children born out of wedlock. The number of live births is also falling with 413,300 recorded in 2010 and 388,200 recorded in 2018. The crucial question this raises is whether the birth rate provides for the simple reproduction of generations. For the time being, it

1. Population, size and structure and vital statistics in Poland by territorial division in 2020. As of 30 Jun. 2021, https://stat.gov.pl/obszary-tematyczne/ludnosc/ludnosc/ludnosc-stan-i-struktura-ludnosci-oraz-ruch-naturalny-w-przekroju-terytorialnym-stan-w-dniu-30-06-2020, 6,28.html (accessed on 4 Jan. 2021), p. 11.
2. Cf. P. Kaczmarczyk, Recent Trends in International Migration in Poland. The 2012 SOPEMI Report, May 2014, http://www.migracje.uw.edu.pl/wp-content/uploads/2016/06/WP71129_2.pdf (accessed on 4 Jan. 2021), pp. 20–31.
3. Act of 24 Jul. 1998, consolidated version: Journal of Statutes 2017, item 682, with subsequent amendments.
4. https://stat.gov.pl/obszary-tematyczne/ludnosc/ludnosc/malzenstwa-i-dzietnosc-w-polsce,23,1.html (accessed on 1 Oct. 2019), pp. 1–2.
5. Concise Statistical Yearbook of Poland, Warsaw 2020. https://stat.gov.pl/obszary-tematyczne/roczniki-statystyczne/roczniki-statystyczne/maly-rocznik-statystyczny-polski-2020,1,22.html (accessed on 4 Jan. 2021), p. 110.

would be difficult to state that such reproduction occurs when the fertility rate does not exceed 2 points. In 1990, the fertility rate dropped below 2.0 points to 1.99 and continues to decrease, amounting to 1.44 in 2018 and 1.41 in 2019. In order to achieve a simple reproduction of generations, the fertility rate should be between 2.13 and 2.15.[6] Statistical data also indicate the increasing age of women with the highest fertility level, which means that married couples decide not to have offspring immediately after the wedding and put off the first child until they reach a satisfactory professional and financial status. The number of divorces and separation cases, the latter institution introduced into Polish family law in 1999, seems relatively low compared to other European states. The divorce rate in 2003 amounted only to 1.2%, covering 47,000 divorced and 3,000 separated couples. In 2008, the number of divorced couples increased considerably and reached the level of 66,000, while the number of separations increased to 4,000. In 2018, there were 62,800 divorces and 1,300 separations. The divorce rate of 1.76% remains rather low when compared to other European countries.[7]

§2. Historical Background of Family and Inheritance Law

3. Family law and inheritance law developed on Polish grounds under highly particular historical conditions, owing to the fact that from the end of the eighteenth century (1795) until 1918, the Polish State had ceased to exist, its territories being divided (the Partitions of Poland) among three invaders: Prussia (later Germany), Austria and Russia. Such state of affairs led to a situation in which the sources of legally binding law on Polish territory were: the Prussian Landrecht, later replaced by the German Civil Code (BGB), the Austrian Civil Code (ABGB) and the Russian Svod Zakonov. Moreover, as a result of the Napoleonic wars, at the beginning of the nineteenth century, the Duchy of Warsaw was created from a sizeable part of the Polish territories and here, the Napoleonic Code was introduced. Later, the Russian-dominated Kingdom of Poland retained the Napoleonic Code, which in 1825 was transformed into the Civil Code of the Kingdom of Poland. Additionally, in some parts of the country (Spisz and Orawa), Hungarian law was in force. Polish lawyers, educated from the great European codifications of the nineteenth century attempted to unify the civil law of Poland throughout the interwar period (1919–1939), but the first unified pieces of legislation appeared only after the end of World War II, in the years 1945–1946. They covered marital law, family law, guardianship law, the law of marital property as well as inheritance law. However, these pieces of legislation proved incompatible with prevailing social conditions which were heading in the direction of a different family model, one which developed after the war and which essentially became a manifestation of the political influence of neighbouring countries on Poland's legal system.

6. https://stat.gov.pl/obszary-tematyczne/ludnosc/ludnosc/malzenstwa-i-dzietnosc-w-polsce,23,1.html, (accessed on 4 Jan. 2021), pp. 5–7.
7. https://stat.gov.pl/obszary-tematyczne/ludnosc/ludnosc/malzenstwa-i-dzietnosc-w-polsce,23,1.html (accessed on 4 Jan. 2021), p. 15.

4. The whole subject of family law relationships was soon regulated within a single legislative, namely the Family Code, which came into force in 1950. This remained in force for a short period of time and was severely criticized, especially for the conciseness of its provisions, in particular the rules on marital property and material relationships between spouses. When it comes to succession law relations, provisions of the Decree on Succession Law of 8 October 1946 very soon turned out to be incompatible with post-war social transformations. This first became apparent with regard to the clear discrimination of extramarital children who could inherit from their mother and her relatives, but not from the father, unless they became acknowledged by their father or properly equalized with marital children. These provisions were derogated on 27 June 1950 along with the entry into force of the Family Code. Works of the Codification Commission appointed at that time (the same type of body was established in Czechoslovakia) paved the way for the enactment of the FGC of 25 February 1964 and the Regulations Implementing the Civil Code. The new statute covered issues of marriage, its formation and legal effects in the area of personal and material relationships, termination and annulment, affinity and relations between parents and children, finally issues connected with guardianship and curatorship. This frequently amended piece of legislation has remained in force to the present day. The FGC regulates family law, which, according to Polish civil law doctrine, forms a part of civil law. In consequence, it does not contain provisions covering personal law, legal capacity and capacity to perform juridical acts (acts in law) by natural persons, or their domicile. These questions are all referred to in the general provisions of civil law incorporated into the Polish Civil Code (PCC).[8] Having regard to the structure of issues covered in this publication, these questions are going to be discussed below, as highly significant to family law.

5. The FGC additionally encompasses guardianship law and rules on curatorship. Their inclusion in this piece of legislation was highly disputable in the course of legislative works. In the view of many authors, these are questions of personal civil law and should be incorporated into the PCC. The decisive argument as to their inclusion in the FGC was that in the event that guardianship should affect adults deprived of the capacity to perform juridical acts as a result of incapacitation, provisions of the FGC on parental authority are to be applied appropriately to the exercise of guardianship. The guardian in relation to the minor, who does not remain under parental authority, replaces necessary activities of the child's missing parents. As regards the incapacitated person, the guardian is a replacement for his or her reasonable action, of which the incapacitated is incapable. The legislator used a specific technical and legal strategy which functions properly in practice.

6. At the time of its preparation, the enactment of a separate FGC was additionally justified by a strong tendency to emphasize the differences between civil law institutions and family law institutions. This tendency was manifested by denying that the conclusion of a marriage forms a civil law relationship of a contractual type. The lawmaker did not provide initially any negative legal results in situations where

8. Act of 23 Apr. 1964, consolidated version: Journal of Statutes 2020, item 1359 with subsequent amendments.

the declaration of entry into a marriage proved defective. It was considered that if the marriage was functioning properly in spite of such circumstances, there was no point in questioning the validity of the declaration of intent. If, however, the marriage had broken down irretrievably, it could be terminated by a divorce. A similar situation could be indicated in the case of adoption, enforced only by means of a court decision and never implemented as a contract between the adopter and adoptee.

7. In addition, it was emphasized that the special position of family law in relation to civil law was justified by the former's broader use of mandatory rules *(iuris cogentis)* and the expanded role of courts and registrars of BMDROs in the creation of legal relationships, as well as the ex officio activity of guardianship courts. Despite all the differences, from the beginning, the strict connection of civil law and family law, expressed in the duty to directly apply PCC provisions to family relationships unless provided otherwise in a special rule, has been acknowledged.

8. Inheritance law, however, was incorporated into the PCC, which entered into force on 1 January 1965. Provisions on inheritance law comprise Articles 922–1087 PCC. Two titles to inheritance were recognized by the legislator: intestate succession and the testament. The lawmaker omitted inheritance contracts which had been admissible in civil law regimes of partitioned Poland, and precisely determined the range of statutory heirs among whom a preferable position of the surviving spouse (widow or widower) is noticeable. Another matter regulated in detail was an issue of crucial importance at the time, namely the inheritance of farms: the appointment of an heir and the heir's necessary qualifications. Other questions covered by the provisions on succession law are acceptance or waiver of the estate, the certificate of estate acquisition, liability for the debts of the estate and finally, division of the estate.

§3. Sources of Family and Succession Law

I. Constitution

9. The Constitution of the Republic of Poland (CRP)[9] is one of the sources of family law, even though it does not regulate family law relationships directly. Beyond any doubt, certain fundamental principles of family law, not formulated directly in the FGC, are derived from Constitutional provisions. The CRP enumerates the following fundamental principles of Polish family law:

(1) marriage as a relationship between a woman and a man;
(2) the protection of marriage as the foundation of a family (Article 18 CRP);
(3) the protection of family (Articles 48 and 53 §3 CRP);
(4) the protection of the interest of the child (Articles 71 and 72 CRP);
(5) durability of the marital bond;

9. Act of 2 Apr. 1997, Journal of Statutes 1997, no. 78, item 483, with subsequent amendments.

(6) equal rights of a man and woman in the area of family law;
(7) special protection of maternity (Article 18 CRP);
(8) intimacy of family life and its protection (Article 48 CRP);
(9) the secular nature of marriage.

10. The CRP does not regulate family law relationships directly but sets out certain directives addressed to the legislator, indicating axiological grounds for certain more precise provisions of law. Article 18 CRP may provide an example of such a directive, stipulating that marriage, maternity, paternity, family are independent values protected by law both within the family and in the individual dimension. This provision bears two functions. The first is to form an element of the constitutional axiology and the second to specify purposes and objectives, which stem from the state's duty to protect and care for the family, for public authorities.[10]

II. Legislation

11. The fundamental piece of legislation which regulates relationships in the area of family and guardianship law is the FGC, which is composed of the following titles:

(1) *matrimony*, comprising regulations of entering into marriage, rights and obligations of spouses, matrimonial property regimes, termination of marriage and separation;
(2) *consanguinity and affinity*, comprising general provisions, issues referring to parents and children, including the problems of the origin of the child and relations between the parents and children, adoption, and the alimony obligation;
(3) *guardianship and curatorship*, covering guardianship over a minor, guardianship over a fully incapacitated person, and curatorship.

12. A separate statute comprises Regulations Implementing the FGC.[11] These contain derogative clauses and amendments to previous enactments, and finally interim provisions.

13. Provisions of the FGC form a part of civil law, even though for technical and legal reasons it was decided that they should be contained in a separate piece of legislation. This does not imply that family law regulations are excluded from the sphere of PCC regulation. Both the PCC and FGC cover certain areas of personal relationships. The PCC regulates personal law in the general part (the notion of a natural person, his or her legal capacity and capacity to perform juridical acts, place

10. Cf. T. Smyczyński, 'Prawo rodzinne i stosunki rodzinnoprawne', in T. Smyczyński (ed.), *System Prawa Prywatnego. Tom 11. Prawo rodzinne i opiekuńcze* (Warszawa: C.H. Beck, 2014), 49–50; S. Kalus, 'Konstytucyjne źródła zasad polskiego prawa rodzinnego', in I. Bogucka, Z. Tobor (eds) *Prawo a wartości. Ksiega jubileuszowa Profesora Józefa Nowackiego*, (Kraków: Zakamycze, 2003), 105–106.
11. Act of 25 Feb. 1964, Journal of Statutes, no. 9, item 60.

of residence, personal interests and their protection). The FGC regulates personal relationships among family members, as well as their material relationships. Issues connected with the notion of a minor and incapacitated person can be found in the PCC, whereas their legal status, protection and legal representation are covered by the FGC. The most important quality of FGC regulation is the civil law method, based on legal equality, since even when the exercise of parental authority is regulated, which refers not only to personal affairs but also to property-related issues, the authority is seriously restricted by the interest of the child and the necessity to take the child's opinion into consideration. Moreover, many provisions of the FGC refer to civil law institutions of property law (co-ownership, joint ownership) and succession law (division of the estate). Connections with these areas of civil law are particularly intense since the whole PCC regulation pertaining to intestate succession is based on the necessity to consider the implied intention of the intestate person, unexpressed in a testament but possible to infer from the principles regulated by the FGC. Hence, the thesis is that succession law is a particular extension of family law relationships and their results in the area of material rights beyond the intestate person's death.[12] It is often stressed that because of the particular nature of family law relations, the provisions of FGC must contain certain differences in relation to other civil law relationships, such as a much broader role of guardianship courts and their supervision over many aspects of functioning of family law relations, indispensable participation of state authorities in the creation of these relationships, vast number of mandatory rules *(iuris cogentis)* accompanied by the impossibility to compulsorily enforce the duties following from the regulated relationships. Nevertheless, the doctrine is almost entirely concordant that these are not reasons which could exclude family and guardianship law from the system of Polish civil law. Moreover, where issues are unregulated in the FGC, the provisions of civil law apply *directly* to family law relationships.[13]

14. The FGC underwent numerous amendments as a result of changes in social and economic relations, and the consequent need to adjust its rules to the EU standards. The most crucial amendments took place in 1975, 1998, 2004, and finally, the most vital one was enacted in 2008. Apart from the FGC, a number of other statutes are significant in the area of family law. These include the Act of 28 November 2014 – Civil Status Registry Law,[14] the Act of 7 September 1991 on the educational system,[15] Act of 26 October 1982 on proceedings in juvenile cases[16] and the Act of 28 November 2003 on family benefits.[17] Undoubtedly, also provisions of the Polish

12. T. Smyczyński, Prawo rodzinne i opiekuńcze (Warszawa: C.H. Beck, 2018) 18–19.
13. S. Grzybowski (ed.), *System prawa cywilnego. Cześć ogólna. Tom.* (Wroclaw – Warszawa – Kraków -Gdańsk: Ossolineum, 1985), 77; J. Winiarz: *Prawo rodzinne* (Warszawa: PWN, 1994), 24–28; A. Stelmachowski, *Wstęp do teorii prawa cywilnego* (Warszawa: PWN, 1984), 43, Smyczyński, *Prawo*, 19 and Supreme Court decision issued on 14 Jan. 1953, *Państwo i Prawo*, no. 12 (1953).
14. Consolidated version: Journal of Statutes 2020, item 463, with subsequent amendments.
15. Consolidated version: Journal of Statutes 2020, item 1327, with subsequent amendments.
16. Consolidated version: Journal of Statutes 2018, item 969, with subsequent amendments.
17. Consolidated version: Journal of Statutes 2020, item 111, with subsequent amendments.

Civil Procedure Code (PCPC)[18] have a considerable impact on the possibilities of enforcement of substantive law rights following from the FGC (the PCPC has also been subject to many amendments, also as a result of enactments modifying both the FGC and civil procedure itself).

15. Provisions of international law – especially those regulating the protection of human rights, once they become ratified or implemented into the national legal system – are an important source of family law. The absolute primacy in this respect belongs to the European Convention on Human Rights and Fundamental Freedoms of 1950, and the Protocols to this Convention. Poland, as a member of the Council of Europe, ratified this Convention and others pertaining to the protection of a human being as a citizen, family member, which set standards binding in most European countries. In particular, one should mention:

(1) European Convention on the Adoption of Children of 24 April 1967.[19]
(2) European Convention on the Legal Status of Children Born Out of Wedlock of 15 October 1975.[20]
(3) European Convention on Recognition and Enforcement of Decisions Concerning Custody of Children and on Restoration of Custody of Children of 20 May 1980.[21]
(4) European Convention on the Exercise of Children's Rights of 1996.[22]
(5) European Convention on Contact concerning Children of 15 May 2003 (currently in the course of the ratification process).
(6) European Social Charter of 18 October 1961 (unpublished).
(7) Convention on the International Exchange of Information Relating to Civil Status of 4 September 1958.[23]
(8) Convention on the issue of multilingual extracts from civil status records of 8 September 1976.[24]

16. Also, the EU regulations are of crucial importance to family law. They are directly applicable in Poland and regulate mostly various procedural and conflict of laws issues. Among these, one should mention Regulation No. 2201/2203 concerning jurisdiction and the recognition and enforcement of judgments in matrimonial matters and the matters of parental responsibility (Brussels IIa); Regulation No. 4/2009 on jurisdiction, applicable law, recognition and enforcement of decisions and cooperation in matters relating to maintenance obligations; Regulation No. 1206/2001 on cooperation between the courts of the Member States in the taking of evidence in civil or commercial matters. It should be noted that Poland did not enter into enhanced cooperation concerning: Regulation No. 1259/2010 on implementing

18. Act of 17 Nov. 1964, consolidated version: Journal of Statutes 2020, item 1575 with subsequent amendments.
19. Journal of Statutes 1999, no. 99, item 1157, with subsequent amendments.
20. Journal of Statutes 1999, no. 79, items 888, 889.
21. Journal of Statutes 1996, no. 31, item 134.
22. Journal of Statutes 2000, no. 107, item 1128.
23. Journal of Statutes 2003, no. 172, items 1667, 1668.
24. Journal of Statutes 2004, no. 166, item 1735.

enhanced cooperation in the area of the law applicable to divorce and legal separation, Regulation No. 2016/1103 implementing enhanced cooperation in the area of jurisdiction, applicable law and the recognition and enforcement of decisions in matters of matrimonial property regimes; Regulation No. 2016/1104 implementing enhanced cooperation in the area of jurisdiction, applicable law and the recognition and enforcement of decisions in matters of the property consequences of registered partnerships.

§4. Courts Administering Justice in Family Law and Succession Law Cases

17. Family law cases are characterized by considerable complexity. Apart from legal knowledge, the judges deciding such disputes, especially guardianship cases, need to have a solid knowledge of psychology and pedagogy, which seem necessary for delivering the proper decision. They should also have extensive professional experience in this field accrued over a long period of time. Consequently, it has been indicated that the practice of assigning family law cases to judges without proper experience in hearing this category of disputes is defective. It has been postulated that a separate division of family law courts should be established on all levels within the system of common courts of law.

18. The Law on the Organization of Common Courts of Law[25] enacted thirty years ago provides in Article 12 for family courts on the district court level. These judicial bodies enjoy a broad spectrum of competence. Pursuant to Article 12 §1 point 3 of this statute, family courts decide in cases:

(1) falling under family and guardianship law, not restricted to proper regional courts (e.g., divorce and incapacitation cases);
(2) pertaining to demoralization and punishable acts of juveniles;[26]
(3) relating to the treatment of persons addicted to alcohol, drugs or psychoactive substances;[27]
(4) referred to the jurisdiction of family courts on the basis of separate statutes.

19. In consequence, family courts decide predominantly in cases falling under the category of family law, guardianship and curatorship law enumerated in Articles 561 PCPC and following ones. These are marital cases pertaining to: permission to enter into matrimony in spite of not having reached the prescribed age, release from

25. Act of 27 Jul. 2001, consolidated version: Journal of Statutes 2020, item 2072 with subsequent amendments.
26. Act of 26 Oct. 1982 on the proceedings in juvenile cases, consolidated version: Journal of Statutes 2018, item 969 with subsequent amendments.
27. Act of 19 Aug. 1994 on the protection of mental health, consolidated version: Journal of Statutes 2020, item 685 with subsequent amendments; Act of 29 Jun. 2005 on counteracting drug addiction, consolidated version: Journal of Statutes 2020, item 2050, with subsequent amendments; Act of 26 Oct. 1982 on education in sobriety and counteracting alcoholism, consolidated version: Journal of Statutes of 2017, item 2277, with subsequent amendments.

the duty to submit to the Head Registrar a document necessary to enter into marriage, decline of the Head Registrar to administer declarations of entry into marriage, solving important questions of the family in the case of differences between the spouses, and the so-called other family and guardianship cases mentioned in Articles 568 PCPC and following ones. Among these, one can enumerate cases related to: care over the child whose interest has become or may become endangered, including cases connected with transplantation of tissues, or acts pertaining to management over the child's property.[28]

20. As a result of the fact that family cases are also decided by other civil court divisions in different kinds of proceedings and modes (both litigious and non-litigious), certain measures have been advocated in order to consolidate the range of cases which belong to the functional competence of family courts. Unfortunately, there have also been proposals to abolish family courts and implant them in the structure of civil court divisions. Such plans evoke harsh criticism among judges, even though the Ministry of Justice envisages in the justification of the draft bill of the amendments that the possible enactment is not going to abolish judicial specialization. On the contrary, the draft sets out that chief justices, by determining the principles of allocation of cases to particular judges, are obliged to take into consideration the judges' specialization and experience in hearing particular types of cases. In this manner, according to the Ministry, the proposed amendments in the organization of courts are not going to override the principle of judges' specialization in particular areas of law and deciding particular types of actions, which essentially has become established solely in the practice of larger courts. However, the opinion of judges sitting in these courts is strongly opposed to the draft, which has been frequently manifested by the Association of Family Court Judges in Poland, who point to the serious concern of the affected judges. As a consequence, for the time being, the old organization of the judiciary in the area of deciding family law cases has been preserved. The Minister of Justice wishes to abandon these proposals.

21. When it comes to succession law cases, they are heard by civil divisions of common courts of law; however, most of these cases are non-litigious in character. Only certain claims deriving from succession law are heard in common litigation, for example, unworthiness to inherit proceedings, a claim for legitim (*see* Part IV).

28. *See also*, H. Haak, Ochrona prawna udzielana przez sąd opiekuńczy, Dom Organizatora TNOiK Toruń 2002, 98.

Part I. Personal Law

Chapter 1. Personal Status

§1. Capacity to Perform Juridical Acts of Natural Persons

I. General Matters

22. Subjects of civil law relationships can be classified in the first place as natural persons, juridical persons (meaning organizational units equipped by law with legal personality) and finally organizational units which do not enjoy legal personality but are equipped by law with legal capacity (Articles 33 and 33[1] PCC). In accordance with civil law provisions, the term 'natural person' refers to every human being, equipped by the Polish legal system with the status of a subject of civil law relationships. Two types of capacity can be differentiated in regard to each natural person: legal capacity and capacity to perform juridical acts.

23. Legal capacity of a natural person arises in pursuance to Article 8 PCC at the moment of the person's birth; however, many special rules provide for earlier legal capacity, setting out the need to respect this capacity in the period before the child's birth (e.g., when it comes to the earlier capacity of *nasciturus*, a child unborn at the moment of death of the intestate person – Article 927 §2 PCC, or acknowledgement of paternity of a child who has not been born at the moment of acknowledgement, but has already been conceived – Article 75 §1 FGC), which leads to the conclusion that both Polish legislation and case law are prone to protect the rights of a conceived though as yet unborn child. The ending point in time of this capacity is delimited by the death of a natural person. The moment of death is determined in the certificate of death issued by a doctor and the subsequent official death certificate prepared by a BMDRO Registrar. Alternatively, it might be determined in a court decision ascertaining the demise or acknowledging somebody's death.[29]

24. Legal capacity denotes that the natural person may be a subject of rights and obligations in the field of civil law, which does not mean however that the person

29. Cf. A. Wolter, J. Ignatowicz, K. Stefaniuk, *Prawo cywilne. Zarys części ogólnej* (Warszawa: Lexis Nexis: 2005), 161 et seq.; S. Kalus, 'Article 29 Commentary', in M. Habdas, M. Fras (eds), *Kodeks cywilny. Komentarz. Tom I. Część ogólna (art. 1-125)* (Warszawa: Wolters, Kluwer, 2018), 144 et seq. M. Pazdan, 'Article 8 Commentary', in K. Pietrzykowski (ed.) *Kodeks cywilny. Tom I. Komentarz* (Warszawa: C.H. Beck, 2018), 81-90.

may be the subject of all rights and obligations throughout all his or her life. Legal capacity undergoes certain restrictions which may derive from various sources. For example, a person who has not reached the specified age of majority cannot enter into marriage (18 years – Article 10 FGC), parental authority cannot be exercised by a person without the full capacity to perform juridical acts (Article 94 §1 FGC).

II. Types of Capacity to Perform Juridical Acts

25. The capacity to perform juridical acts of a natural person determines his or her ability to make juridical acts by means of declarations of intent and to acquire rights and obligations thereby. This type of capacity is no longer universal, because of the requirement that the natural person should attain a sufficient level of mental maturity which comes only with a particular age. Also, a judicial decision may deprive a person of his or her capacity to perform juridical acts as a result of the situation in which the person in question suffers from mental illness or mental deficiency, and is unable to control his or her conduct.

26. A natural person's capacity to perform juridical acts rests on two premises, that is, age and lack of incapacitation. Taking into consideration these two factors, one can distinguish persons:

(1) without the capacity to perform juridical acts;
(2) of partial capacity to perform juridical acts;
(3) of full capacity to perform juridical acts.

27. Lack of capacity to perform juridical acts means that a person falling in this category (minors under 13 and persons fully incapacitated) cannot participate in legal transactions on their own, except when concluding contracts regarding minor things common in everyday life, in which case the act is effective when performed, unless it should blatantly harm the incapable person (Article 14 §2 PCC). As a result, juridical acts on behalf of these individuals must be made by their statutory representatives, meaning parents or guardians. When it comes to the performance of juridical acts exceeding the scope of ordinary management of the affected persons' assets (which correspond to more important acts of asset management), the statutory representative needs additional court permission.

28. A much broader scope of possibilities to independently make legal acts concerns persons of partial capacity to perform juridical acts. These include:

(1) minors over 13;
(2) partially incapacitated persons;
(3) persons for whom a temporary advisor has been appointed for the period of incapacitation proceedings.

29. Such people are in a relatively complicated legal position because with regard to certain juridical acts they are treated as equipped with full capacity to perform juridical acts, which means that in this respect legal acts can be made freely (Article 17 PCC *a contrario*, Articles 20, 21, 22 PCC). Other juridical acts require the consent of the statutory representative (parents, guardian or curator if the FGC envisages the possibility to appoint one in the circumstances set out in Article 102 FGC). There are also juridical acts in the case of which persons of partial capacity are treated as persons deprived of the capacity to perform juridical acts, which leads to invalidity of the juridical act made without valid consent of the statutory representative (as far as unilateral juridical acts are concerned, there is a statutory requirement of the representative's consent – Article 19 PCC).

30. The first of the situations presented above concerns juridical acts of such persons which are neither acts of disposition nor contracting obligations. Persons of partial capacity to perform juridical acts can also conclude contracts in minor matters of everyday life, dispose of their own earnings, dispose of chattels entrusted to them for free use (Articles 20–22 PCC). As a result, persons of partial capacity to perform juridical acts may independently appropriate nobody's things, conclude contracts classified as generally entered into in minor common matters of everyday life (purchase of food or school accessories), dispose of their own earnings (unless the court excludes such possibility) and they may dispose of assets given to them for free use by the statutory representative (as long as these are acts where consent of the statutory representative is sufficient, without court's permission).

31. In the second of the depicted situations – where validity of a juridical act made by a person of partial capacity to perform juridical acts requires the consent of the statutory representative and such consent has not been given – there arises a situation where the contract concluded by the person of partial capacity makes an incomplete act whose validity is suspended. If the contract becomes confirmed by the statutory representative, or should the person himself or herself affirm the act once he or she acquires the full capacity to perform juridical acts – the act becomes enforceable. This provision protects the person of partial capacity because the other contracting party cannot invoke the lack of consent of the statutory representative, although he or she may mark a period of time in which the statutory representative should endorse the juridical act of the person of partial capacity to legal acts. This other contracting party becomes released of its obligation upon ineffective expiry of the term (Article 18 PCC).

32. The last of the legal situations described above, where the juridical act made by a person of partial capacity to perform juridical acts is invalid because of the lack of consent of the statutory representative, takes place when such a person on his or her own makes a unilateral act which requires consent of the representative (Article 19 PCC).

33. Undoubtedly, the fullest possibility of participation in legal transactions relates to persons of full capacity to perform juridical acts. These are majors (either as a result of turning 18 or earlier entry into marriage) not incapacitated, either partially or fully. They may entirely freely (without consent of a third party) make all juridical acts, although within the limits of their legal capacity. As a consequence, these persons are the most frequent actors in commercial transactions. They act both as consumers and businesses.[30]

III. Minors, Juveniles and Persons of Age

34. Minors are natural persons before they reach full age. In Polish civil law, there are two ways in which a minor can become a person of full age (attain majority): by turning 18 (Article 10 §1 PCC) or entering into marriage before that age has been reached (Article 10 §2 PCC). Article 10 of the FGC stipulates that a marriage may be concluded once the couple turns 18, but provides for an exceptional situation where the court driven by important reasons (most importantly pregnancy of the bride-to-be) may allow a minor girl who is at least 16 years of age to enter into marriage; in addition, the circumstances of the case must indicate that the conclusion of the marriage is going to be concordant with the interest of the newly founded family (Article 10 §2 FGC). By entering into the marriage such a woman becomes a person of full age. She does not lose the age of majority even if the marriage is later annulled or dissolved by divorce or the other spouse's death. Similarly, if a man who is not of an age to marry brings about a situation in which he enters into marriage (e.g., by forging his birth certificate), the marriage shall still entail his majority and this majority, even if the marriage is later annulled or dissolved by divorce or the other spouse's death, is not going to be cancelled even though the requirement of majority was not fulfilled at the time the marriage was concluded (Article 10 §2 PCC second sentence).

35. Since the competence of family courts covers not only cases relating to minors and persons of full age, but also juveniles, it should be explained who exactly is referred to by this category. This has been defined in a statute whose legal status seems interesting. Until the 1980s, it has been considered that these issues are a matter of criminal law, and the provisions of the statutes regulating criminal proceedings applied also to judicial proceedings in juvenile cases. However, the situation changed as a result of enactment of the Act of 26 October 1982 on the proceedings in juvenile cases. Presently, these questions belong rather to the area of civil law protection of a certain category of persons. Also, the measures envisaged in the statute, apart from placement in a reformatory, are analogical to measures applied for the purpose of protection of minors. Additionally, provisions of the PCPC apply to matters unregulated by the discussed statute.

30. Cf. Wolter, Ignatowicz, Stefaniuk, *Prawo*, 165 et seq.; S. Kalus, 'Commentary to Art. 10 and 11', in M. Habdas, M. Fras (eds) *Kodeks cywilny. Komentarz. Tom I. Część ogólna (art. 1-125)* (Warszawa: Wolters, Kluwer, 2018), 66–70 et seq.; Pazdan, 'Article 11 Commentary', in K. Pietrzykowski (ed.) *Kodeks cywilny. Tom I.*, 92–93.

36. Article 15 of the statute refers juvenile cases to the competence of family courts unless a special provision should stipulate otherwise. This is a consequence of the statute's function since the legislator specified in the preamble that the aims were to counteract demoralization and criminal conduct of juveniles, to create conditions enabling the juveniles' return to normal life, to strengthen family and facilitate its care and educational function, and the sense of obligation in the family for the upbringing of juveniles to become responsible members of society aware of their duties.

37. Similarly, as with cases involving minors, the legislator also invokes the principle of the interest of the child in juvenile cases, which remains common for both these relations, by imposing in Article 3 the obligation on the part of the courts to follow in the first place the juvenile's interest and the need to achieve beneficial effects in the personality and conduct of the juvenile, with a reservation similar to Article 95 FGC, that the court is to frame the parents' or guardian's responsibilities towards the juvenile in such a way as to consider both the child's interest and the public interest. Moreover, Article 3a of the statute provides for the analogical possibility as the one envisaged in the PCPC rules to refer the juvenile case to mediation, regulated relatively extensively in the PCPC after the amendment of 2 July 2004.[31]

38. In the understanding of the Act on the proceedings in juvenile cases, a juvenile is a person under 18 who displays symptoms of demoralization, or is threatened by demoralization (avoids the school obligation, remains in a criminal or demoralized environment), which results in the need to apply to him or her measures leading to prevention or counteraction of this demoralization. These are also persons between 13 (which makes the upper limit of non-liability) and 18 who have committed within that time span a punishable act, and who in pursuance of norms of the Criminal Code did not commit a crime, and persons in relation to whom educational or corrective measures have been adjudicated, no longer, however, than until they reach the age of 21.

39. Legal measures that can be applied by the family court in relation to the juvenile are: admonishment; obligation to specified conduct, in particular, to compensate the inflicted damage; obligation to perform specified works or renditions to the benefit of the aggrieved party or the local community; apologize to the disadvantaged person; take on studies or work, participate in educational, therapeutic or training meetings; and refrain from staying in particular environments or places, quit alcohol or drugs. The measures frequently applied are: establishment of responsible supervision of the parents, guardian or curator, or a trustworthy person who supports the juvenile; referring the juvenile to a curator centre; adjudicating forfeiture of items obtained in connection with the commitment of a punishable act; ordering a ban on driving a vehicle; and finally placement of the juvenile in a foster family, juvenile education centre or reformatory, as well as enforcement of other measures envisaged in the FGC.

31. Journal of Statutes 2004, no. 172, item 1804.

40. Certain measures which the court may apply to the parents of the juvenile have a family character since most frequently demoralization or poor socialization follow from omissions of the parents or guardians. Within the limits prescribed in Article 7 of the discussed statute, the family court may oblige the parents or guardian to improve the conditions of education, existence or health of the juvenile, to cooperate strictly with the school attended by the minor, psychological and pedagogical counselling institution or other specialist centre, the employer of the juvenile, a physician or health care institution. The court may also oblige the parents or the guardian to repair the damage inflicted by the juvenile and refer to proper institutions or units of self-government for necessary assistance. Non-compliance with the court's order on the part of the parents or guardian results in the penalty of a fine ranging between PLN 50 and PLN 1,500 (Article 8 s. 1 Act on proceedings in juvenile cases).

IV. Consent to Medical Treatment of a Child

41. The problem of consent of a particular person to medical examination or provision of certain medical services is regulated in Poland in the Act on the profession of the physician and the dentist.[32] Article 32 of this statute stipulates that the physician may examine the patient or provide other medical services subject to the patient's consent. However, if the patient is a minor or a person unable to independently express consent, the statute requires the consent of his or her statutory representative. If the patient is a child under parental authority, consent is given by the parents. If the child remains under parental authority of neither of the parents, the statutory representative shall be his or her guardian. Similarly, where the patient has been incapacitated, consent must be given by the guardian or curator. If the physician cannot contact persons whose consent is necessary, the consent may be given by the guardianship court. Manifestation of consent on the part of the parents or guardians is an element of the entitlement and obligation to care for the child or incapacitated person, which is a constituent part of parental authority or guardianship.

42. Where a medical examination or provision of a medical service is potentially dangerous to the patient, i.e., when there is a possibility of negative health consequences, it should be concluded that the consent qualifies as an important act falling under the scope of care. As a result, pursuant to Articles 109 and 156 FGC, the statutory representative should obtain the consent of the guardianship court before proceeding to give consent to the attending physician. A certain enhancement of the child's or incapacitated person's rights is visible in Article 32(4) and (5) of the Act on the profession of physician which provides that where the child is at least 16, or the incapacitated person acts insightfully, his or her consent is also required. Such a patient's refusal to consent may be problematic when it comes to

32. Act of 5 Dec. 1996, consolidated version: Journal of Statutes 2020, item 514, with subsequent amendments.

particular medical procedures. On such occasions, judicial consent shall be necessary together with the regular consent of the statutory representative. The Act also regulates the question of consent where the examination or provision of another medical service takes place under such circumstances that timely medical aid is necessary for the patient's well-being, but the patient is unable – because of his or her age, or health condition – to give such consent personally and at the same time there is no possibility to approach the patient's statutory representative or actual caretaker. In such circumstances, Article 33 of the Act allows for medical procedures without such consent, but only after consultation with another physician and recording this fact in the patient's medical documentation. When it comes to the performance of surgical procedures, there is a requirement of consent of the same persons in writing. This refers to all types of treatment in which the risk incurred by the patient is increased.

43. Under such circumstances, the legal interest of the minor or incapacitated person is duly protected. In the case of damages inflicted on such patients as a result of medical maltreatment, their statutory representatives may on their behalf bring respective actions before the court against the persons responsible for the damage.[33]

V. Civil Law Tortious Liability

44. In Polish law, the parents (or guardians) are liable for the acts of minors remaining under their parental care. Similarly, guardians shall be held responsible for the deeds of fully incapacitated persons entrusted to them. This makes one of the cases of liability for other people's acts imposed on persons who by force of law (parents), or by force of a judicial decision (guardians) are obliged to make sure that the dependent persons, because of their age or mental condition resulting in insufficient perceptive skills, should not inflict harm upon third parties. This type of liability is not based on the principle of fault dominant in civil law, since the minor, especially when under 13, or person fully incapacitated because of his or her abnormal mental condition, cannot be ascribed with fault. The representative's liability is based on the principle of risk. The person who supervises the child or the incapacitated should assure proper control of the dependent person, and once the latter inflicts damage upon a third party, the event is most frequently a consequence of faulty supervision *(culpa in custodiendo)*. Article 427 PCC, covering this problem, envisages the presumption of fault in supervision, and the aggrieved party need not demonstrate this fault. On the contrary, the dependent person's parent or guardian should prove the lack of fault in supervision, namely that the damage would also have been inflicted had the dependent person been properly supervised.

---

33. Cf. W. Czachórski et al., *Prawo zobowiązań. Zarys wykładu* (Warszawa: Lexis Nexis, 2009); M. Nesterowicz (ed.), *Ustawa o prawach pacjenta i Rzeczniku Praw Pacjenta* (Warszawa: Instytut Problemów Ochrony Zdrowia, 2009); L. Ogiegło (ed.), *Ustawa o zawodzie lekarza i lekarza dentysty. Komentarz* (Warszawa: C.H. Beck, 2010); S. Kalus, 'Liability for Medical Damages', in e *Tort Law In Poland, Germany and Europe*, ed. B. Heiderhoff & G. İmij (München: Sellier, 2009), 47 et seq.; S. Kalus, 'Patient Rights Protection and Premises of Efficacy of Patient Consent for Medical Procedures', *Humanistyczne Zeszyty Naukowe*, no. 13 (2010): 118 et seq.

45. The following rule, Article 428 PCC, envisages in certain situations the direct compensatory liability of a child or fully disabled person. This occurs when there are no persons obliged to supervise the perpetrator of damage, and the circumstances, especially comparison of the financial position of the aggrieved party and the perpetrator, lead to the conclusion that such a solution is justified by principles of social cohabitation. In consequence, this liability is based on the principle of equity.[34]

§2. Representation of Minors

46. Representation of the minor constitutes an element of parental power and, as long as the child remains under parental authority, both of his or her parents are the statutory representatives. Sometimes there is only one parent entrusted with parental authority. If the child does not remain under parental power of either parent, or when it comes to a fully incapacitated person, the statutory representative is the guardian appointed by the court. Representation makes an element of personal care, which is also a constituent part of the relationship of guardianship.[35]

47. The entitlement to represent the child or incapacitated person has been vested in parents or the guardian since the directly involved persons either enjoy no capacity to perform juridical acts or their capacity to perform legal acts is partial, which leads to a situation in which many of their juridical acts require the consent of the statutory representative, who is obliged to take care that these acts should not be detrimental to the represented person (Article 17 PCC). Representation of the child or person under guardianship boils down to the entitlement under which parents or guardians may act on the child's behalf, and realize his or her interest with legal effects affecting directly the represented person, both when it comes to performing juridical acts of civil substantive law and within judicial procedures, or before other state authorities, especially administrative bodies.

48. As mentioned above, the scope of the child's representation depends on his or her age, since at the stage when the child has no capacity to perform juridical acts the range is very broad and encompasses all legal acts apart from minor everyday contracts which can be effectively concluded under the conditions specified in Article 14 §2 PCC by a minor without the capacity to perform juridical acts (as well as a fully incapacitated person). The scope of representation is narrower where juridical acts are made by a minor over 13 (and a person partially incapacitated), thus as far as a person of partial capacity to perform juridical acts is concerned. On such occasions, as already suggested, there are a handful of legal acts that can be made by the directly interested person independently, without necessary consent of

---

34. Czachórski et al., *Zobowiązania*, 219–221, M. Habdas, 'Tortious Liability in Polish Law for Damages Caused by Minors', in B. Heiderhoff &G. İmij (eds), *Tort Law In Poland, Germany and Europe*, (München: Sellier, 2009), 105–121.
35. S. Kalus, 'Article 12 Commentary', in M. Habdas, M. Fras (eds) *Kodeks cywilny. Komentarz. Tom I. Część ogólna (art. 1-125)* (Warszawa: Wolters Kluwer, 2018), 71–72.

the statutory representative. Moreover, as a result of a recent amendment to the FGC the principle has been introduced in Article 95 §2 FGC that as far as juridical acts are concerned in relation to which no consent is required, the child should merely pay attention to the parents' opinion and indications as to the act. Such juridical acts do not have to be made by statutory representatives and the child is not under the duty to follow parental guidelines and warnings.

49. However, the right to represent a child undergoes certain restrictions in situations where unlimited exercise of representation on the part of the parents could be detrimental to the minor. In certain specific circumstances, provisions of the FGC shall exclude the right of any of the parents to represent the child. In the first place, this would be the case of juridical acts between children who both remain under control of the same parents, where a possibility emerges to privilege one of the children to the detriment of the other one. On similar grounds, in order to eliminate possible detriment to the child, juridical acts between the child and one of the parents or a parent's spouse (where the child comes, for instance, from a previous marriage of the parent who exercises parental authority). Such representation shall still be admissible in cases which do not result in a breach of the child's interest, namely the following situations:

(1) where the juridical act consists in the child's gratuitous enrichment, which in practice may refer to donations without any additional command;
(2) where the juridical act concerns alimony independent of the other parent (conclusion of a respective contract with the other parent, representation of the child in alimony proceedings) – Article 98 §2 FGC.

50. When it comes to representation of the child in proceedings referring to determination of his or her origin (establishment of motherhood or its denial – Article 61,[10] denial of marital paternity – Article 70, annulment of paternity acknowledgement – Article 80, judicial ascertainment of paternity – Article 84 §4 FGC), courts generally recognize in this respect the right of representation by one of the parents, but such representation is redundant, since such actions may as well be brought by the parents in their own name. Additionally, after reaching full age, the child may, once the parental authority expires, initiate the proceedings on his or her own motion.[36]

---

36. Smyczyński, *Prawo*, 220; K. Piasecki, 'Article 84 Commentary', in K. Piasecki (ed.), *Kodeks rodzinny i opiekuńczy. Komentarz* (Warszawa: Lexis Nexis, 2011), 689–695; Wolter, Ignatowicz, Stefaniuk, *Prawo*, 336 et seq.

Chapter 2. Registration of Civil Status

§1. Bodies Administering the Births, Marriages, Deaths Register

51. As pointed out above, one of the principles of Polish family law is the participation of an official factor in the formation and modification of family law relationships. The official shall most frequently be the Registrar of a BMDRO who performs acts in the area of registration of civil status pursuant to Article 9 of the Act of 28 November 2014 – Civil Status Registry Law (CSRL).[37] These acts have a very crucial character since certificates from the register of civil status make the exclusive evidence of the conditions entered in the registry, and their non-conformity with the actual state of affairs may be proven solely in judicial proceedings (Article 3 CSRL). Moreover, many acts which create legal relationships entered into the register are made in the presence of the Registrar, before whom the parties make respective declarations. As far as the legal position of the Registrar is concerned, he or she cannot be considered a mere administrator of the parties' declarations of intent. These declarations undergo verification on the part of the Registrar, who may decline their administration or refuse to pass over a document, for example, certifying the lack of circumstances excluding entry into marriage. Where doubts exist, the Registrar may refer the case to the court for judicial decision.

52. Among the certificates from the register, which bear fundamental significance in the area of family law, one should enumerate the certificates of birth, marriage and death. They are issued by the Registrar, competent for the place where the respective registered event took place. When it comes to reporting the birth of a child where neither parent resides within the range of territorial competence of the BMDRO proper for the birth, such an event may be reported in the BMDRO of the place of residence of both parents, or one of them. In exceptional cases, death of a natural person may be reported in the BMDRO of the last place of residence of the deceased or the place of his or her burial.

53. When it comes to the conclusion of marriage in the BMDRO, the legislator has abandoned the former strict rules of territorial competence of the BMDRO proper for the place of residence of one of the spouses and accepted instead that matrimony can be formed in a BMDRO of the parties' choosing. As far as the marriage certificate is concerned, this is prepared by the BMDRO officiating the wedding ceremony.

54. There are certain exceptions to this rule in which the competent BMDRO shall be the BMDRO proper for the Śródmieście district of the capital city of Warsaw. This shall be the case where:

(1) the birth of a child took place on a Polish registered seagoing vessel or aircraft – as regards the certificate of birth;

37. Consolidated version: Journal of Statutes 2020, item 463, with subsequent amendments.

(2) judicial ascertainment of death or pronouncement of death has taken place;
(3) death took place on a Polish registered seagoing vessel or aircraft;
(4) a soldier on active service or some other person dies while allocated to a military unit;
(5) death concerns a person killed in, or who died as a result of, military action.

55. Moreover, many declarations of crucial importance in family law can be made in any BMDRO. This refers to such declarations as a statement concerning the acknowledgement of paternity or giving a child the surname of the mother's husband, the statement of a divorced spouse regarding her return to the use of her former surname and a petition for entry in the certificate of birth that the child's parents formed a marriage.[38]

56. The question of competence of the BMDRO is specifically framed in a situation where a man acknowledges paternity of a conceived but unborn child, or where the paternity of a child already born has been acknowledged before a consul. The entry of the declaration of the child's father in the registry and preparation of the certificate of birth takes place in the BMDRO of the mother's place of residence, and where the child has already been born – in the BMDRO where the birth certificate was prepared. Persons who are without a permanent place of residence in Poland, which is now a frequent occurrence in relation to illegal immigration, too are capable of making family law acts which have to be concluded in a BMDRO. For them, the competent office shall be the BMDRO serving their last place of residence in Poland. Where there was no previous place of residence, or where a consul applies for the entry, the competent office shall be the BMDRO for the Śródmieście district of the capital city of Warsaw.

§2. BMDRO and Certificates

57. Registers of civil status are administered separately for each category of certified events. Consequently, there are registers of births, matrimonies and deaths (Article 19 CSRL). They also include documents and declarations made simultaneously or after the preparation of a civil status certificate, as well as documents handed over to the offices by courts and other state authorities. These documents make the basis of entries into the register of civil status. As a result, courts and other state authorities are obliged to send to the BMDRO respective copies of binding and final decisions. Without these, it would be impossible to properly administer the civil status registry, modify entries or make respective remarks in the content of an existing certificate in the case of events which affect the content or validity of an entry.

58. The preparation of entries in the register of civil status, certificates of birth or death are usually triggered by oral reports of the interested parties, or by written

38. Cf. A. Czajkowska & E. Pachniewska, *Prawo o aktach stanu cywilnego. Komentarz.* (Warszawa: Lexis Nexis, 2009), 40 et seq.

reports originating from state authorities, health care institutions, physicians or midwives. The Registrar is obliged to make an evaluation of these reports and, in particular, to request corroborative evidence confirming the verity of the data reported in order to make a respective entry in the births, marriages and deaths register. As an example, when a death is reported, before preparing the death certificate, the Registrar must first examine the certificate of death issued by a physician in which he or she can find the data concerning the deceased person and confirmation of the date of death, as well as its precise time expressed in hours and minutes or, where the deceased died before the discovery of the remains, the estimated date and time of death certified by a coroner.

59. Registers of civil status are not registries open to public scrutiny. Exceptionally, and only with the consent of the Registrar of the BMDRO, they can be made available to authorized representatives of state authorities, and to scientific institutions for research purposes.

60. Registers of civil status bear the feature of durability since it is inadmissible to make any changes other than corrections to obvious typographical errors. There may also arise a situation in which an entry in the births, marriages, deaths register requires to be cancelled. This is carried out by a body of higher rank than the Registrar of the BMDRO who, for example, made the later entry in a case where two entries were made for the same event. Another reason for cancellation of an entry in the register is a condition where the entry certifies an event that is untrue, or where in the preparation of the entry certain irregularities took place which served to lessen its force of evidence. In the case of a mistaken or imprecise formulation of an entry, the entry is rectified. Moreover, it is possible to formulate the proper content of the entry where it has been cancelled out and is to be replaced with a new one, or where the certificate of birth or marriage has not been prepared and/or cannot be made in the manner prescribed in the provisions of the CSRL. All of these issues are decided upon by a court in non-litigation mode, at the request of an interested person, public prosecutor or BMDRO Registrar.

61. If the whole or a part of a particular register becomes lost or perished, the need to reconstruct the content of the register emerges, together with additional remarks. The motion for reconstruction of the births, marriages, deaths register can be submitted by interested parties or by state authorities (Article 133 CSRL). The reconstruction may also take place ex officio, in accordance with the provisions contained in Article 35 CSRL. An entry in the births, marriages, deaths register may be supplemented where it fails to contain all relevant data which should be included therein. Cancellation of an entry is yet another option.

62. The CSRL prescribes in much detail the periods to report events referred to in the certificates of birth, marriage and death, names the persons obliged to report these events, envisages data which should be entered in the register and the grounds for preparation of the particular type of entry (Articles 52–95 CSRL). Another crucial question is the problem of issuing copies of the entries and certificates. Out of the register, the following can be passed over: complete and abridged copies, certificates concerning entries in the civil state register or their lack, as well as certificates concerning the loss or destruction of an entry in the births, marriages and deaths register. Copies and certificates pertaining to particular entries are issued at the request of a court or other state authority, a person whose civil status has been recorded in the register, his or her descendants, ascendants, siblings, spouse or statutory representative. When it comes to copies of the entries in the births, marriages, deaths register and certificates of particular entries or their lack, they can be issued as well at the request of other persons if they demonstrate their legal interest, as well as at the request of a non-governmental organization if it is justified by the statutory aims of such organization and favoured by important public interest. Certificates stating particular entries or parts thereof in the births, marriages, deaths register that have been lost or destroyed may also be issued at the request of other interested persons.[39]

39. Cf. Czajkowska & Pachniewska, *Prawo o aktach*, 244 et seq.

Chapter 3. Personal Interests of Natural Persons

63. One of the most crucial legal regulations relating to natural persons are the rules on personal interests (included in Articles 23 and 24 PCC), which are enumerated in the Code in a non-exclusive manner in Article 23 PCC, and which can be derived from international conventions to which Poland is a party, oftentimes from additional protocols attached to and forming part of those conventions. This provision points to certain exemplary personal rights of a natural person, including in particular health, liberty, dignity, freedom of conscience, name or pseudonym, image, secrecy of correspondence, inviolability of property including place of residence and various types of creation. Other personal interests, even though not expressly set out in the discussed provision undergo legal protection as well; these could be, among other things, intimacy, privacy of personal life, sense of belonging to a particular sex, life in proper environmental conditions and memory of a deceased member of family.

64. Personal rights of natural persons are protected by law, which protection safeguards individuals from their unlawful violations. In a situation where these interests are threatened, the person so entitled may demand that the offending party cease and desist such action unless the act itself is not unlawful. Once personal interests have actually been breached, the offended person may demand that the party responsible for the breach remedy the effects of the violation, which may consist in the form of a public apology (published in the media), or the payment of a monetary sum in compensation, or the donation of a monetary sum to a social cause specified by the offended party. If the breach of personal interest brings about tangible loss on the part of the offended person, he or she may claim respective compensation on general grounds (Articles 415 PCC and following).

65. Personal interests are protected not only by remedies set out in the PCC but also in further provisions, for instance, in authorship law, which gives the overall protection a multidimensional character.

Chapter 4. Name and Surname

§1. Composition of Name and Surname of a Natural Person

66. Names and surnames are used to identify natural persons as individuals. In Poland, as indeed elsewhere in the world. forenames alone bore that function long before surnames came into being, although often suffixed with a secondary title to differentiate one 'John' from another 'John' living in the same community Such secondary titles were typically derived from the individual's place of birth, their trade or profession or a particular physical characteristic and they differed from surnames in the contemporary sense, insofar that they did not pass from one generation to another, nor to the spouse.

67. In Polish literature and legislation, it has been accepted that a surname in its contemporary understanding must be preceded by one or two forenames. Both names play an important role in the life of a natural person, not only relating to his or her individualization but also in making a statement as to their physical existence, belonging to a particular family or civil status. As personal interests of an individual, they undergo civil law protection. A specific role of the surname cropped up in the contemporary economic environment, where the forename and surname of an entrepreneur make in light of Article 43^4 PCC, the commercial name of a natural person acting as a business.[40]

68. The dominant stance in the literature is that the surname makes a formal, external and permanent quality of a human being which in connection with the forename determines the individual's identity, and constitutes an important part of a person's civil status. The surname identifies the individual in the public context. The forename, just as the surname, enables the individualization of a human being. It forms a vital element of personal identity but not an element of the person's civil (family) status. It forms a part of personal status instead. As opposed to surname, the name bears in the first place the function of private individualization. It should be added that the name points to another element of the personal status of a natural person, that is gender. Traditionally, under the provisions of Polish law, the first name of a female person should end in 'a', which marks the difference between a woman and man (e.g., a man: Stanislaw, a woman: Stanislawa'), although there are exceptions to this.

---

40. Cf. P. Ruczkowski, *Ustawa o zmianie imienia i nazwiska. Komentarz* (Warszawa: ABC, 2010); P. Pinior, 'Article 43^4 Commentary', in M. Habdas, M. Fras (eds) *Kodeks cywilny. Komentarz. Tom I. Część ogólna (art. 1-125)* (Warszawa: Wolters Kluwer, 2018), 318 – 319.

§2. SURNAME

I. Acquisition of Surname

69. The acquisition of surname constitutes an individual within the family and is linked either to the exercise of parental authority over the child or a judicial decision related to the determination of the child's origin. Also, the person preparing the certificate of birth may choose the surname where the child's parents remain unknown. More deliberations on this issue can be found in the chapter on the child's origin.

70. It should be, however, mentioned that although 'surname' is a legal concept, there is in fact no legal definition of this term in the provisions of law. Some scholars define it as a formal, external and permanent feature of a person, making a constituent part of his or her civil status, which in combination with the forename individualizes the natural person and determines his or her identity.[41]

71. These issues are interesting since one can only agree with the opinion that surname is a concept relevant to various branches of law: civil and family law, administrative law, constitutional law and public international law.

II. Change of Name

72. The statute regulating the administrative law mode of change of name was enacted on 17 October 2008.[42] New legislation in this respect was connected with the necessity to adjust provisions of Polish law to EU standards, as well as the norms of the International Convention on Civil Status, and the CSRL.

73. The statute retained the binding status of the fundamental principles concerning names and surnames, supplementing these by a number of new solutions. Just as before, the change of either name may take place only at the request of the party whom the change concerns or a child's statutory representative. In any case, the capacity to initiate proceedings does not relate to third parties or public administrative bodies which could act ex officio. This would constitute an excessive intervention in the personal situation of an individual. In the new statute, it has been clearly stipulated what information must be included in the petition for change of name and what documents should be attached to this petition. The legislator also envisaged the duty to justify the motion. However, the catalogue of persons entitled to change their name has broadened. Apart from Polish citizens and stateless persons with a place of residence in Poland, it now also includes foreign nationals who

41. Z Duniewska, 'Zmiana imion i nazwisk', in M. Stahl (ed.), *Materialne prawo administracyjne- poje ̨cia, instytucje, zasady*, (Warszawa: Difin, 2005), 73, *See also*, S. Łakoma, 'Rejestracja i zmiana nazwiska', *RPEiS*, no. 4 (2008): 65.

42. Consolidated version: Journal of Statutes 2020; item 707, with subsequent amendments.

have acquired refugee status in Poland, which allows them to hasten their assimilation into Polish society. However, in their case, a change of name is only admissible where connected with a threat to the applicant's right to life, health, freedom and personal safety.

74. Another crucial issue regulated in the new statute concerns the interpretation of the terms 'change of forename' and 'change of surname'. The former denotes a change to another name or modification to the spelling of an existing one. The latter refers to the replacement of the old surname by a new one, change in the spelling of the surname or adjustment of the surname to the grammatical form proper for the female or male gender.

75. Just as it was the case in the previous legal condition, the new statute provides for the admissibility of changing the name or surname with the view to important reasons. The previous prerequisites, such as a surname which sounds like a forename or sounds like a foreign surname, have been crossed out. However, the legislator added as a premise a previous unlawful change of a forename or surname and enabled adjustment of either to the one borne in accordance with another state's legislation if the applicant is also a national of that country. The introduction of such possibility has been dictated by the necessity to adjust Polish legislation to EU law. In addition, it accounts for the recent serious problem of labour migration of Polish citizens abroad, connected with the impossibility to use Polish fore or surnames because of the difficulties concerning their pronunciation in another country (e.g., surnames like: 'Brzeszczykiewicz' or 'Drzaszcz'). The Act on the change of names and surnames also protects historical surnames, by excluding the possibility to change a person's surname to a historical one, renowned in the area of culture, sciences, political, social or military activity, unless the applicant has members of the family of the particular name (Article 5 of the Act). The above regulation is to enhance the protection of names which form a part of the nation's cultural heritage.

76. Change of name may be allowed only for important reasons, which must be significant to the applicant alone and not to other persons. Nonetheless, the evaluation of his or her premise must be based on objectified criteria. In particular, this might be the case where the application concerns:

(1) a name or surname of ridiculing character or incompatible with human dignity;
(2) a foreign-sounding name or surname;
(3) a surname which sounds like a forename;
(4) a name or surname borne in accordance with the law of a foreign state where the applicant is also a national of that state (Article 4 section 1 of the Act).

77. The application shall be dismissed in the lack of the 'important reasons' envisaged in statutory provisions, or where the negative premises set out in Article 3 of the Act are at play.[43]

43. Łakoma, 'Rejestracja', 75.

Chapter 5. Nationality

78. In Polish law, nationality signifies a legal bond between a natural person and the state or the belonging of a particular person to a given state. This quality has a crucial significance in the law of conflict as the basic personal connector in the sphere of Private International Law (PIL) rules pertaining to the capacity to perform juridical acts of a natural person, family law and succession law relationships. Provisions of the Hague Convention of 12 April 1930 on Certain Questions Relating to the Conflict of Nationality Law[44] envisage that the problem of whether a person is a national of a particular state is decided by the law of that state. In practice, various countries specify these issues according to completely different principles. Most frequently, the relevant factor is the origin of citizens of a particular country, but nationality may also be determined by reference to the fact of birth on the territory of the respective state, as well as on seagoing vessels and aircraft operating under its flag. Another ground for nationality is marriage with a citizen of the country or running for a position in some elected authority in the respective state.

79. In light of the Act of 2 April 2009 on Polish citizenship,[45] Polish nationals are persons who enjoy Polish citizenship, and the entry into marriage with a foreigner does not result in automatic acquisition of the spouse's nationality. Upon birth, a child acquires Polish nationality if at least one of the parents is a Polish citizen. A child born on Polish territory to unknown parents or parents whose nationality cannot be identified or who are stateless acquires Polish citizenship. If a minor child is found on Polish territory and his or her parents are unknown, he or she also acquires Polish nationality. In addition, a child of no more than 16 years of age adopted by at least one Polish national, acquires Polish nationality.

80. Another possibility of acquiring Polish nationality is naturalization by the President of the Republic of Poland. A foreigner may be naturalized if he or she has filed a request, which among other information, contains statements concerning knowledge of the Polish language, professional achievements, political and social activities, and sources of income. Awarding Polish citizenship to such a person results *ex lege* in the naturalization of the children who have been submitted to his or her exclusive parental authority. The same effect is going to be produced if the other parent gives consent before a proper authority to the acquisition of Polish citizenship by the child. Polish nationality may also be acquired by persons who have lived in Poland for a specified number of years on the basis of special permits (Articles 30–37).

---

44. Journal of Statutes 1937, no. 47, item 361.
45. Consolidated version: Journal of Statutes 2020, item 347, with subsequent amendments.

Chapter 6. Domicile and Residence

81. The place of residence of a natural person is significant to the legal position of the individual. The notion has nothing to do with administrative law registration. Residence is designated (pursuant to Article 25 PCC) by the locality where the natural person resides with the intent of permanent stay. It makes not only the central point of life interests of every human being but also an element which constitutes, along with nationality, the personal connector of a natural person which points to the law proper for evaluation of personal status. In accordance with Article 28 PCC, a natural person may have only one place of residence.

82. It is noteworthy that certain persons have a so-called derived place of residence, independent of their will. In particular, pursuant to Article 26 PCC the place of residence of a child under parental authority is the place of residence of the parents or of the parent who exercises parental authority. As a result, the child's parents often contest with one another for parental control over their child, most frequently in divorce proceedings where, because they cease to live together, each wants the child to stay with them as opposed to with the other parent. Moreover, this decision is crucial for resolving which of the spouses and to what extent is going to be awarded the right to the matrimonial home. If both parents exercise parental authority equally, and they have separate places of residence, their child's residence is the place where the child normally resides on a permanent basis (Article 26 §2 sentence 1 PCC). If the child stays with neither parent on a permanent basis, his or her place of residence shall be determined by the guardianship court (Article 26 §2 FGC, sentence 2). When a natural person remains under guardianship (a child who does not undergo parental authority of either parent or a person who is fully incapacitated), his or her place of residence shall be the place of residence of the appointed guardian (Article 27 PCC).

83. Domicile is of primary importance not only in substantive law. There are many provisions of conflict law which provide for the connector of the place of residence of a natural person, both as an independent connector and auxiliary one taken into account for lack of nationality. It should be borne in mind that – as with the nationality of a given person – the place of residence is also dependent on national legal systems, and the fact which national law (if any) dictates that the person has a place of residence within the respective country. In consequence, residence as a connector is an independent concept of PIL and should be treated autonomously, not on the basis of national law and internal definitions binding in particular states.

Chapter 7. Mentally Handicapped Persons

84. Neither Polish civil law nor family and guardianship provisions use the notion of mentally handicapped persons, which does not mean that these persons fall outside the range of interest of these two branches of private law.

85. First of all, provisions on consent allow in the most general way to capture the situation of such persons, especially when consent was given with lack of awareness or discretion (Articles 82 and 945 §1 point 1 PCC). These provisions stipulate that a declaration of intent of a given person is invalid if it comes from a person who, for whatever reason, was in a condition excluding conscious or free decision and manifestation of intent. Article 82 PCC sets an exemplary list of causes of such a condition: mental sickness, mental deficiency or other disturbances, even temporary in nature, of mental capacities. They must occur at the time of making the juridical act, that is the statement of intent which makes an obligatory, though not always sufficient, element of any juridical act. Beyond any doubt, this vice of consent may be invoked not only by mentally handicapped persons but also by persons temporarily placed in such a condition (e.g., high fever, brain damage, alcohol intoxication, drug abuse).

86. Slightly more significant is the psychological situation of a natural person in the area of family law, especially in questions related to marriage. In this case, the rule of Article 12 §1 FGC provides that a mentally ill or mentally deficient person cannot enter into marriage. This means that a person before whom the marriage is concluded, i.e., the Registrar of a BMDRO, the priest of a church with which the Polish State made a respective agreement, or a Polish consul abroad, has the right to refuse to accept the declaration of entry into marriage if he or she suspects that a mental deficiency exists. If the official concerned fails to spot this mental condition of the potential spouse, marriage is formed effectively, although it may subsequently be annulled.

87. Since various cases of mental illnesses and various levels of mental deficiency can be distinguished, the FGC provides for the possibility of entry into marriage by a person suffering from such an illness without danger of annulment if the court grants permission to form a marriage including such a person. When making a decision in this respect, the court takes into consideration whether the health or mental condition of the person involved does not pose a threat to the marriage or future offspring, or whether the betrothed has not been fully incapacitated because of the illness or deficiency. Quite often mental sicknesses are hereditary in nature and on such occasions, the court shall deny permission on eugenic grounds, even though the formation of marriage is purposeful and beneficial bearing in mind its effects, especially for the sick person. Another situation refers to a fully incapacitated person. In light of Article 11 FGC, such persons cannot enter into marriage, and if such marriage becomes formed, it may subsequently be annulled. The mental condition of a person willing to enter into matrimony is meaningful at the moment the person makes the declaration of intent to enter into marriage. As a consequence, if at this particular moment the betrothed was in a condition excluding conscious manifestation of his or her will, the betrothed may demand annulment of the marriage concluded in the described circumstances. However, he or she may not initiate annulment proceedings after the lapse of six months from the date of expiry of the mental condition vitiating consent.

88. Where conditions such as mental illness or deficiency, or other disturbances, affect particular persons to such an extent that they are unable to control their behaviour, or if there arises a need of assistance for that person in matters of everyday life, the possibility emerges to deprive them of the capacity to perform juridical acts by means of full incapacitation or to restrict their capacity to perform juridical acts by way of partial incapacitation. These issues are covered by provisions of personal law which have been placed by the legislator in the PCC (Articles 13 and 16 PCC), in the PCPC, which regulates the procedure in incapacitation cases (Articles 544–560^{1} PCPC), as well as questions of guardianship and curatorship over such persons, regulated in the FGC, under Title III: Guardianship and Curatorship.[46]

46. S. Kalus, 'Article 145 Commentary', in K. Piasecki (ed.) *Kodeks,* 1014 et seq.; S. Kalus, *Opieka nad osobą całkowicie ubezwłasnowolnioną* (Katowice: Wydawnictwo Uniwersytetu Śląskiego, 1989).

Part II. Family Law

Chapter 1. Marriage

89. Legal regulation covering the formation of marriage contained in the FGC has undergone a significant evolution. Initially, as long as until 1993 when the Concordat between Poland and the Holy See was concluded, church marriages were allowed, but only if the parties had previously entered into a civil marriage before the Registrar of a BMDRO, which solution was based on the principle of the secular character of matrimony. A priest who officiated the conclusion of a church marriage prior to the civil marriage could be fined. Only the conclusion of the Concordat brought about legal grounds to accept that the formation of a church marriage could produce civil law effects. Moreover, it has been accepted that there is no reason to deny other church matrimonies of different denominations the same legal effects as marriages formed before a Catholic priest, as long as a particular statute covering the relations of a particular denomination to the Polish State so provides. Thus presently, entering into marriage before a priest does not involve just Catholic priests but also the priests of such churches as the: Polish Autocephalous Orthodox Church, Evangelical-Augsburg Church and Evangelical and Reformed Church. Formation of an effective marriage before a priest became possible only after the amendment of Article 1 FGC by the Act on the amendment of Acts: FGC, PCPC, CSRL and on the relation of the State towards the Catholic Church in the Republic of Poland and certain other statutes.[47]

90. Unfortunately, the provision of Article 10 of the Concordat with the Holy See has not, it seems, been properly formulated. The rule provides that from the moment of entry into marriage, the canonical matrimony produces the same legal effects as a civil marriage under Polish law if:

(1) there are no matrimonial impediments between the betrothed which derive from Polish law;
(2) the betrothed have declared that they wish their matrimony to bring about civil law effects;
(3) the entry into marriage has been entered into the births, marriages, deaths register at the request passed to the Registrar of the BMDRO within five days from the formation of matrimony.

47. Journal of Statutes, no. 117, item 757.

91. This rule has been improperly drafted since the provision makes matrimony dependent on whether or not there are impediments to matrimony provided for in Articles 10–16 FGC. Such an approach is wholly incorrect, as in Polish secular law a violation of matrimonial impediments never results directly in the non-existence of the marriage. Lack of this type of violation does not even amount to a prerequisite of matrimonial validity, since Polish law provides for only one type of sanction for breaching the impediments, namely the possibility to annul the marriage, but not its automatic invalidity. In fact, it is difficult to understand how or why a violation of the impediment of age, full incapacitation, mental sickness or mental deficiency, affinity or blood relation, adoption, maintenance of previous matrimony and finally vitiated power of authority, should result in the non-existence of civil law results of a church matrimony. The formulation of the discussed provision appears still more ill-considered when we take into account that vitiated consent on the part of the betrothed does not pose any impediment to a valid matrimony. In light of secular law, the results shall be precisely the same as in the case of statutory impediments, the possibility to annul the marriage is going to arise.

92. This issue was captured more accurately by the statutes on the relation of the Polish State to respective denominations where the text stipulates that matrimony concluded in the form provided by church law produces also the same civil law effects as marriage concluded before the Registrar of a BMDRO as long as the requirements (and not impediments) set out in the FGC are met. Below, the prerequisites of the existence of matrimony, without the fulfilment of which a marriage cannot be considered as legally formed, are presented in more detail.

93. It should be emphasized that Polish law knows three alternative forms of marriage conclusion. These are:

(1) secular wedding – the marriage is concluded before the Registrar of a BMDRO and produces the effects envisaged by Polish law (Article 1 §1 FGC);
(2) the so-called concordat wedding – which is not the most fortunate name, since the marriage can be concluded before any priest entitled to administer declarations of intent to enter into marriage by way of an agreement between a particular congregation or church and the Republic of Poland. The act becomes subsequently registered by the Registrar of a BMDRO and, likewise, produces secular effects, as provided for in Article 1 §2 FGC. In the case of denial to register the marriage on the part of the Head Registrar, for instance, where the statutory period provided for the priest to report the marriage has expired, the matrimony shall have an exclusive canonical character and shall not produce civil law effects;
(3) wedding before a consul – marriage concluded by Polish citizens abroad, before a Polish consul or other person entitled to perform the functions of consul (Article 1 §4 FGC).

§1. Capacity to Enter into Marriage

I. Prerequisites of Marriage Formation

94. Prerequisites of marriage formation have been formulated in the first place in Article 1 §1 FGC. This provision enumerates the following premises:

(1) gender difference between the betrothed, which implies inadmissibility of matrimony not only between persons of the same sex but also between a hermaphrodite and a man or hermaphrodite and a woman;
(1) simultaneous presence of the betrothed;
(2) their declarations of intent concerning entry into marriage;
(3) made before the Registrar of a BMDRO or the priest of a respective church;
(4) if the matrimony is concluded before a priest, the marriage must be registered by the Registrar of the BMDRO who, on his or her own initiative, may refuse to register the marriage if the priest should fail to deposit the requisite declarations of the betrothed with the BMDRO within the five-day period prescribed.

95. Non-fulfilment of any of these prerequisites results in the condition where the matrimony cannot be considered as concluded – it is a so-called *matrimonium non existens*. If the certificate of marriage has been drafted in the absence of any of these prerequisites, anyone who has a legal interest is entitled to bring an action to determine the non-existence of matrimony. In a situation where such a certificate has not been prepared at all, there is no reason to institute such action since, pursuant to Article 4 CSRL, the registers of civil status constitute exclusive evidence to support the events entered into the registry. Their inconformity with the truth may be proven only in judicial proceedings. As regards the prerequisite mentioned in para. 94 (4) above, one should additionally invoke Article 87 section 5 CSRL, pursuant to which the Registrar of the BMDRO may refuse to issue a marriage certificate for matrimony formed in compliance with Article 1 §2 FGC if the five-day period prescribed for the priest to deposit the requisite documents with the Registrar (Article 8 §3 FGC) has not been observed. Where this occurs, the interested party may refer the case to a competent court serving the district in which the BMDRO is situated and apply for a decision whether the refusal to register the marriage on the part of the Registrar was justified in light of the circumstances of the case.

96. Another important prerequisite is the simultaneous presence of the betrothed while making their declarations of intent to enter into marriage. The only exception to this concerns the situation where one of the betrothed is unable to be present and the matrimony is concluded by proxy. In this instance, the simultaneous presence of the attendant betrothed and the proxy of the absent betrothed is required.

97. The betrothed must make a declaration before a proper person concerning their entry into marriage. No other declarations, for instance, about the non-existence of impediments to marry are necessary to make during the wedding ceremony. As far as the person before whom the statements must be made is concerned, he or she is not the addressee of the declarations only the commissioner. Provisions of law stipulate extensively who the person entitled to commission declarations of intent to marry may be. As far as the Registrar of a BMDRO is concerned, the special requirements which refer to this official derive from the CSRL. In the case of a church matrimony with civil law effects, the list of posts entitled to commission the declarations of the betrothed and draft a notice which serves as a basis for the entry into register and elaboration of the marriage certificate is contained in the Announcement of the Minister of the Ministry of the Interior and Administration of 21 February 2008.[48] The Announcement sets out the categories of entitled persons within the respective churches and congregations. It follows from the list that the respective rights are vested in persons holding particular posts in the Catholic Church, Polish Autocephalous Orthodox Church, Evangelical-Augsburg Church, Evangelical and Reformed Church, Evangelical Methodist Church, Christian Baptist Church, Seventh-Day Adventists, Polish Catholic Church, Association of Jewish Religious Communities, Old Catholic Mariavite Church, and the United Pentecostal Church.

98. When it comes to the last of the required prerequisites of marriage existence, its inclusion by the legislator was to reconcile the possibility to enter into church marriage with civil law effects and the principle of the secular character of matrimony. Here, one may speak of civil law effects only once the matrimony becomes registered by a BMDRO Registrar. The role of this official is not confined to the mere act of registration. Before entry into a church marriage, the betrothed are obliged to present themselves to the Registrar in person and to declare that no legal impediments to the matrimony are known to exist. The priest, for his part, may not proceed to commission their statements of intent to marry before the betrothed present a respective notice issued by the Registrar.

99. The declarations referred to above delimitate the starting date of the mandatory one-month period provided for in Article 4 FGC, which has to elapse before the actual declarations of intent to enter into marriage can be made. This is the so-called *tempus deliberandi* or cooling-off period; a time for the betrothed to reconsider their respective positions and decide whether to proceed with the marriage or withdraw from it. Such period was intended to serve as a regulated substitute for the institution of engagement, which is unknown to Polish law. While true that in certain areas of society, engagement is accepted as a normal practice preceding the wedding, it nevertheless remains an informal undertaking that has not been regulated in any provision of law.

---

48. Monitor of Laws 2008, no. 18, item 191.

100. Wedding ceremonies constitute a costly undertaking and particularly so in Poland where they tend to be quite lavish events catering to many people. Consequently, should one of the betrothed withdraw from the marriage near to or after the conclusion of those preparations, it can leave the other party and/or their immediate relatives facing considerable financial loss. The person or persons so harmed may demand compensation for such loss on general grounds, Article 415 PCC. However, they would have to demonstrate before the court that the loss incurred was the result of a tortious act on the part of the jilting party and show an adequate causal link between the loss and that party's conduct. Polish law does not differentiate whether the defaulting party acted intentionally or not. In both instances, his or her liability will be the same.

II. Capacity to Perform Juridical Acts and Capacity to Enter into Marriage

101. The capacity to perform juridical acts has no direct impact on the capacity to marry, whereas the capacity to marry may influence an individual's capacity to perform juridical acts. For example, a minor of at least 16 years of age who enters into marriage, regardless of the impediment of age on the date of matrimony, becomes a major with full capacity to perform juridical acts.

102. If we are to consider premises of the capacity to perform juridical acts, these come down to age and lack of incapacitation. As far as the age impediment to marriage is concerned, a person under 18 is not capable of entering into matrimony. However, as illustrated above, this provision does not make the capacity to marry directly dependent on full age, and the full age itself may be acquired by earlier matrimony. Moreover, this majority does not disappear even if the marriage terminates or is annulled. Notwithstanding, in a situation where a woman who acquired majority as a consequence of marriage wishes to enter into a new matrimony if the former has terminated (for instance, as a result of the death of the other spouse), the new marriage requires judicial consent in the manner of Article 10 §1 FGC if that woman has not yet turned 18. Such an example defines the difference between acquisition of the capacity to marry and acquisition of the capacity to perform juridical acts.

103. Similarly, the second of the premises of the capacity to marry, lack of incapacitation, depicts the difference between the capacity to marry and the capacity to perform juridical acts. As far as partial incapacitation is concerned, such a situation has no direct influence on the capacity to enter into marriage. Only full incapacitation constitutes an impediment to matrimony, but if the betrothed was incapacitated prior to the matrimony and the Registrar of the BMDRO failed to detect this condition, the marriage still remains valid as long as it has not been annulled. However, any juridical act of such person (except contracts referring to minor and common affairs of everyday life) is absolutely invalid. Where the marriage is entered into by a partially incapacitated person, his or her incapacitation does not affect the matrimony unless this person suffers from mental sickness or mental deficiency, in which case, the impediment set out in Article 12 FGC becomes applicable. If the partial incapacitation has been adjudicated as a result of mere mental disorders of the affected person, there are no legal grounds to annul the matrimony he or she entered into. Such a person is also going to enjoy partial capacity to perform juridical acts in the understanding of the PCC provisions. He or she has to acquire consent of the statutory representative for any juridical act which results in acquiring an obligation or disposing of an asset, but the statutory representative has no right to make any act or give consent as far as the matrimony itself is concerned. At most, the court may give consent for such a person to enter into marriage pursuant to Article 12 §1 FGC.

104. The norms of international law, especially Article 12 of the European Convention on Human Rights, establish a fundamental right of a man and a woman to enter into matrimony and form a family. Consequently, the problem of conditions of matrimony set out in national laws is not entirely left to the discretion of states party to the Convention. While it is true that the possibility of establishing certain restrictions on the part of the countries is unquestioned, the margin of freedom in this respect should be defined quite narrowly. This follows from two decisions of the European Court of Human rights (ECtHR) in the cases *Frasik v. Poland* and *Jeremowicz v. Poland.*[49] While these limitations may be based on universally acknowledged principles of public interest, in particular pertaining to the capacity to enter into marriage, consent, prohibited degree of consanguinity, or the need to counteract bigamy or fictitious marriages, state authorities cannot and should not be authorized to make the evaluation as to which relationship deserves protection and legalization as matrimony if matrimonial impediments envisaged in the statute are not in evidence.

III. Matrimonial Impediments

105. Matrimonial impediments provided for in the FGC are of a particular character. They exist to prevent the formation of marriages which: lack the prospect of proving successful (marriages formed at too early an age); violate the basic tenets of Poland's legal order (such as the principle of monogamy and non-recognition of incestuous relationships); show evidence of disparity between the intended and communicated will of the betrothed (vices of consent, defective power of proxy and the like). These impediments are obviously different in character, depending on the consequences of their violation. They are so-called irremovable impediments (e.g., lineal consanguinity or collateral kinship to a particular degree between siblings) or removable ones: by judicial consent (e.g., to matrimony of a minor woman who has already attained the age of at least 16 years) or by dissolution of the relationship which poses the impediment (e.g., dissolution of adoption). The emergence of any of these impediments and resultant awareness of the Registrar of a condition which excludes matrimony entitles this official to refuse to commission the declarations of intent to enter into marriage and, if doubts exist regarding such condition, he or she ought to refer the case to the court. Such circumstances also justify a refusal by the

49. Judgment of ECtHR of 5 Jan. 2010, LEX no. 534227, and of the same date LEX no. 534230.

Registrar to issue a notice certifying the non-existence of impediments to marriage which is required to be presented to the priest before a church wedding can proceed.

106. When it comes to a situation in which the Registrar has doubts as to whether matrimony can be formed and if any impediments occur which justify his or her refusal to commission a declaration of intent to enter into marriage, the court, after hearing the facts of the case, delivers a respective decision pursuant to Article 564 PCPC. This provision stipulates that refusal on the part of the Registrar may concern the following catalogue of situations: commission of the declarations of entry into marriage, issue of the notice on the non-existence of impediments to marriage which is to be handed to the priest before the conclusion of church marriage, as provided for in Article 4^1 FGC, granting permission to enter into marriage without complying with the statutory one-month cooling-off period preceding the submission of declarations of intent to marry, drafting the marriage certificate following a church wedding, and certification that a Polish citizen or a foreigner living in Poland who lacks citizenship is allowed to enter into marriage abroad in compliance with Polish law.

A. Age Impediment

107. Article 10 FGC, currently provides that a person under 18 cannot enter into marriage. Before the entry into force of the amendment of the FGC of 1998,[50] this provision was formulated in a slightly different way, setting an additional age threshold for men, who had to be at least 21 years of age. For women, it sufficed to have turned the age of 18. This derived not from unequal treatment of men and women but from the fact that the legislator took into consideration the compulsory requirement for many young men to serve in the military, which did not bring about the best prospects for a marriage formed before the period of such military service had come to an end. Also, in respect to the possibility of judicial consent to an earlier marriage, it was stipulated that an application may be filed by a man who was at least 18 years of age and a woman after turning the age of 16. Nowadays, particularly with a view to international conventions, it has been admitted that the provision breaches the principle of equality of the parties. In addition, compulsory military service has since been abolished, which proved decisive when it came to the need for amendment of the age prerequisite and introduction of an equal age threshold for both prospective spouses.

108. The current version of Article 10 §1 FGC provides for the possibility of judicial permission for earlier matrimony, but only in respect to a woman who has turned 16, and only where ‘important reasons’ for the formation of marriage emerge, i.e., where the circumstances of the case indicate that the matrimony is going to be concordant with the interest of the family. Judicature demonstrates that the most frequent reasons in this regard are pregnancy of the wife to be, the birth of a child to

50. Act of 21 May 1999, Journal of Statutes 1999, no. 52, item 532.

parents in an informal relationship and an existing state of cohabitation between the parties which leans toward the possibility of the woman conceiving a child.

109. Judicial proceedings leading to such permission take place before the guardianship court competent on the basis of the applicant's place of residence and in the non-litigation mode provided for in Article 561 §1 PCPC. In urgent situations (e.g., danger to the life of one of the betrothed), the competent court shall be the court serving the applicant's place of stay. In the proceedings leading to the grant of respective permission, the court hears the applicant, the other spouse to be and, where necessary, also the relatives of the future spouses. The testimony of these relatives, who do not necessarily have to be the statutory representatives of the minor wife to be, is a crucial element in determining whether the intended marriage will be in conformity with the interest of the family and public interest.

110. These general clauses are interpreted in such a way that it should be determined whether the marriage gives prospects for the future, what the mutual attitude of the future spouses is if they are sufficiently mature to take on family roles and how the maturity of their conjugal life is likely to develop. Moreover, the court examines if the prospective spouses have a chance to live together, whether they have sufficient funds to found the common family and support it, or if their relatives are able and willing to provide them with indispensable aid, both financial and personal.

111. In the proceedings, in order to fully shed light on the situation and in particular to determine the conditions in which the applicants for judicial permission live, the court may order a probation officer's report (Article 561^1 PCPC) to obtain specific information which allows to objectively determine the circumstances on which the decision in respect to granting the permission depends. If the court decides to award permission, analogically as in the case of other permits to marry in spite of a particular impediment, the court (as provided for in Article 561 §3 PCPC) should name the person with whom the marriage is to be concluded, which means that the permission would no longer be effective if the spouse to be wanted to use the decision for the purpose of entering into matrimony with another party.

B. Impediment of Full Incapacitation

112. Article 11 FGC provides for the inadmissibility of entry into marriage by a person fully incapacitated. Moreover, the Code does not allow for any form of judicial permission for matrimony with respect to such persons. The decision with regard to full incapacitation only concerns a person who is mentally sick, suffers from mental deficiency or mental disorders, has attained the age of at least 13 years (below this age the need to incapacitate does not arise) and remains unable to control their conduct. Such a person offers little by way of prospects for future functioning in marriage and due condition of matrimony. What also needs to be taken into consideration is that where incapacitation is adjudicated after the marriage has been formed, the mental condition of the spouse, especially mental disorders deriving from alcoholism, frequently leads to the breakdown of conjugal life. Thus, under such circumstances, it is better not to allow a marriage in which the prospects of durability are judged to be minimal.

113. It should be noted that only full incapacitation results in the inadmissibility of matrimony. As far as partial incapacitation is concerned (which is adjudicated in a situation where a minor over the age of 13 on the same grounds as in the case of full incapacitation is not quite fully incapacitated but requires assistance in conducting his or her affairs), this legal condition does not constitute an impediment to matrimony. Should full incapacitation be replaced by partial incapacitation after a marriage has been entered into, pursuant to Article 11 §3 FGC, that marriage cannot be annulled, even if it was concluded when the impediment was still fully active. Notwithstanding, if the marriage continues to function improperly, and if such condition should lead to a complete and permanent breakdown of conjugal life, divorce must be adjudicated if the spouses are willing to terminate the marriage.

C. Impediment of Mental Sickness or Mental Deficiency

114. This impediment is not superfluous in relation to the impediment covered by the previous provision. In the first place, one needs to recognize that in Polish society it is difficult to convince people of the protective function of full incapacitation. As a consequence, the attitude of relatives of a person suffering from mental disorders or mental deficiency is more often than not expressed in the form of caution and reserve. It is frequently claimed that full incapacitation, as a condition leading to deprivation of the capacity to perform juridical acts, constitutes a sui generis civil death of the affected person. One also has to take into consideration that the condition of a mentally sick person tends to fluctuate, between a remission period and one of complete lack of awareness – which establishes the grounds for incapacitation. That is why there is an abundance of people at large who have no control over their conduct whatsoever but have not been declared incapacitated. Nevertheless, the impediment of Article 12 seems correct, since it not only decreases the risk of forming a matrimony which does not offer the prospects of durability but also serves as a means to mitigate the risk of bringing offspring into the world affected by genetic disorders, as some mental sicknesses and deficiencies are frequently hereditary.

115. In addition, it should be emphasized that mental disorders are also a frequent reason for full incapacitation, particularly in relation to disorders stemming from alcohol addiction or drug abuse. They are not, however, by themselves an impediment to enter into marriage following from Article 13 FGC. They are going to influence the capacity to marry if the court, after implementing proper procedures, concludes that adjudication of full incapacitation is the correct solution taking into account not only the psychological and psychiatric nature of the particular disorder but also the fact that the affected party is of a particular age (at least 13) and remains unable to control his or her conduct. These are premises of full incapacitation.

116. The existence of the impediment discussed here is additionally justified by the fact that in the Polish legal system there is not only the possibility to adjudicate full incapacitation but also partial incapacitation. A person partially incapacitated is not restricted in the possibility to enter into marriage; still, such a person's mental sickness or mental deficiency may serve to engender negative effects in terms of everyday functioning within marriage. The impediment thus provides a specific tool to obviate such negative effects by preventing matrimony.

117. The impediment is not absolute, irremovable in nature. Pursuant to Article 12 §1 FGC, the court may grant permission to marry a person who is mentally ill or suffering from a mental disorder. However, certain conditions must be met to enable this to occur. It is admissible only if the condition of health or mind of such a person does not pose a threat to either the marriage or health of future offspring and he or she has not been fully incapacitated. Evaluation of this condition depends primarily on expert opinion. The expert is to explicate what the prospects are as to the functioning of the person within marriage. The person's prevailing condition is deemed to pose a threat if it excludes fulfilment on the part of the spouses of the roles and functions typical of an average matrimony, or disables the emergence of a durable emotional, physical and economic bond upon which conjugal life is dependent.

118. The professional assessment of personality is not confined to the impaired matrimonial candidate. It also involves the prospective partner and in a way that is of crucial importance in the decision-making process. Examination of the partner consists of establishing whether that person is calm, trustworthy and capable of the long-term acceptance of a spouse suffering mental disorder; if he or she has learnt sufficient about that person, is conversant with the behavioural swings associated with the disorder and will be able to cope with them.

119. As far as the second of the prerequisites is concerned, which must be examined concurrent with the foregoing one, this comes down to assessing the risk of the impaired spouse's mental illness or disorder producing negative effects to the health and well-being of future offspring from the marriage. Judicature of the Supreme Court depicts that the threat to the health of the potential offspring should be considered in such a manner that it refers not only to the possibility of hereditary transfer of the sickness to the future child but also the question of whether the mental condition of a particular person does not exclude the correct upbringing of children, conforming with the accepted standards and principles, as well as the proper exercise of parental authority.[51] It must be added that many mental sicknesses or conditions brought about by such ailments produce direct or indirect effects on the spheres of intellect and emotional life of the affected parties.

D. Impediment of the Existence of a Previous Marriage

120. This impediment is expressed in Article 13 FGC which provides in §1 that a person remaining in an existing marriage cannot enter into new matrimony. The regulation concerns marriages with civil law effects. In consequence, the impediment is not the case where the betrothed (one or both) remains a spouse in an exclusively canonical (church) marriage. This is a manifestation of one of the fundamental principles of the Polish legal order, namely the principle of monogamy. The discussed provision is strictly connected with the norms of the Polish Penal Code (PPC),[52] which provides in Article 206 PPC for the crime of bigamy, the formation of a marriage while remaining in matrimony with another person. The court is bound in civil proceedings with the determinations of a binding judgment of a criminal court which convicted the person in question for bigamy, and the binding decision of the civil court establishing a right or a legal relationship (e.g., annulment of marriage) shall be binding to a criminal court pursuant to Article 8 §2 PPC.

121. Bigamy should be differentiated from a situation where spouses whose previous marriage did not produce civil law effects (e.g., a sole church marriage), manifest their intent to enter into marriage. The precondition of a successful legal action for the annulment of marriage is the existence of a previous matrimony and not its validity or invalidity. Since in earnest there is no general category of an invalid marriage, the problem of whether the marriage had been formed despite a legal impediment remains insignificant for the prohibition of bigamy, as long as it is an existing marriage, which means here that the premises following from Article 1 FGC have been met. Another relevant question is whether or not the previous matrimony was extinguished (adjudication of divorce or annulment of marriage, death of a spouse or pronouncement of his or her death). When it comes to divorce and marriage annulment delivered by courts of the EU Member States, their effectiveness is determined in Council Regulation (EU) No. 2201/2203 of 27 November 2003, concerning jurisdiction and the recognition and enforcement of judgments in matrimonial matters and the matters of parental responsibility.[53]

122. The fact that the conclusion of a bigamous marriage violates fundamental principles of Poland's legal system sometimes produces far-reaching consequences

51. Supreme Court judgment issued on 29 Dec. 1978, II CR 475/78, OSPiKA 1980/7-8/141; Supreme Court judgment issued on 5 Apr. 2013, III CSK 228/12, LEX no. 1353197.
52. Act of 6 Jun. 1997, consolidated version: Journal of Statutes 2020, item 1444, with subsequent amendments.
53. OJ 2003, L 338.

which breach the interests of a spouse who innocently enters into a bigamous marriage unaware of the impediment's existence. In the majority of cases, it is impossible to attribute bad faith to that person. Notwithstanding, annulment of the marriage may subsequently expose them to many unfavourable outcomes, particularly in relation to pension rights, inheritance law and entitlement to alimony owed from the other spouse. Judicature consequently denies such a spouse the right to invoke Article 5 PCC and dismiss the action for annulment of the marriage on grounds of violation of the spouse's fundamental and socially justified interests or principles of social cohabitation.[54]

123. A particularly difficult situation arises where matrimony was entered into by a person whose previous marriage expired following the pronouncement of their former spouse's death and where, after the formation of a new marriage, it subsequently comes to light that the former spouse is still alive. Pursuant to Article 55 §1 FGC, in the case of pronouncing the death of a spouse, it is presumed that the marriage came to an end at the time and date of death specified in the pronouncement ruling. However, the pronouncement of death does not serve as an instrument to nullify the previous marriage. It merely allows the surviving spouse the freedom to enter into a new marriage in good faith, meaning that both parties to the new marriage genuinely believe the former spouse to be deceased. Thus, in the situation described above where the former spouse is found to be still alive, the new marriage concluded in good faith will not be annulled. Where the new marriage has been concluded in bad faith, i.e., the parties to it either knew or suspected that the former spouse still lived, the new marriage will also not be annulled, but this does not release either party from criminal responsibility.[55]

E. *Impediment of Consanguinity or Affinity*

124. The impediments provided for in Article 14 FGC are of varying natural weight. The reasons for their introduction differ as well. The impediment of consanguinity is based on serious eugenic grounds and should be associated with the fundamental principles of Poland's legal order. The point is to prevent matrimonies which transfer hereditary diseases to their children, which is a frequent occurrence in marriages concluded between close relatives. The other impediment, direct affinity, makes only a manifestation of morality accepted in society. This impediment follows from moral principles of the society and is not treated as restrictively as the impediment of consanguinity. This becomes especially manifest when it comes to the possibility of judicial consent to such marriage in spite of the occurrence of the impediment. Since the impediment of consanguinity is so highly important, it has been treated in the FGC as absolute, which means that judicial permission may not

54. Supreme Court decision issued on 4 Jan. 1971, II CR 601/60, *Gazeta Sądowa i Penitencjarna* 1971/12/2 and of 13 Apr. 1973, II CR 106/73, LEX no. 7246.
55. Supreme Court judgment issued on 3 Feb. 1970, II CR 517/ 69, OSNCP 1971/2/ 26.

be delivered in the case of consanguinity between the betrothed. The situation looks different where the impediment of affinity is concerned. More on this can be found below.

125. The first of the two impediments shall be treated relatively narrowly, since the prohibition of marriage between relatives concerns only lineal cognates without further restrictions (children, parents, grandparents and grandchildren), and collateral cognates to the degree between siblings. Direct consanguinity in light of Article 61^7§1 FGC is the case when one person descends directly from the other; secondary consanguinity is at stake where the related persons descend from the same ancestor and are not direct cognates.

126. It should also be mentioned that the impediment regards cognates consanguinity with whom follows from the births, marriages and deaths register as long as it does not become effectively denied, for example, as a result of denial of motherhood or paternity, irrespective of the register's conformity with the factual, natural state of affairs. However, in our opinion, consanguinity refers also to persons whose family status does not follow from the births, marriages and deaths register if they are naturally connected with consanguinity links. As a consequence, where the paternity of a child has not been determined, the prohibition of matrimony is going to concern both the biological father and the child, and the father named on the child's certificate of birth or judgment of a court, as well as the act of recognition of paternity on the part of the father who has not been included on the certificate of birth. Again, in our opinion, this follows from the eugenic grounds for the introduction of this impediment which are at play regardless of whether or not the consanguinity has been officially reported, and whether or not the particular persons are considered as cognates in the legal sense.

127. However, this is a procedurally complicated issue, and we agree with the opinion that the court in the course of proceedings leading to the annulment of a matrimony concluded between parties whose consanguinity does not follow from the births, marriages and deaths register, cannot by itself determine *ad usum* a condition contrary to the register. Nevertheless, if the content of the register indicates something suspicious, the court is in a position to stay the proceedings until other proceedings are accomplished leading to the determination of a family relation, and adjudicate only after delivery of the binding decision of the court as to the establishment of the groom's paternity of the bride.

128. It should be borne in mind, however, that many doubts may derive here from different reasons. Until recently, we have not had the opportunity to draw certain conclusions about the child's paternity, largely due to the unreliability of biological evidence. It sufficed that the proof of blood type could not exclude paternity of a given man and the court would establish paternity based on this. Obviously, this sometimes led to decisions that were blatantly incorrect, results which did not correspond to the factual consanguinity relations.

129. The same concerns consanguinity between siblings. It often occurs that children sharing the same natural parents are separated and adopted into different families. The so-called full adoption introduced in Poland in 1975, conducted on the basis of anonymous consent of the child's parents, and currently also a judicial decision in the case where the parents are either deceased or unknown, led to the protection of secrecy of adoption, where the previous certificate of birth was made secret and a new one issued bearing the names of the adoptive parents. This procedure gave rise to the rather obvious risk that if the children were of the opposite sex that they could, at some future date, unwittingly enter into an incestuous matrimony.

130. In spite of such possibility, in light of Article 20 of the European Convention on Adoption, preservation of the secrecy of adoption is admissible. This provision sets out that national laws may provide for procedures leading to adoption with the exclusion of openness. The adoptive parents and the adoptee may obtain documents from the births, marriages and deaths register which certify the date and place of birth of the adopted child without disclosing the fact that the child was adopted and without disclosing the names of the natural parents.

131. The impediment of affinity in a direct line is less significant. Affinity, in light of the new content of Article 61^8§1 FGC, derives from matrimony and holds between one of the spouses and relatives of the other spouse. As a result, there is no family relationship between relatives of one spouse and relatives of the other. Affinity survives even if the marriage from which it was established terminates. The character of this impediment entails as well, the admissibility of judicial permission to matrimony between the affected persons if the court decides that there are important reasons which support such a course of action. Proceedings leading to the grant of such permission take place in accordance with Article 561 §2 PCPC, at the request of each of the betrothed, who should indicate in the motion the nature of the reasons which apply in their particular case.

132. The criteria for evaluation in this regard might be circumstances such as the personal situation of the persons applying for the permission, their age, health condition, necessity of assistance of one spouse on the part of the other, prospects of normal functioning of their matrimonial life and the like. It cannot be ignored that occasionally there is a considerable age difference between the spouses whose marriage is the reason behind the emergence of affinity. For example, where a much older wife survives the death of a young husband and subsequently develops a close relationship with the late husband's father, the court may well take the view that the prospects for marriage between the two are such as to warrant granting its permission.

F. Impediment of Adoption

133. This impediment has been defined in Article 15 FGC as referring to the relationship between adopter and adoptee. There is no restriction when it comes to the possibility of marriage between the adoptee and a natural descendant of the adopter or some other of his or her relatives. While it is true that pursuant to Article 121 §2 FGC, full adoption gives rise to the acquisition on the part of the adoptee of the rights and obligations following from the consanguinity relationship in relation to relatives of the adopter, this is not tantamount to the emergence of the relationship of consanguinity. However, even though in such instances the rights and obligations deriving from the relationship of consanguinity expire between the adoptee and his or her natural relatives, the matrimonial impediment holds among such natural cognates on the basis of Article 14 §1 FGC (impediment of consanguinity).

134. One cannot speak of matrimonial impediments, even if the identical legal effect is produced, namely, the possibility to annul the marriage, if the following circumstances exist at the time of marriage formation: vices of consent concerning declarations of entry into matrimony exhaustively enumerated in the FGC, and vitiated power of proxy in the situations where the marriage was concluded by a proxy.

G. Defects of Consent Regarding the Declaration of Entry into Marriage

135. Until the entry into force of the Act of 24 July 1998,[56] which took effect on 15 November 1998, the FGC did not contain any provisions covering these problems. In the literature, it was raised at the time that entry into marriage is not a common juridical act in the field of civil law, and its evaluation cannot be performed on the basis of principles provided in the PCC regarding the validity of juridical acts. Many authors were of the opinion that it is insignificant in what conditions the declaration of intent to enter into marriage was made, and that the correct question was whether or not the matrimony formed in particular conditions functioned properly.

136. Where, in spite of a defect of consent, the matrimony fulfilled its social functions and the spouses remained in conjugal life, there were no reasons to question the validity of marriage formation. If the defects were so essential that the spouses either had not entered into common conjugal life or their conjugal life had been extinguished in a complete and permanent way, there were grounds to dissolve the marriage by divorce, which is the normal way of breaking the marital bond in a situation that has become too unbearable for the spouses to endure.[57]

137. The amendment introduced by the above statute was a result of transformations which took place in Poland after the collapse of the previous political regime. More attention was paid to the social consequences associated with divorce than to the annulment of marriage. Finally, ideological shifts were also crucial with more attachment to religious beliefs than previously.

---

56. Journal of Statutes 1998, no. 117, item 757.
57. H. Trammer, 'Czy wada oświadczenia woli nupturienta jest przyczyną unieważnieniamałżeństwa', *Nowe Prawo*, no. 1 (1966): 55; K. Pietrzykowski, 'Wpływ wad oświadczenia woli nupturientów na ważność małżeństwa', *Studia Prawnicze*, no. 3 (1980): 125.

138. In consequence, pursuant to Article 15^1§1 FGC, marriage may be annulled if the declaration of intent to enter into matrimony, as well as the expression of intention that a church marriage should produce civil law effects, were made for any reason in a condition excluding conscious manifestation of will, be it because of a mistake as to the identity of the other party, threat of the other spouse or a third party, a situation where the person expressing intent had reasons to assume that he or she, or some other party is seriously endangered.

139. This regulation differs from the defects of consent covered in the PCC in Articles 82 and the following ones. First of all, the PCC knows four, not three, types of defects of consent, providing for false declarations and exploitation. Additionally, the legal effects of these defects are going to differ. In the case of lack of awareness and freedom (not awareness alone) as well as feigned consent, results in absolute invalidity of the juridical act made in the condition of a respective vice, which must be taken into consideration by the court ex officio. Any person with a legal interest in the case may invoke this invalidity and the juridical act cannot be validated.

140. The remaining defects of consent provided for in the PCC include mistake (not only as to the identity of the other party, but a mistake concerning the content of juridical act essential in weight, unless the mistake was a result of deceit (where any mistake is considered relevant) and threat (illegal and serious, but not restricted to a threat of violating a personal or material interest of the party or a third person). These defects result only in relative invalidity which follows only from the intent of the parties. The court may consider such conditions only at the request of a party. The act may be validated. The last of the defects of consent referred to in Article 388 PCC covers exploitation. The consequence of this vice is merely the possibility to raise a claim to equalize disproportions of renditions extorted by the abuse of a party's unfavourable position, incompetence or lack of experience. Should the equalization prove too difficult, the entitled party may claim annulment of the contract.

141. First among the defects listed in Article 15^1§1 FGC, is that a marriage may be annulled if the declaration of intent to enter into marriage was submitted by a person who, for any reason, was in a state excluding conscious expression of will. Mental sickness does not automatically trigger this provision, since there are periods of remission when the party concerned remains aware of the declaration of intent entered into despite the impairment, and there are no grounds on which to annul the marriage. The same may also be said of a condition relating to severe somatic sickness, physical pain or post-surgical disorder, as well as the effects of alcohol intoxication or drug abuse.

142. Matrimony produces legal effects in a situation where a person submits a declaration of intent to enter into marriage without the actual intention to undertake conjugal life, hence making a false declaration. This is so because the FGC does not recognise this particular defect as a prerequisite of marriage annulment.

143. As far as the defect of mistake is concerned, the only significant type is *error in persona*, which excludes *error in qualitate personae*. Moreover, this has to be a mistake as to the physical identity of the spouse, and not as to his or her family or other features of the spouse. The interpretation of the mistake is thus very restrictive, in practice amounting only to a situation in which someone marries the wrong identical twin. In academic writings, there seems to be a reluctance in accepting that the mistake concerning the identity of the spouse should also include cases of identity fraud. As a consequence, the introduction of this impediment has not served to effect any changes, as the provision has yet to find an application in practice.[58]

144. The defect of threat, in order to constitute a legally relevant vice, must itself constitute an illegal act. Nevertheless, one must agree with the argument that any threat used to force a person to enter into marriage bears the feature of illegality since marriage by definition is a voluntary relationship in which coercion by either party is unacceptable. The threat must also stem from a specific person or persons; it cannot be the result of a particular arrangement of affairs. The threat must be serious and evoke justified concerns that non-compliance with it shall bring about negative personal consequences to the other party or to a third person. For instance, the threat may concern the disclosure of circumstances compromising not only the betrothed but also some of his or her close relatives, danger to life or health, physical integrity or violation of such personal interests as freedom or dignity.

H. Defective Proxy

145. The last of the grounds for annulment of a matrimony may occur where the marriage is entered into by proxy. Polish law approaches this form of marriage formation with a certain degree of reserve. In consequence, pursuant to Article 6 FGC, it is admissible to make a declaration on entry into marriage or production of civil law effects in the case of church matrimony by proxy, but only with judicial consent and only where sufficiently important reasons exist to warrant such consent. In accordance with a well-established opinion of the judicature, the court may accept only such circumstances as important reasons which in light of the principles of social cohabitation justify the exemption from the obligation of the simultaneous presence of the betrothed before the Registrar of a BMDRO in order to make concordant declarations of intent to form a marriage. The reasons behind this procedure cannot be as simple as a situation in which one of the spouses lives abroad permanently or has some difficulties in arriving in Poland.[59] Situations which do qualify as being important reasons may include: where one of the betrothed is on active overseas military duty from which leave is not possible; where an intended spouse has to stay abroad as a result of severe incapacitation; where the matrimony is additionally justified by the pregnancy of the future wife to be, etc.

58. See M. Nesterowicz, 'Błąd co do osoby jako przyczyna unieważnienia małżeństwa (uwagi de lege ferenda)', *Państwo i Prawo* no. 4 (2009): 27–30.
59. Supreme Court resolution issued on 6 Jun. 1970, III CZP 27/70, OSNCP 1971/1/2.

146. The premises for annulment of a marriage pursuant to Article 16 FGC, shall be circumstances such as the formation of a marriage by proxy without judicial consent or where the power of proxy is either invalid or has been withdrawn. Since granting the power of proxy is a civil law juridical act, its invalidity may result from the breach of any prerequisite of validity of a juridical act. Among these one can enumerate: lack of capacity to perform juridical acts, formal defects of the power of proxy, vitiated consent concerning the expression of intent to grant the power of proxy, and finally, contradiction with legislation or the principles of social cohabitation. Most frequently, invalidity of the power of proxy follows from non-fulfilment of the formal conditions set out in Article 6 §2 FGC, although it remains disputable whether both conditions mentioned in this rule refer to the form of the juridical act of empowering a proxy. Undoubtedly, a formal condition is the requirement that the power should be given in writing endorsed with an officially certified signature. The other requirement concerning the content of the power of proxy is that the document must indicate the name of the person with whom the matrimony is to be formed. One cannot grant the power of proxy to enter into marriage to a person selected by the appointed proxy. The name of the prospective spouse is to be included in the power. Moreover, there are grounds for annulment of matrimony if the power of proxy has been effectively withdrawn, and despite this fact, the proxy made a declaration of intent on behalf of the principal to enter into marriage or to bring about civil law effects in the case of a church matrimony.

IV. Annulment of Marriage

147. Entry into marriage despite one of the impediments discussed above shall not directly result in the nullity of the matrimony, it only provides the possibility to annul such a marriage. There are, however, exceptions to this principle which derive from the fact that the provisions regulating matrimonial impediments provide in certain cases for the possibility of entering into matrimony with court's permission. Such permission is provided for in Article 10 §1 FGC, since the court may allow a woman (but only a woman) who is at least 16 years of age to enter into marriage if it is justified by 'important reasons' and formation of the matrimony shall be concordant with the interest of the family.

148. Also in the case of mental sickness or mental deficiency of one of the betrothed, legal rules provide for the possibility of granting judicial consent to enter into marriage provided that the condition of health and mind of the affected person does not pose a threat to the future marriage or to the health of any future offspring, and such person has not been fully incapacitated (Article 12 §1 FGC).

149. The next case where the possibility exists to remove the impediment by judicial consent is a situation where important reasons arise to allow marriage between parties linked by the relation of affinity (Article 14 §1 FGC). Another context in which judicial consent to matrimony appears does not relate to lifting an impediment. Rather it opens the possibility for the betrothed to enter into matrimony in absence of their simultaneous presence before the Registrar at the time of declaring intent to form a marriage, this by way of concluding the marriage by proxy. Proceedings leading to the award of the judicial consents previously mentioned do not involve litigation. The procedure is regulated in the provisions of Articles 561 PCPC and the following ones and initiated at the request of the entitled person.

150. When it comes to proceedings on the annulment of marriage, again they take place in non-litigation mode and make one of the separate proceedings prescribed by the PCPC, among which one can distinguish proceedings in marital cases. The course of action is regulated in Article 425 PCPC and following ones. The action is brought by a person entitled on the basis of respective provisions to institute the process. A case may also be brought before the court by a public prosecutor. The power to sue a given party depends on the nature of the impediment which has been breached. As far as the impediment of age is concerned, each of the spouses may claim annulment of marriage. However, if the woman has already become pregnant, pursuant to Article 10 §4 FGC, it is not permissible for the husband to sue for annulment. Nevertheless, a public prosecutor may bring such a case before the court instead of the husband. Where the marriage was entered into with a person fully incapacitated or suffering from mental deficiency and remaining in the relation of affinity, annulment of marriage may be claimed by either spouse (Articles 11, 12, 14 §3, and 15 §2 FGC).

151. A specific issue, insufficiently discussed in the literature, is the question of the power to sue in a situation where the interested spouse is fully incapacitated and lacks the capacity to sue. Provisions of the PCPC allow such a person to make certain acts in the proceedings but only exceptionally. However, proceedings on the annulment of marriage do not refer to cases mentioned in Article 573 PCPC. Moreover, it is disputable if the action could be brought by the affected person with permission of the guardianship court, or by a public prosecutor. Here, one would indeed question the possibility of divorce proceedings being instituted by a public prosecutor involving a fully incapacitated person. Pursuant to Article 22 FGC, the public prosecutor does have the capacity to sue in every case of marriage annulment and determination of its existence or non-existence, but this is not exercised on behalf of a spouse and the prosecutor's capacity does not extend to involvement in divorce cases.

152. Broader capacity to sue for the annulment of matrimony is going to be the case in situations where the marital impediments are especially significant because the circumstances they refer to are contradictory to the fundamental principles of Poland's legal system, which means a case of consanguinity between the spouses or that one of them remains in a former marriage. In either case, the capacity to sue for annulment of the marriage can be exercised by any person who has the legal interest in doing so, regardless of whether this interest is personal or material.

153. Narrowing the capacity to sue to a particular person shall nevertheless be the case, apart from the situation in which the woman has become pregnant, if the declaration of intent to enter into marriage or to produce civil law effects in the event of church marriage was vitiated by one of the defects envisaged in Article 15[1] §1 FGC, since only the spouse who filed the defective declaration may sue for annulment of the marriage (Article 15[1]§2 FGC). One may speak of a similar situation where the matrimony has been concluded by proxy without respective judicial permission or where the power of proxy was invalid or withdrawn (Article 16 FGC). In the latter case, the only person allowed to claim annulment of such marriage is the spouse represented by the proxy.

154. The possibility to annul matrimony is additionally restricted by certain periods or legal events which bring about validation of the marriage. It is no longer possible to annul the marriage on the grounds of age impediment if the affected spouse reached full age before court proceedings were initiated. Likewise, one may not annul matrimony on grounds of mental illness if the affected spouse no longer suffers from it. A bigamous marriage cannot be annulled if the previous matrimony ended as a result of the death of the spouse of the bigamist, but not the demise of the bigamist themself. Some scholars perceive this as a specific legalization of bigamy. Finally, it is impossible to annul a marriage concluded in the conditions of vitiated power of proxy where the spouses have engaged in some form of conjugal life. If just one of the bonds which constitute the concept of conjugal life has existed between them (physical, emotional or economic) the marriage cannot be annulled.

155. Marriage concluded in the conditions of a declaration affected by one of the defects of consent envisaged in Article 15[1]§1 FGC, cannot be annulled after the expiry of a six-month period calculated from the termination of the condition exempting the spouse's lack of awareness, detection of mistaken identity and cessation of fear arising from threat. Notwithstanding, such a claim cannot, in any event, be raised after the lapse of three years from the date the marriage was formed. This is to prevent a condition of uncertainty as to the fate of the matrimony and to remove potential difficulties that may arise in evidence hearing, particularly with regard to the testimony of witnesses for whom the lapse of time entails uncertainty about the facts they are supposed to shed light on.

156. The annulment judgment is without doubt constitutive in character. The marriage is considered concluded until the judgment becomes binding. The decision creates a new legal situation and produces (with certain exceptions) *ex tunc* effects (retrospective ones). This does not affect the majority gained by a spouse as a consequence of entering into a marriage which remains unaffected by the subsequent annulment of matrimony.

157. As a consequence of annulment:

(1) both spouses return to the civil status they held prior to entering into marriage;
(2) the relation of affinity terminates between the spouse and relatives of the other spouse (which shall not be the case where the marriage is terminated by divorce);

(3) the spouse who has changed his or her name as a result of the marriage returns to the use of their former surname (or maiden name as the case may be).

158. Nevertheless, some legal effects of matrimony cannot be affected by the judicial decision which annuls the marriage, since certain results of matrimony cannot be deemed non-existent. The effects, whose force is only prospective, in other words, *ex nunc*, are that:

(1) the presumption of origin of a child born in marriage from both spouses does not expire;
(2) the situation of children should be determined anew in respect to their upbringing and right of contact (just as in the case of divorce);
(3) the community of property extinguishes between the spouses, both community of statutory and contractual origin (based on a settlement); this community institutes one of the types of joint co-ownership, which is always based on a special principal relationship between the co-owners, which in this case shall be marriage. If the marriage terminates, also the co-ownership must be extinguished and transformed into co-ownership expressed in fractional parts, as a result of which the co-ownership may be divided;
(4) if the spouses shared a common matrimonial property, the court decides as well about the future of that property, that is the way of using it by the spouses or its division;
(5) the court also adjudicates in regard to alimony between the spouses in accordance with the principles set out in Article 60 FGC.

159. Consequently, these are the same effects as brought about in the case of a divorce judgment (Article 21 FGC). Also, the principles elaborated by the doctrine and judicature concerning the interpretation of provisions which prescribe the effects of a divorce judgment, are to be applied respectively. In the case of divorce adjudication, one of the crucial factors is the determination of fault for the breakdown of a marriage. Similar solutions apply also to the annulment of matrimony in pursuance with Article 20 FGC, where the court is to determine whether and which of the spouses entered into matrimony in bad faith. The spouse in bad faith is the one who, at the time of entry into marriage, knew about the condition which instantiates a matrimonial impediment resulting in the possibility to annul a marriage. There is also an opinion found in jurisprudence and judicature that, as far as mental sickness and full incapacitation are concerned, if doubts should arise among the psychiatrists as to the mental condition of the spouse, it is difficult to ascribe bad faith to such person.[60]

160. Such a point of view should not be accepted. It cannot be ignored that Article 20 FGC speaks precisely about the moment of entry into marriage, and the mental condition of a natural person is only rarely constant. In practice, even a person suffering chronic mental illness experiences periods of remission, so-called

60. Cf. Smyczyński, *Prawo*, 69, Supreme Court decisions issued on 20 Jun. 1968, II CR 232/68, OSNCP 1969/4/ 75 and on 6 Feb. 1981, IV CR 533/80, OSNCP 1981/11/215.

lucida intervalla, where they are fully aware of their conduct or the situation they are in. Also, provisions regulating incapacitation do not require that the condition of incapacity to control one's conduct should be permanent, without periods of remission. In consequence, one should be very careful about expressing such statements.

§2. Formalities Connected with Entry into Marriage

I. Acts Preceding Conclusion of Matrimony

161. Conclusion of marriage, both in the secular and the religious form, the latter pursuant to Article 1 §2 FGC, as well as marriage concluded before a consul, are preceded by certain necessary formalities. These are envisaged in Articles 3 FGC and following ones, as well as in the CSRL. These formalities protect against entry into marriage in a way which violates the law while at the same time assuring proper solemnity of the occasion. As a consequence, the Registrar of the BMDRO or consul should exercise care in the examination of the requisite documents involved, so as to preempt the possibility of a faulted marriage emerging that may subsequently require to be annulled.

162. In order to facilitate the betrothed access to the BMDRO, the legislator renounced the necessity to observe the territorial competence of particular offices. Instead, the parties are free in their choice of office (Article 15 section 1 CSRL). In the BMDRO, the parties who intend to enter into marriage are required to confirm their identity and present documents on the basis of which the Registrar may determine their age, civil status (birth certificate, court decision on the dissolution or annulment of a previous marriage, certificate of death of a previous spouse, judicial permission to enter into marriage, etc.).

163. In the case of foreign nationals, they should present documents which confirm their capacity to marry in accordance with the provisions of their national law. This is of special significance in a situation where a number of countries still recognize polygamy. As a consequence, by evaluating the capacity of a foreign national to enter into marriage in Poland with a Polish citizen, in the course of proceedings on the exoneration of a foreigner from the duty of submitting such a document (the need for such proceedings follows from the fact that in certain national systems – Albania, Australia, Croatia, Estonia, Greece, Spain, Yugoslavia, Lithuania, Macedonia, Malta, Romania and Ukraine – provisions of law do not envisage the issuance of certificates confirming the capacity to enter into marriage), the Polish court should not only take into consideration the content of national law of the betrothed, but also the principle of public order following from Article 7 PIL.[61] The clause on public order provides that foreign law cannot be applied where its enforcement could produce results contrary to the fundamental principles of the legal order in

61. Act of 4 Feb. 2001, consolidated version: Journal of Statutes 2015, item 1792 with subsequent amendments.

the Republic of Poland. Thus, if the award of capacity to marry for the affected foreigner should result in total dependence of the Polish citizen on the foreign spouse, such an award would stand in opposition with the principle of Poland's legal order which envisages full equality of rights between the spouses, thereby opening up room for the clause to be applied. It is also important to note that Poland has not adopted Council Regulation (EU) No. 1259/2010 of 20 December 2010, implementing enhanced cooperation in the area of the law applicable to divorce and legal separation.

164. If the marriage is concluded by proxy, in accordance with Article 6 FGC and Article 76 section 3 CSRL, the Registrar should be shown the power of proxy to conclude matrimony on behalf of the principal. Apart from that, the parties are required to provide a written declaration that they are not aware of the existence of any matrimonial impediment. Where one of the betrothed was previously in a marriage, but the marriage has been dissolved by divorce or annulled, at the time of making this declaration the divorce decision must already be binding. If the prospective spouse was in a marriage in a foreign country and the marriage has been dissolved or annulled in that country, the decision must be acknowledged in Poland in the manner of Article 1145 PCPC, unless Council Regulation (EU) No. 2201/2003 applies. Judgments/decisions issued in non-EU states or issued in EU states before Poland joined the EU must therefore be recognized according to Article 1145 PCPC. Certain difficulties may occur when it comes to the recognition of foreign divorces adjudicated in an administrative capacity. Currently, in compliance with the widespread interpretation of Polish courts, backed in particular by the Supreme Court, the position has been accepted that the requirement that the foreign decision should be judicial is to be understood in such a way that where foreign law so provides, a decision coming from a body other than a court may be treated in the same way as a judicial decision.[62]

165. As mentioned before, with the intention of enabling candidates to a marriage to reconsider their position and think the decision through, Article 4 FGC imposes a one-month 'cooling-off' period. Such period is calculated from the day the betrothed submit their written declarations that they are unaware of the existence of any impediments to matrimony, and the period must be served in full before the parties can then proceed to make their respective declarations of intent to enter into marriage. This requirement has nothing in common with the church institution of bans, since the period does not serve the purpose of either publicly announcing the intent to conclude marriage or informing the Registrar of issues that might preclude matrimony. Notwithstanding, it may transpire that during this same period the Registrar may learn of circumstances which could justify a refusal to administer the declarations of intent to enter into marriage. While the one month term is mandatory, the Registrar may, at his or her discretion, allow for matrimony within that time if 'important reasons' favour such a solution, which may, for example, cover an

62. Supreme Court decision issued on 20 Sep. 1983, II CR 278/83, OSNCP 1984/4/61.

advanced stage of pregnancy of the future bride, illness exposing danger to the future spouse's life or the necessity of imminent departure and subsequent long-term absence of the spouse.

166. Where a couple intends to conclude a church matrimony with civil law effects or marriage before a consul, prior to the wedding they are required to present to the priest or consul a certificate issued by the Registrar certifying; the absence of circumstances excluding marriage, the content and date of the statements of the future spouses concerning their surnames after marriage and the surnames of their children (Article 4^1§1 FGC). The certificate is valid for a period of six months from its date of issuance (Article 4^1§2 FGC). Hence, the certificate should also include the date up to which the certificate remains valid. Where a certificate expires prior to the marriage taking place, a new certificate requires to be issued again valid for a period of six months.[63] The certificate serves only the purpose of evidence and by itself does not produce substantive law effects, which means that if the parties should violate the term, this would have no consequences as to the validity of the marriage. The only consequence is that the body administering the declarations of intent to enter into marriage may refuse such administration due to lack of respective notice. Another duty of the Registrar is to inform the parties of the further acts necessary to conclude a marriage (Article 4^1§3 FGC), which is presented orally.

II. Wedding Ceremony

167. Provisions referring to the conclusion of marriage are located in Articles 7–9 FGC. They regulate the ceremony of entry into marriage before the Registrar and before a priest. First of all, they require compliance with the public and solemn form of this legal event before the Registrar or priest in the presence of two witnesses. The witnesses do not play a special role in the wedding ceremony, in particular, they do not make any statements of intent. However, they should be persons capable of understanding the essence of the ceremony. Any defects in this respect, lack of capacity to perform juridical acts or even the absence of witnesses at the ceremony, bears no influence on the formation of marriage itself.

168. Where the marriage is to be concluded before a Registrar, Article 15 section 1 CSRL provides that this may take place in a BMDRO of the prospective bride and groom's choosing. There are no provisions which allocate territorial competence to a particular registry office and neither can such competence in any way be linked to the places of residence of the respective parties. Furthermore, although the current regulation of the FGC does not stipulate so expressly, the Registrar may, under the specific circumstances envisaged in Article 9 FGC and previously described in 165 above, not only proceed with the marriage without observing the

63. J. Strzebińczyk, 'Zawarcie małżeństwa wyznaniowego podlegającego prawu polskiemu', *Rejent*, no. 4 (1999): 9 et seq.

statutory one-month cooling-off period but also, where the need arises, conduct the ceremony outside the premises of the BMDRO, e.g., in a hospital, nursing home or prison.

169. The conclusion of marriage is conducted with solemnity. The Registrar, while administering the declarations of intent to enter into matrimony, wears an official badge of office the pattern of which and proper place of display on the person is specified by the Ordinance of the Minister of the Interior. While the betrothed are delivering their declarations of intent, all persons present, including the Registrar, shall stand (Article 85 CSRL).

170. Further procedure consists of the Registrar asking the betrothed individually whether they intend to enter into marriage, by which each of them is provided with a final opportunity to withdraw. If both answer the question in the affirmative, the Registrar then calls upon them to make declarations of intent to enter into marriage and state the future surnames they intend to adopt for themselves and their children (Article 7 §2 FGC). Subsequently, the betrothed make their declarations of entry into matrimony by repeating after the Registrar the prescribed text, or by reading from the written text out loud. Following this the betrothed sign the certificate of marriage which is prepared in advance (Article 7 §3 FGC). Finally, with the formalities completed, the Registrar pronounces that as a consequence of concordant statements by both parties they have successfully formed a marriage (Article 7 §4 FGC).

171. This last provision was interpreted in the doctrine of family law in different ways. According to one group of authors, the pronouncement is of crucial character since without it no marriage is formed. The vast majority of scholars and judicature are of the opposite opinion, which to our way of thinking is well-grounded in the content of the provision. One should bear in mind that the Registrar pronounces that the marriage has been concluded as a result of concordant declarations of intent by both parties; hence, the declarations themselves account for the essence of the legal event which by the will of the legislator results in the formation of marriage. Even if the Registrar had omitted to make the respective pronouncement, there would be no grounds upon which to claim that the matrimony has not been concluded. Also, the refusal or incapacity of a spouse to sign the certificate of marriage does not produce any binding effects.

172. The certificate of marriage drafted as a consequence of the conclusion of marriage contains the elements envisaged in the CSRL (Article 88). The certificate has a serious evidential significance since, pursuant to Article 3 CSRL, the registry of births, marriages and deaths is exclusive proof of the events included in the register; their inconsistency with the truth may be proven only in judicial proceedings. As a consequence, where at a wedding ceremony a certificate of marriage has not been produced, the need to sue for the determination of non-existence of marriage does not arise since is there is no evidential proof to show that a marriage had been formed.

173. Where the conclusion of marriage takes place before a priest, in principle the priest may not commission declarations of intent to enter into marriage before he is presented with the certificate issued by the Registrar certifying the non-existence of matrimonial impediments. Only in the situation envisaged in Article 9 §2 FGC, where there is an imminent threat to the life of one of the parties, is the priest entitled to disregard this certificate. The betrothed are required to make an oral statement directed to the priest that they do not know of any circumstances excluding the conclusion of a marriage. The priest then prepares a notice confirming that the declarations were made in his presence at the conclusion of marriage undergoing the internal law of the church or other congregation. This notice is subsequently signed by witnesses present at the time the declarations were expressed.

174. The priest's notice, together with the certificate issued by the Registrar prior to the conclusion of the marriage, requires to be returned to the BMDRO by registered post within five days from the date the marriage was formed. Should the five-day period be exceeded and the priest be unable to demonstrate that breach was the result of force majeure, which would occasion an extension of the term period, the Registrar is obliged to refuse to register the marriage. When calculating this five-day period, days recognized by statute as state holidays are not included.

§3. Effects of Marriage

175. Upon entry into marriage, serious changes take place in the factual and legal situation of both spouses. This concerns their civil status, the marriage being the source of consanguinity of the offspring born within matrimony, and grounds for the relation of affinity. Moreover, independent of the intention of the spouses, new personal rights and obligations arise based on the principle of their full equality. In addition, a new material situation is established for them. This situation is to some extent dependent on the intention of the spouses since they can either accept the statutory property regime or conclude a marriage settlement stipulating the regime of extended community, limited community property separation or separation with common earnings. Further results brought about by the formation of marriage concern the spouses' surname. The spouses have certain limited freedom in this regard. Finally, they acquire the right to intestate succession upon the death of the other spouse.

176. All of these regulations conform with international and European standards. Equal status of the spouses follows both from the European Convention on Human Rights of 1950 and Protocol No. 7, to the Convention of 1984. Specific recommendations in this area are to be found in the Resolution of the Committee of Ministers of the Council of Europe No. (78) 37 of 1978, which envisages that civil law in the EU Member States should not privilege one of the spouses and entrust that spouse with the superior role of the head of the family, or the exclusive right of representation or decision making concerning the other spouse.

177. As to the question of surname, the above-mentioned provisions of international law recommend lack of restriction and freedom of choice of the spouses in the matter of surname selection. Moreover, the Resolution proposes to give the spouses equal position in deciding about the commonplace of residence, safeguarding at the same time the right of each spouse to dwell separately, as long as the national legislator has provided for such possibility. The problem of determining the commonplace of residence of the spouses is highly significant from the point of view of the conflict of laws since in most legislations it is applied as the connector determining the proper law for divorce and separation in the absence of a common national law of the spouses. The above international legislation also provides for equality of rights of the spouses to conduct business or work professionally, study and undertake further vocational training.

178. Also regarding the conflict laws rules, Resolution No. (77) 12 of 1977 of the Council of Europe, recommends that its Member States should facilitate the acquisition of nationality of the state of citizenship of the other spouse, regardless of gender. This is about shortening the period of expectancy for the acquisition of citizenship, and safeguarding the spouses' freedom to choose nationality and acceptance of that nationality should be common to the whole family established by the spouses. The Council of Europe's legislation also pertains to the problem of guarantees of the spouses' rights and obligations in the family household, especially in terms of their rights to the family home.

179. In particular, the Council of Europe envisages specific suggestions as to the family home in Recommendation No. R (81) 15 of 1981, and aims to protect the spouse who does not enjoy legal title to the shared property. The document recommends that a juridical act by one spouse which affects the right of the other to use the property should only be made with the affected spouse's consent and that in case of demise of the spouse holding title to the property, the surviving spouse should be able to continue living in it. Moreover, the Recommendation also envisages protection of the spouses' right to use the contents of the household and the inadmissibility of a juridical act relating to any item of the contents by one spouse to the detriment of the other's rights.

180. These Council of Europe regulations were reflected in the amended version of Article 28^1 FGC, which provides that where the title to the family home is vested in one of the spouses, the other is entitled to use of the premises for the purposes of fulfilling family needs. Appropriately, This provision also applies to the contents of the household.[64]

181. Personal rights and obligations of the spouses have a particular character in relation to civil law rights and obligations. First of all, they arise *ex lege* as a result of the formation of matrimony and cannot be freely shaped by the spouses. Their agreement that certain of the obligations are not going to be binding for them (e.g., conjugal fidelity) do not have in any respect any legal force, and the spouse who

64. M. Sychowicz, 'Article 28^1 Commentary', in K. Piasecki (ed.), *Kodeks,*170–172.

violates the statutory obligations, even though in accordance with such agreement, shall be acknowledged as guilty of the breakdown of marriage in case of divorce proceedings between the spouses.

182. Even if the obligations of each spouse encumber as well the other party, they do not have the character of mutual obligations (as defined in the PCC), in particular, it becomes inadmissible to apply Article 488 PCC concerning the possibility to withhold the mutual performance in mutual obligations on the part of the debtor towards the other party, where that other party fails to comply with his or her mutual obligation. Nevertheless, the Supreme Court has stated in one of its rulings, that a spouse can be released from the responsibilities imposed on him or her by Article 23 FGC where it is justified by the conduct of the other spouse as a result of mental illness.[65]

183. Another highly characteristic feature of the personal rights and obligations of the spouses is the fact that unlike the majority of other subjective rights in the field of civil law, they are not enforceable by coercion. One cannot agree with the opinion that some of these personal obligations are of material character. Even the duty to contribute to the satisfaction of the needs of the family does not have, in our opinion, a purely material character. The needs of the family as such are not restricted to financial affairs. On the contrary, they also encompass direct care over the members of the family, satisfying the needs of personal security and love.

184. This was spotted in full by the legislator who envisaged in Article 27 FGC, that compliance with this obligation may consist as well in part or in full in personal efforts to bring up children and work in the common household of the spouses. Moreover, one cannot agree with the thesis that the fulfilment of this obligation may consist exclusively in pecuniary renditions for the benefit of the family. The needs of the family are generally of a non-material character and the mere incurrence of costs in this regard does not make for proper cooperation for the interest of the family. Quite conversely, it can frequently lead to alienation of the spouse and his or her pangs of conscience about the increased financial renditions.

I. Duty of Common Conjugal Life

185. This duty is first expressed in the FGC, since the legislator is of the opinion that common conjugal life is the basic obligation which gives rise to all other obligations and whose exercise makes a foundation for the creation by the spouses of a particular community, covering three bonds: emotional, physical and economic. The emotional bond denotes not only mutual respect between the spouses but also trust, honesty, loyalty, leniency, understanding and respect for the needs of the other one, his or her personal features, readiness to concede or compromise,

65. Supreme Court decision issued on 18 Mar. 1999, I CKN 1050/97, OSNC 1999/10/177.

finally feelings connected with the special character of mutual love – not just friendship, willingness to reach compromise and observance of the other spouse's opinion.[66] The physical bond consists not only in marital intercourse but also closeness in everyday contact. Whether this actually triggers the necessity for the spouses to share a common place of residence remains disputable.

186. The opinion of judicature in this respect is relatively well-grounded and follows from the belief that the spouses should in principle live together unless there are justified reasons for their living separately. Among these one can enumerate the unavailability of a common family home, being employed in a distant location, the need to take care of an ailing member of the family (mother or father), or where a situation arises that the conduct of one or other of the other spouses, or both, renders living together with an unbearable or impossible experience.[67]

II. Duty of Fidelity

187. This obligation signifies not just the necessity to refrain from having sexual intercourse with a person other than the spouse, but also the need to withhold from all forms of relations of an erotic and emotional nature with a third party. Some judgments of the Supreme Court envisage that in order to violate the duty of fidelity it is sufficient to create appearances of an infringement, for example, to evoke jealousy on the part of the other spouse.[68] In scholarly writings, such a situation is treated as an infringement of the duty of loyalty towards the other spouse, rather than infidelity.

188. In addition, the courts have also examined whether remote forms of contact, for example, via social media or chat sites on the internet, undertaken specifically for erotic purposes and the achievement of physiologic results associated with sexual fulfilment, could also be treated as an infringement of the obligation of matrimonial fidelity if it leads to deterioration of the emotional bond with the other spouse – especially since the provision of Article 23 FGC does not define a separate obligation of fidelity in this regard. Therefore, if it can be demonstrated that in a particular case the online conversations with other persons were of an erotic nature and this was responsible for the deterioration of emotional bonds in the marital relationship, such conversations should be thoroughly considered from the point of view of the discussed matrimonial duty.

66. Supreme Court judgment issued on 6 Feb. 2002, V CKN 741/00, LEX no. 424457.
67. Supreme Court judgment issued on 5 Dec. 1997, I CKN 597/97, OSNC 1998/6/99.
68. Supreme Court judgment issued on 19 Dec. 1950, C 322/50, *Państwo i Prawo*, no. 11 (1951): 803.

III. Duty of Mutual Aid

189. Mutual aid is a highly important obligation of the spouses, the proper exercise of which constitutes a certain guarantee of cooperation in various spheres of marital life. It stands in opposition to the encumbrance of just one person bearing the weight of nearly all duties and responsibilities for the proper functioning of the household. Such assistance encompasses all factual actions of one spouse supporting the other in the performance of various activities connected with care for close and more distant family members, satisfying the needs of the family, help in the performance of professional work or education, as well as providing psychological assistance and moral support. The duty concerns a variety of activities, starting from the basic ones of everyday life in a household to addressing the many complicated and unpredictable life situations that arise.

190. The exercise of this duty may also consist in assisting the spouse in the performance of their professional work or economic activity (running a business). However, the spouse may only expect such assistance where the other spouse has the necessary skills, capacity and time for its performance. It has to be understood that assistance in the spouse's work, no matter how provided, is ultimately for the mutual benefit of both spouses and the family. It does not constitute a master/servant relationship and consequently, both spouses should see and treat each other as equals. Moreover, the assisting spouse does not become a party to the contract under which the spouse is performing work and therefore the former does not acquire any right to remuneration from the spouse's employer.

IV. Duty to Cooperate for the Interest of the Family

191. This obligation is strictly connected with the previously discussed duty of mutual aid, even though the statute introduces it separately. It can also be treated as a subordinate category in relation to the obligation to contribute to the satisfaction of family needs, which has been formulated in Article 27 FGC. However, we do not agree with the thesis that the duty is of material character. The obligation consists in part of the provision of means to support the family, but certainly cannot be restricted to such a form of contribution. This seems predetermined by the wording of Article 27 FGC, which entails in the first place that the duty encumbers both spouses, each of whom not only according to his or her powers but also according to his or her earning and property income capacities, should contribute to the satisfaction of needs of the family established by the formation of marriage. Undoubtedly, one cannot speak of such duties in informal relationships, since the statute expressly provides so.

192. The extent to which each of the spouses performs the obligation depends above all on the spouse's strength and capacity. One cannot require him or her to fulfil the obligations in respect to contribution to the needs of the family to the extent surpassing his or her physical or intellectual capabilities. Moreover, since the object of satisfaction is the needs of the family, the scope of the duty depends as well on the type and condition of the family. Even if the spouses are without children, they form a family as a result of matrimony. The needs of such a family, however, are going to be much less than the needs of a family with children, especially in a situation where their support and satisfaction of their needs becomes exceptionally difficult because of sickness, invalidity or other hardships which appear in the process of their upbringing. The notion of family, in light of the discussed provision, encompasses the spouses themselves, not just their minor children but also adult children who are unable to support themselves independently. Status equal to the children originating from both spouses is also to be enjoyed by children adopted commonly by the spouses and children raised by them together even if not adopted, as well as the children of one of the spouses raised commonly but not adopted by the other spouse.

193. The second sentence of Article 27 FGC seems highly significant as it points to the non-material character of the duty. In that sentence, the legislator envisaged that compliance with the analysed obligation may also consist, in whole or in part, in personal care for the upbringing of children and domestic work in the common household. In this way, the importance of insufficiently appreciated domestic work for the interest of the family and satisfaction of its needs has been emphasized. The legislator equalized such activities with professional work.

194. Other delimitating factors of the scope of the discussed duty are the earning capabilities or financial capacities of the spouse. Factually acquired incomes do not really justify the spouse in this respect if he or she is capable of earning more and it is necessary for the satisfaction of needs of the family to put more effort on his or her part to become more intensely engaged in work, by sacrificing free time if need be for the achievement of higher incomes necessary to the family. In order to cover the family needs, each of the spouses ought to not only make avail of his or her earning capacities, but also property resources. If one of the spouses is in possession of personal property capable of generating particular incomes (e.g., by leasing it out), the spouse should take steps to conclude respective contracts generating income in order to cover the family's needs.

195. The FGC also envisages certain facilitations regarding the coverage of family needs by the spouses, especially in a situation where shortcomings in this respect follow from improper conduct of one of the spouses, which amounts to the failure to cooperate for the purpose of covering the needs of the family. If the spouses remain in conjugal life, on the basis of Article 28 FGC the other spouse may apply to the court for a judicial order that the remuneration for work and other receivables due to the former spouse be paid in whole or in part to him or her in person. Since the couple remains in common conjugal life, their needs are going to be covered by the spouse who has received the earnings. The notion of 'other receivables' seems quite capacious, because it includes not just, for instance, remuneration for the performance of certain services by the spouse but also amounts gained as rent in the relationship of lease or payment for a specific item of work. Still, the judicature is opposed to the extension of this category to such receivables which cannot be considered incomes of the spouses, for example, money deriving from insurance, compensation for expropriation of the spouse's immovable property and the like.

V. Duty to Co-decide about Crucial Questions of the Family

196. Such a duty, and not entitlement, is envisaged in Article 24 FGC. The provision restricts the freedom of spouses to decide about important issues of the family as a whole, without excluding the total freedom of decision on the part of each spouse in personal questions. The duty follows directly from the principle of equality between the spouses, each of whom should have the right to know what kind of important issues arise in the family, be able to express his or her statement in that matter, and oppose careless solutions suggested by the other spouse. The obligation is, however, exempted if communication with the other spouse is impossible or raises insurmountable difficulties (e.g., migration abroad for the purposes of work in conditions of uncertainty as to if and what job is going to be undertaken by the migrating spouse, or where his or her location is unknown), where the other spouse suffers from mental illness or remains fully incapacitated.

197. The notion of family affairs encompasses situations concerning both the family as a whole and its individual members, sometimes just one of them. Such situations must have an impact on the situation of the family as such. These can be property-related issues and non-material ones. The term may concern a juridical act or only factual action. The criteria that should be taken into account if one wishes to determine whether a given question is crucial are the significance of the issue and its impact on the situation of the family – should be considered assuming the standard of an average family. Obviously, this evaluation depends on the circumstances of the particular case, but on the whole, one can state that ordinary questions of a family which belong to the sphere of everyday life are not going to be considered crucial issues. It is, however, undoubted that among crucial questions one can include: residence of the spouses or one of them, change of this residence, the way of use of the marital home, questions of use of things encompassed by personal property of a spouse, or belonging to the common property in a situation where one of the spouses leaves the marital home and the objects are necessary for the remaining members of the family. Very often important questions of the family involve children, for example, selection of a child's name, determination of the child's location, profile of education or choice of profession.

198. One problem which has not been acknowledged as a crucial issue of family life is the question of the wife undertaking paid employment or if already in employment, the temporary discontinuation of such work,[69] which, in our opinion is a serious oversight. Especially if a family assumes the traditional model of role division, in which the organizational and upbringing role is played by the wife, such a solution is not accurate. However, we believe that courts should treat analogically

69. Supreme Court resolution issued on 7 Aug. 1974, III CZP 46/74, OSNCP 1975/12/160.

the situation in which the issue described affects the husband, which could be connected with his change of job or other payable activities (establishing his own business or migration abroad for work).

Chapter 2. Divorce

§1. Divorce Prerequisites

199. In Polish secular law, the principle of durability of marriage, stemming from the Polish Constitution and being one of the fundamental principles of national family law, does not necessarily mean its inseparability. However, it is generally agreed that marriage is not only the result of a free consensus of the parties. The parties are not in a position to entirely freely shape their situation when it comes to the formation of marriage, rights and obligations within marriage, or whether they remain a married couple or the marriage disintegrates resulting in its dissolution. Undoubtedly, matrimony is a highly specific juridical act of personal character. It initiates a certain arrangement of rights and obligations specified by provisions of law. In order for a matrimony to produce legal effects, the presence of an official body – the Registrar of a BMDRO or consul – shall be necessary. If so, also termination of marriage and legal effects produced by this termination are decided not by the parties themselves but by a state authority: a common court of law which represents the state.

200. While deciding about the dissolution of marriage or dismissing divorce action, the court must in the first instance take into consideration and establish whether a permanent and complete disintegration of marriage can be observed and if any negative divorce prerequisites are evident.

201. When it comes to the basic premise of divorce, namely the complete and permanent disintegration of marriage, this refers to a situation in which all bonds which constitute the conjugal life of the spouses: the emotional, physical and economic bonds have ceased to exist. Courts assume that in a situation where a scant economic bond holds between the spouses, arising, for example, from the need to maintain the marital home, such state of affairs does not contradict the assumption that the disintegration is full in character. Similarly, where the spouses remain on friendly terms with one another, but marital emotions have expired, such circumstances do not stand in opposition to the recognition of full dissolution of marriage.

202. Disintegration of the marital bonds is a continuous process stretched over time that progressively deteriorates the marriage. When disintegration becomes complete and permanent, the spouses may obtain a divorce. The period of progressive marriage disintegration does not necessarily have to be a long one, although it is probably true to say that in the majority of cases the marriage had been breaking down for a substantial amount of time. A marriage may be treated as permanently disintegrated when one cannot reasonably expect that the spouses will return to normal conjugal life. The experiences of judges demonstrate that a short conflict, but caused by serious reasons, suffices to instantly break the marital bond (for example, one of the spouses committed a serious crime). There are also situations in which one spouse has de facto already established a new competing family and there is no possibility of a return to the previous status quo. In such circumstances, the disintegration of marriage acquires the quality of permanence rather quickly, usually immediately after these circumstances become obvious to the other spouse. However if one may reasonably expect that there are chances that the spouses' may return to common conjugal life, the court may attempt to rectify the marriage. Currently, the divorce court no longer appoints a conciliatory meeting but instead refers the parties to mediation. Judicial mediators, who frequently are psychologists trained to mediate and guide the parties to an agreement, may find arguments in a way more effective than before in favour of reconciling the parties and enabling their consideration of the results of the possible dissolution of marriage both for the spouses themselves and their children. Such mediation may result in a real attempt to reconcile their differences.

203. According to Article 56 FGC, despite the complete and permanent disintegration of marriage,[70] divorce is inadmissible if, as a result of its adjudication, it would damage the well-being of the common minor children of the spouses or should for other reasons be contrary to the principles of social coexistence. The issues that should be taken into consideration by the court while deciding whether such contradiction between the potential divorce and the interest of the spouses' common minor children exists (according to the stable line of adjudication of the Supreme Court and doctrinal statements) are:

(1) whether and to what extent the child is going to suffer as a result of the divorce, the separation of parents, or discontinuance of contacts with the child's siblings from the same parents;
(2) whether it is necessary for the parents to continue to cooperate on a day-to-day basis for the better good of the child (a child suffering severe disability);
(3) whether the stance of one of the spouses regarding the exercise of parental authority after divorce might lead to separation of the child from the other parent or the child's grandparents.

204. When evaluating these circumstances, the court not only has to take into consideration the age of the child, his or her sensitivity, relations with each of the parents thus far, relations with siblings and more distant relatives, his or her health condition, as well as how the tension stemming from the breakdown of marital bonds between the parents influences the child, whether it is more beneficial for the child to dissolve the marriage by divorce than further subject it to the constant friction between the parents, quarrels or sometimes even physical violence. In practice, the interest of common minor children of the spouses is not found to preclude divorce from being adjudicated. More often, courts see this negative prerequisite as an additional argument to support the inadmissibility of divorce when they have already established that due to the lack of a complete and permanent breakdown of marital relations divorce cannot be adjudicated.

70. A. Szpunar, 'Rozkład pożycia jako podstawa rozwodu', *Nowe Prawo*, no. 4 (1954); T. Sokołowski, 'Rozkład pożycia a rozpad rodziny', in *Rodzina w świetle prawa i polityki społecznej*, ed. T. Smyczyński (Poznań: UAM, 1990).

205. When it comes to the notion of common, minor children of the spouses whose interest is to be considered, one should understand by this term that it includes not only children whose paternity is pointed to by the presumption of the child's origin from the mother's husband, as well as children whose origin was established by a court decision, and those children who were jointly adopted by both parents, or offspring of one of the parents adopted by the other.

206. The second negative prerequisite is that divorce would violate rules of social coexistence. This would include situations in which the interest of a child who is no longer a minor but suffers from a serious illness requires care on the part of both parents and consequently for them to remain married. Another reason would be unjustified harm of a spouse, resulting from reprehensible conduct of the other spouse, where the divorce would be a specific bonus for neglecting marital and family duties. In such circumstances, adjudication of divorce would stand in opposition to the principles of social coexistence (Article 56 §2 FGC). As in the case of the previous negative prerequisite, in practice, it is not utilized as the sole reason for the refusal to adjudicate divorce but serves as a supplementary circumstance supporting the court's finding that the breakdown of the marriage is not complete and permanent. The third of the mentioned negative prerequisites of divorce is a manifestation of the doctrine of recrimination. It will be the case where the divorce claim comes from the spouse who is exclusively guilty of the disintegration of marriage, and the innocent spouse does not agree to divorce unless the lack of consent could be considered in the particular circumstances of the case as a breach of the principles of social coexistence (Article 56 §3 FGC).[71]

207. At the same time, it is crucial that Article 57 §1 FGC does not differentiate between various degrees of the spouses' guilt. The basis for assuming a spouse's guilt is the determination that his or her conduct has contributed to the emergence or escalation of decomposition. It is irrelevant to what degree each of the spouses contributed to this decomposition. Inequality in the degree of guilt of the spouses does not pose any hindrance to the acknowledgement of their common guilt in the decomposition of conjugal life. The spouse who is guilty of the emergence of one of many reasons for the decomposition must be deemed guilty, even if the other spouse committed numerous and more severe acts leading to disintegration of a marriage. If the guilt of a spouse leading to the decomposition of marriage is a consequence of his or her violations of responsibilities following from family law provisions, which stem from universally accepted moral principles, the ascertainment of guilt does not require further evaluation as to whether such conduct is morally unacceptable. However, reference to moral values is necessary in order to assess the spouse's guilt if the illegality of his or her acts stems from non-compliance with the

71. Z. Krzemiński, *Rozwód. Praktyczny komentarz. Orzecznictwo. Piśmiennictwo. Wzory pism* (Warszawa: Wolters Kluwer, 2007); K. Gromek, *Kodeks rodzinny i opiekuńczy. Komentarz* (Warszawa: C.H. Beck, 2018), 591–593; T. Smyczyński, 'Prawo rodzinne i stosunki rodzinnoprawne', *Studia Prawa Prywatnego*, no. 1 (2007).

principles of social coexistence.[72] In consequence, it should be concluded that sickness of a spouse not only does not and should not cause permanent decomposition of conjugal life, it also imposes on the other spouse the obligation to use all accessible means in order to restore health and aptitude to comply with marital duties towards the sick spouse. Conduct contrary to this contradicts the generally accepted principles of morality.[73]

208. The guilt must be connected with a violation of statutory marital duties binding the spouses as a result of matrimony. The above-mentioned duties comprise common conjugal life, fidelity, mutual support, cooperation for the benefit of the family, or co-deciding about important questions concerning the family. This covers in particular adultery of one of the spouses, disregard of the other spouse, violation of his or her dignity, battery, physical or psychological tormenting, alcoholism of a spouse with all negative results of the addiction pertaining to the personal situation of the family members.

209. All these types of behaviour, since contradictory with statutory provisions, are unlawful in nature. If there is a possibility in the particular circumstances of a case to accuse one of the spouses of objectively improper conduct, the conduct may be evaluated as blameworthy. The provision quoted above stipulates that divorce is going to be admissible should the innocent spouse give his or her consent to the divorce, or if the spouse's denial of consent should be considered by the court as contradictory with the principles of social coexistence.

210. A stable line of adjudication of the Supreme Court establishes that the denial of consent to divorce on the part of the spouse innocent of disintegration of marital bonds is generally in conformity with the principles of social coexistence, but this presumption can be rebutted by the proof of specific circumstances which indicate otherwise. Such a situation is going to take place, for instance, if the denial of consent derives solely from the willingness to spite the guilty spouse out of vengeance, eagerness to repress, or no rational and morally acceptable reasons behind the denial of consent have been demonstrated.

211. Judicial examination of the circumstances depicted above in actual divorce cases demonstrates usually that the extinction of conjugal life, hence a situation where disintegration of marriage is of complete and permanent character, affects not only the personal situation of spouses, but also causes frequently psychological rejection of children, treating them as an obstacle that stands in the way of realizing one's own personal purposes. The issue at hand in this particular situation is to strive after at least restricting or minimizing threats to the child and violations of the child's interest. Decomposition of marital bonds between parents, their separation,

72. Supreme Court judgment issued on 29 Jun. 2000, CKN 323/00, LEX no. 52485.
73. Judgment of the Administrative Court in Białystok issued on 6 Mar. 1997, I ACa 48/97, OSA 1998/10/45.

always implies a lack of uniform patterns and stability of the upbringing environment, as well as the lack of regular educational impact of both parents, who frequently fight in addition for a dominant position towards the child, which can render the maintenance of the child's proper relations with the parents impossible. Moreover, an extremely negative influence is exerted on the parting spouses and their children by the duration of divorce proceedings. Psychological research described in Polish and foreign literature on the subject demonstrates that the situation shaped as a result of disintegration of conjugal life and divorce brings about an escalation of stress and tension for all the members of the affected family, the family's entrance into a deep crisis which leads to malfunctions in all areas of family life: on the psychological and physiological level. In addition, the situation brings about deterioration of internal relations between all members of the family, which necessitates transformations as to the structure and function of the affected family.

§2. Procedure

212. Divorce proceedings belong to the group of separate procedures regulated in the provisions of the PCPC starting from Article 436. The divorce procedure was seriously amended by the Acts of 28 July 2005[74] and 17 December 2009.[75] New enactments regulate, in a way different from what was the case before, certain important procedural aspects of divorce. Divorce cases are heard by Regional Courts in the first instance, and in the second one by the Courts of Appeal. Provisions of PCPC introduce a new form of conciliatory proceedings, pending not before the court (as was the case before), but a mediator to whom the court may refer the parties if there are prospects for the preservation of marriage, or where the judicial proceedings have been suspended, which generally takes place when the court becomes convinced that there are certain prospects for preservation of the conjugal life between the spouses, but the process of reconciliation requires a certain amount of time. The amendments provide as well certain principles of evidence hearing, its purpose and possibilities of reduction, which facilitates mutual relationships and mitigates conflicts between spouses. They also touch upon certain securities for the period of divorce proceedings, especially when it comes to spouses' duty to contribute to the maintenance of family within that period and the exercise of parental authority, as well as contacts with the child.

213. Divorce proceedings bear certain characteristics and specific features:

(1) it is a procedure of strictly personal character, which bars the legal representative of a spouse from initiating the proceedings (guardian or curator), which also applies to public prosecutors;
(2) it is exclusive in nature, which means that in the course of this proceeding separate actions cannot be brought before the court concerning the satisfaction

74. Journal of Statutes, no. 172, item 1438.
75. Journal of Statutes, no 7, item 45.

of family needs, alimony, restricting, suspending or deprivation of parental authority. All these issues are decided by the divorce court as such;

(3) the judgment issued in the particular case is characterized by integrity, which means that particular decisions contained in this judgment make a certain whole and are mutually interdependent. This signifies, for instance, that a partial appeal against the judgment pertaining to the dissolution of marriage by divorce causes its repeal also in relation to the remaining questions, thus parental authority or contacts with the child. This principle does not apply only to additional questions decided in the judgment, which results in the situation in which the judgment may be repealed in particular as to the alimony adjudicated for the benefit of the child or a spouse, and in the part relating to the dissolution of marriage, parental authority or contacts with the child remains in force, unless it was appealed against as regards the very dissolution of marriage.[76]

214. Divorce proceedings themselves produce multiple effects, legal, factual, parental, emotional and identity-related among members of the family. The literature confirms the thesis that the longer divorce proceedings last, the greater the destabilization of the emotional situation, frequently also the material stance of children, which stands in gross opposition with the best interest of the child. Unfortunately, it is not uncommon to observe a phenomenon of children being used instrumentally in the struggle between the parting spouses who compete for the children's emotions. While this trait is especially detectible among women, it concerns men as well.

215. It is a pity that in instances where the parents do strive to maintain relative stability and continuity in the everyday life conditions of their children in relation to themselves, contact with siblings, more distant relatives, especially grandparents and other persons significant for the child, are relatively rare. Legal and psychological academic writings indicate that it is extremely crucial not only to assure stability for the sake of the child in this respect but also to minimize conflicts between the parents in the course of the pending divorce case. The parents' cooperation is necessary with regard to deciding questions related to the upbringing of the child, adjustment of means to the child's development, compromising on contacts of both parents and other persons with the child. Unfortunately, model situations are seldom observed in this respect, which in turn may lead to serious difficulties concerning potential decisions on the parental authority and contacts with the children within the divorce judgment.

---

76. B. Czech, 'Article 58 Commentary', in K. Piasecki (ed.), *Kodeks,* 464–465; A. Czeredecka, *Rozwód a rywalizacja o opieke nad dziećmi* (Warszawa: Lexis Nexis, 2010), 19.

§3. Divorce Judgment

I. Termination of Marriage

216. The divorce judgment decides whether the matrimony between the parties terminates (which becomes effective as the judgment acquires its binding force) or continues on if the court dismisses the action. The decision contains as well a resolution on the spouses' guilt unless they petitioned for a divorce without deciding the question of guilt. Further elements of the divorce judgment, in the case of which the court is obliged to decide ex officio, concerns parental authority over the common underage children of the parties, as well as many other relevant questions discussed below. Scholarly writings emphasize that the divorce judgment is of constitutive character, effective *erga omnes*, yet it does not reinstitute automatically the legal situation from before the matrimony. The divorce does not cancel the relation of affinity which emerged as a result of marriage. Children of the spouses retain the status of marital children, and the judgment only shapes new relations between the divorced spouses.

217. Scholars enumerate the following effects of a divorce decision:

(1) the judgment is effective in relation to all, hence it frames a new situation of the spouses in relation to third parties, enabling a new matrimony on the part of the divorced spouses (Polish law does not provide for any intermediate period during which a new matrimony would be inadmissible);
(2) the decision determines new alimony relations between the divorced parents which expire upon the entry into a new marriage by the spouse entitled to alimony, or on the expiry of the period specified in Article 60 §3 FGC;
(3) the regime of joint matrimonial property expires and transforms into co-ownership expressed in fractions. The FGC itself provides for the presumption of equal shares in the co-owned assets, but allows at the same time in Article 43 §3 FGC for the possibility of a motion for settling unequal shares if such a solution is justified by important reasons (most often it is the case of the lack of due contribution to the generation of the said assets, their squander, gambling, etc.);
(4) the judgment determines anew the exercise of parental authority and contacts with the child;
(5) interim measures issued in the divorce proceedings are repealed, such as the interim decision regarding contribution to satisfying the needs of the family, custody over the child, ways of use of the common home, or providing access for the spouse leaving the home to chattels which are necessary to him or her.

II. Content of the Divorce Judgment Pertaining to the Exercise of Parental Authority and Contacts with Children

218. Depending on the relations between the divorcing spouses or between both of them and their children, the court may deliver various decisions. The court may preserve the parental authority of the parties as enjoyed thus far if the parties demonstrate in the course of proceedings that they can act harmoniously, without harm to the child and his or her upbringing, thus in the best interest of the child. In such cases, the parents continue to exercise parental authority over the child in the full range, both when it comes to personal care and control over the child's assets. Unfortunately, it must be admitted that such resolutions are not frequent, because the parents usually are in conflict with one another and are unwilling to cooperate in the best interest of the child.

219. A very interesting regulation in this respect was introduced in the recent amendment of the FGC by the inclusion of the new Article 58 §1 which stipulates that by deciding about parental authority and the right of contact with the child, the court shall enforce an agreement between the spouses concerning the way of exercising parental authority and contacts with the child after the divorce, unless the agreement is contrary to the interest of the child, and taking into account the principle that siblings should live together unless the interest of the children necessitates another solution. In Polish literature on the subject, it was proposed that as a part of the interpretation of the term 'interest of the child', the court should accept a certain interpretive directive pursuant to which separation of siblings is generally contrary to the child's interest unless there are special reasons which oppose to this kind of solution. This can be wrong, for instance, in a situation of a considerable age difference between the siblings, conflicts among them, competition for the parents' emotions, or when it comes to siblings of half-blood. In sentence 3 Article 58 §1 it is currently expressly stated that siblings should be raised together unless the interests of the child require otherwise.

220. Another significant amendment introduced to the FGC by the same statute concerns the obligation on the part of the court to hear the child and the child's wishes as regards parental authority and the right of contact. Such a duty follows directly from Principle 3 of the annex to Recommendation R(84) 4 regarding parental responsibility, delivered by the Committee of Ministers of the Council of Europe on 28 February,[77] which provides that opinion of the child is necessary whenever a proper authority is to make a decision concerning fundamental interests of the child, as long as the age of the child and maturity level allows him or her to understand the character of the problem, and if it does not inflict harm on the child. Also, other European documents[78] provide that to the extent that the child is treated by national law as sufficiently perceptive, he or she should enjoy in judicial proceedings rights (the child may also demand the following on its own motion) such as the right to be informed on all relevant issues, to be asked opinion and to be able to express their own stance. The child must be informed about the possible results of expressing his or her stance, as well as the possible effects of any decision.

77. M. Safjan, *Standardy prawne Rady Europy. Teksty i Komentarze* (Warszawa, 1994).
78. For example, Strasburg Euroconvention of 26 Jan. 1996, Journal of Statutes 2000, no. 107, item 1128.

221. The same legal document specifies numerous obligations on the part of the judicial body deciding about a child. In the first place, there appears the question of proper consideration whether the body has all necessary and sufficient information to make a decision which is to be optimally in accord with the interest of the child. If necessary, the judicial body is to call for additional information, make sure whether the child has been thoroughly and properly informed. If the court deems it necessary, it shall hear the child either directly or with the aid of third parties (psychologist, mediator) in the manner corresponding to the perceptive capacities of the child, enabling the child to present his or her statement in the conditions of respect towards that statement. These principles have been implemented in Polish law and became manifest also in the amended Article 216^1§1 and §2 PCPC, as well as Article 576 §2 PCPC. We are witnessing currently a discussion within the Polish doctrine concerning the mode of such hearing. Scholars generally agree that the hearing should take place outside the courtroom and without official judge robes being worn; still, it remains highly disputable how the testimony of the child as to relevant matters should be recorded, and which of the child's representatives and parents should be allowed to participate in such a hearing.

222. Divorce court decisions concerning parental authority and the right of contact with the child also cover other resolutions. First, if the parents have not reached an agreement concerning the manner of exercising parental authority, the court takes into account the child's right to be raised by both parents and resolves for parental authority to be performed jointly and for contacts with the child to be awarded equally to both parents (Article 58 §1a, sentence one FGC). If both parents make a unanimous request, the court will abstain from resolving the matter of contact with the child (Article 58 §1b FGC). These two provisions are a recent addition to the FGC[79] which seems to suggest a move towards rulings that allow parents to alternately take care of the child for specified time periods.[80] If the above conditions do not exist, the court may entrust the exercise of parental authority to one of the parents, restricting the other parent's authority to particular rights and obligations in relation to the child. This type of solution is the one which up until now has been the most frequently enforced in practice, yet there are certain differences between particular judicial decisions. In the overwhelming majority of cases, courts have entrusted parental authority over the child to the mother, while the father's authority becomes limited to certain rights and obligations, for example, concerning co-decisions about the direction of the child's education, sports done by the child, medical therapy. More and more often courts decide on these issues only after a thorough examination of the child's relations with both of the parents thus far, with whom the child has stricter emotional bonds and which of the parents is more willing and ready to devote more time and energy to everyday care for the child. It is

---

79. Journal of Statutes 2015, item 1062; the amendment came into force on 29 Aug. 2015.

80. For more on joint physical custody in Polish family law, *see* M. Habdas, 'The Evolution of Joint Parenting in Poland: The Legal Perspective on Lessons Learned and Still to Be Learned', *International Journal of Law, Policy and the Family* vol. 33 (2019), 337–359, DOI: https://doi.org/10.1093/lawfam/ebz010.

insignificant in this respect which of the parents can assure a better material position to the child, since the financial situation may always be equalized by court decision adjudicating alimony and obliging the better-conditioned parent to a higher contribution to satisfying the child's needs than the other one.

223. Such distribution of parental authority is not equivalent to its restriction within the meaning of Article 109 FGC. This does not denote that the court may not, during divorce proceedings, restrict, suspend or even deprive one or both of the parents of parental authority, should the prerequisites of such resolutions emerge, as provided for in provisions regulating these remedies. If the court determines that the interest of the child is endangered, the court may restrict parental authority by respective orders set out (in a non-exhaustive manner) in Article 109 §2 FGC. Should the court determine that in the case of one or both of the parents there occurs an impediment as regards the exercise of parental authority (e.g., moving abroad to work), the court may suspend the authority. If the proceedings indicate that parental authority cannot be exercised by the parents because of a permanent impediment or instance of abuse of the power on the part of the parents (for instance, forcing the child into prostitution or theft), or if they blatantly neglect their duties towards the child (the child is malnourished, parents indulge in drinking without paying attention to the child and his or her needs, are away from the house for long periods leaving the child to fend for itself unsupervised and without care), or if the parents, in spite of the aid they receive, remain permanently disinterested in the child – in such circumstances, the court may deprive them of parental authority within the divorce judgment (Article 112 FGC).

224. As a result of the amendments to the FGC, another obligatory element of the divorce judgment is the decision concerning the right of contact with the child. As has already been mentioned above, this matter will not be decided by the court upon the unanimous request of the parents (Article 58 §1b FGC). The amended Code provides that the contacts are independent of parental authority. In the same way that the alimony cannot be considered an element of parental authority, contacts also remain a separate issue. The introduction of this institution in Polish law reflects the implementation of European legal standards, especially those following from the Convention on the Rights of the Child. The Convention's treatment of the matters related to contacts with the child and their inclusion as the child's right to maintain personal and direct contact with the parents is extremely important. Exceptions are delimitated by situations where such contacts could be contrary to the best interest of the child. It should be emphasized that Article 10 of the Convention stipulates precisely that the child has the right to maintain regular personal relations with both of the parents, except in certain rare and extraordinary situations. The Convention gives examples of situations where state authorities are to limit the right of contact by a decision of a proper body. This concerns the following circumstances: maltreatment of the child or neglecting the child. Article 113 §2 FGC specifies the basic scope of elements which amount to the notion of contacts:

(1) spending time with the child (the Convention mentions the examples of visits, meetings, taking the child away from his or her place of residence);

(2) direct communication with the child;
(3) mail correspondence;
(4) use of alternative means of distant communication, including measures of electronic communication.

225. This enumeration is only exemplary since the provision itself uses the term 'in particular'. Other means of personal contact may qualify as well if the court accepts them as necessary for not only the interest of the child but also its parents. Academic sources quote such a measure as the obligation to inform the person entitled to contacts about the child. The right to unsupervised contacts is in principle allowed unless such entitlement should be contrary to the interest of the child. Also, the right of the child's contact with other persons apart from his or her parents is recognized, which concerns, for instance, grandparents.

226. The specification of means of maintaining contact is regulated in Article 113^1 FGC, which provides that where the child stays by one of the parents the way of exercising the right of contact by the other shall be determined by both parents together, guided by the interest of the child and taking into account the child's reasonable wishes. Unfortunately, the parents are not able to settle this by themselves. In such instances, the case must be decided by the court. This principle is followed as well where the child remains under guardianship, has been placed in a foster family, or in a care and education centre. Also under such circumstances, the parents should stay in touch with the child; on the contrary, it should be noted that it is not in the best interest of the child to force him or her to maintain contact with the parents if the child consciously and deliberately opposes such meetings.

227. Frequently, preservation of contacts is not possible without previous preparation of both the parents and the child to such a situation. What is more, it seems obvious that the court cannot confine itself to a general clause that the parents are entitled to contacts with the child. The court should, taking into consideration the circumstances of the case, determine in a precise manner the realization and frequency of contacts, and cooperate with the parents in order to determine the way of realization of the entitlement which could be optimal from the point of view of the interest of the child.

228. It is also feasible, whenever the interest of the child dictates so, to restrict the child's contacts with the parents pursuant to Article 113^2 FGC. This provision sets out certain ways of restricting the entitlement. This statutory list is not exhaustive. Such a restriction may take the form of the ban on meeting the child, prohibition of taking the child away from his or her habitual residence, permission to encounter the child only in the presence of the other parent or third parties appointed by the court (guardian, curator), restricting contacts to specific ways of distant communication, or finally a ban on distant communication.

229. One cannot exclude the possibility that the court might be forced to deprive the parents of the right of contact completely. This shall take place in a situation where the court determines that the contacts endanger the interest of the child. This might be the case, for instance, in a situation in which the parents demoralize the child, force him or her to beggary, consumption of alcohol, doing drugs, or commitment of penalized acts, or where the child has been sexually abused or maltreated by the parents who suffer from a sickness or mental disorder, or if the parents are addicted to alcohol or drugs.

230. Since contacts with the child are not an element of parental authority, Article 113^6 FGC contains a norm according to which provisions on the right of contact with children apply appropriately to contacts with persons who are not the child's parents at all. This refers to such parties as siblings, grandparents, who, in Polish conditions, still bring up their grandchildren if both parents are professionally active, or other persons who provided care for the child over a period of time. This has already found manifestation in a body of court decisions which confirm grandparents' right of contact with their grandchildren.[81]

III. Alimony Obligation after the Divorce Concerning the Needs of the Spouses' Children

231. Another highly important question covered by the divorce judgment is to what amount the parents are obliged to contribute to the child's maintenance and upbringing costs. The court decides on the particular value of the alimony obligation for each of the divorcing spouses. If the care of the child is entrusted to one of the parents, the court does not determine the value of his or her contribution, which remains a manifestation of the principle that the fulfilment of the alimony obligation does not have to consist in the provision of a particular sum of money, but may boil down to personal efforts and care for the child, and satisfaction of the child's needs in the area of upbringing and maintenance (Article 27 FGC).

232. The court's decision in this respect does not depend in any way on the spouses' guilt or will. Neither of the spouses may become obliged to exclusively incur the total costs of the child's maintenance. It is also impossible for one of the spouses to forfeit the right to alimony for the child for the benefit of the other spouse. Moreover, while delivering the judgment, the court is not bound in any way by a settlement between the spouses as regards the distribution of costs of the child's maintenance. The decisive factors are the needs of the child (depending on his or her age, state of health, educational needs, etc.) and earning capacity of the parents as well as their assets.

81. Supreme Court resolution issued on 14 Jun. 1988, III CZP 42/88, OSNCP 1989/10/156.

IV. Decisions Concerning Common Accommodation of the Spouses after the Divorce

233. The problem of deciding about the common matrimonial home of the spouses, division of their common property and alimony obligation between the divorced spouses are optional elements of the divorce judgment.

234. When it comes to the common matrimonial home, the court decides about the use of the premises only where the spouses live together in a single dwelling, regardless of the title to the property. This issue is adjudicated by the court ex officio, but it only concerns the manner of using the matrimonial home and not any proprietary or contractual rights to the home. However, the issue of who should retain the right to the matrimonial home may also be resolved by the court. The problem itself is a very difficult issue, especially in the period of deficit and high costs of residential property. It is practically negotiable between the spouses who may reach a compromise and settle on the division of the property or leave the property to one of the spouses while the other agrees to abandon the premises without the right to substitute lodgings. On such occasions, the court shall deliver the judgment in this matter only upon a unanimous motion of the parties. Unfortunately, in many cases, the situation occurs where one of the spouses makes common living impossible (picking brawls under the influence of alcohol, maltreatment of the other spouse or children, bringing home third persons who misbehave, etc.). In such a situation, eviction of the trouble-making spouse may be ordered if the other spouse petitions for such a solution.

V. Elements Concerning the Common Property of the Spouses

235. Another decision which may be included in the divorce judgment is the division of community property of the spouses. The court divides the assets at the request of one of the spouses only in a situation where such a division does not lead to unnecessary protraction of the proceedings. In practice, the division most often takes place in separate proceedings, after the divorce judgment has become binding. If the spouses agree as to the necessity of its implementation, especially where the property is not considerable, the court may divide the whole community property of the spouses or a selected part of it. It is obvious, however, that such a division is going to be effective only once the divorce judgment becomes binding, since the common character of the spouses' assets amounting to the common property may terminate only upon termination of the basic relationship, namely the legal relationship instituted by marriage.

VI. Alimony Between the Spouses after the Divorce

236. Pursuant to Article 60 FGC, a divorced spouse who has not been found solely responsible for the breakdown of the marriage and who is in need (i.e., cannot satisfy his or her basic and justified living expenses), may request the other divorced spouse to provide means of subsistence to the extent corresponding to their justified needs and the earning and financial capabilities of the other spouse. A spouse who has been found solely responsible for breakdown of the marriage (the exclusively guilty spouse) can never demand alimony from the completely innocent spouse. Where one of the spouses has been found solely guilty for breakdown of the marriage and the divorce entails a significant deterioration of the material situation of the innocent spouse, the court, at the request of the innocent spouse, may determine that the guilty spouse is obliged to contribute to the needs of their former partner, even if they are not in need. This denotes that the exclusively guilty spouse may be sued for alimony even though the other spouse is capable of satisfying his/her basic and justified needs, however, as a result of the divorce his/her material/financial situation has significantly worsened. The obligation to provide for the divorced spouse's livelihood expires in the event of that spouse entering into a new marriage. Otherwise, the obligation of a spouse who has not been found guilty of causing the breakdown of the marriage (that is either a spouse who has been found to be completely innocent, or both spouses were found to be at no fault for causing the marriage breakdown, or both spouses are assumed to be innocent because they have requested for the court not to consider fault in the divorce proceedings) expires after five years from the date of the divorce decree unless, due to exceptional circumstances, the court, at the request of the entitled party, sees fit to extend the five-year period.

§4. Separation: Prerequisites, Mode of Proceedings and Differences in Relation to Divorce

237. Separation of spouses was known to all legal systems binding on Polish territories in the period of partitions and between the two World Wars. Shortly after the Second World War, in the decree of 25 September 1945,[82] this institution was introduced in the unified law under the name 'division of spouses', but soon, as a consequence of entry into force of the 1950 Family Code, separation was removed from Polish family law. Under the influence of opinions expressed at the time in neighbouring countries belonging to the so-called Bloc of Socialist Republics, it was considered that the sufficient form of deciding matrimonial conflicts which result in the decomposition of marriage should be a divorce and keeping up the appearances of the continuance of the marital bond was unnecessary. The goal was, in particular, to free family law from the impact of Canonic law, forgetting that the vast majority of marriages in Poland had been formed not only before the Registrar of a BMDRO but also before a priest in a church.

238. The first legislative initiatives leading to the introduction of the institution of separation, with the view to take into account persons who on religious grounds refuse to accept the institution of divorce, were brought in 1992, but the draft prepared at the time was rejected, which was also the case of the next draft of 1994. In 1998, there appeared a new bill, which did not differ much from its predecessors.

82. Journal of Statutes 1945, no. 48, item 270.

After its rejection, the Polish Commission for the Codification of Civil Law (PCCCL) elaborated a new draft bill which was finally enacted by the Parliament in 1999. Separation was introduced into the FGC directly after the provisions regulating divorce. In the same way, the new institution has been established with the function of not only a certain durable division between the spouses but also organizing the life of the separated spouses with the intention to alleviate their conflicts over time and the possibility to eventually return to common conjugal life. It was, however, not the intention of the drafters to make separation an introduction to a further divorce claim or as a means to replace divorce. It is not entirely clear whether separation, as an institution that caters to the needs of persons who, for religious reasons, reject the possibility of divorce (e.g., Roman Catholics) was a sensible solution. It must be reiterated that divorce in a civil court does not in any way influence the religious status of a marriage, so by obtaining a civil divorce the spouses do not change their obligations following from the principles of their religion. Practice has shown that separation, as it is currently regulated, is an institution rarely applied in practice. According to statistical data, in 2018 there were 62,800 divorces and 1,300 separations,[83] which denotes that the latter institution has little practical significance.

239. The provisions of Article 61^{1-6} FGC envisage a single positive prerequisite of separation and two negative premises. In relation to divorce prerequisites, the positive precondition that must be proven if the court is to adjudicate separation is the complete disintegration of conjugal life, though not necessarily decomposition of a permanent nature. However, among negative premises, the legislator maintained the prerequisite of contradiction of the separation with the interest of common minor children of the spouses and contradiction of the separation with principles of social coexistence. In the case of separation, the legislator did not decide to include the negative premise of the divorce claim coming from the spouse exclusively guilty of the decomposition of marriage and justified denial of consent to divorce on the part of the innocent spouse. The idea behind such regulation was that the examination of fault for the decomposition of conjugal life would antagonize the spouses unnecessarily, disabling the possibility of their return to common conjugal life.

240. Another manifestation of the willingness not to escalate the conflict between the spouses is Article 61^{1}§3 FGC, which stipulates that where spouses who have no common minor children unanimously apply for separation, the court may adjudicate separation on the basis of that request. In such instances, further facilitation of the separation process has been provided for. While the court must determine whether there really is complete disintegration of conjugal life between the spouses, the court may base this determination on a mere hearing of the parties and omit further evidence, the allowance of which usually serves to antagonize the spouses. Beyond any doubt, the hearing of the parties is predominantly of formal

83. https://stat.gov.pl/obszary-tematyczne/ludnosc/ludnosc/malzenstwa-i-dzietnosc-w-polsce,23,1.html (accessed on 4 Jan. 2021), p. 15.

significance, but the court should evaluate the testimony of the parties and examine whether the separation claim is fictitious and only aimed at achieving, e.g., certain financial gains.

241. The prerequisites of separation are treated analogically as prerequisites of divorce. That is why we shall not discuss their essence and understanding at this point. Decision concerning separation may be delivered in two ways before a regional court: in separate proceedings, just as in the case of divorce, or in a non-litigious mode, when the parties have no common, minor children and have applied for separation unanimously (Article 41 PCPC and 567^1 PCPC).

I. Separation Effects

242. The biggest difference as to the legal effects of a separation judgment as opposed to divorce judgment is that despite separation the marriage maintains as such, and neither spouse is in a position to enter another marriage nor return to the surname they used prior to the matrimony. There is indeed a general tendency to draw similarities between the effects of separation and divorce, but there are certain differences as well. Separation lifts the duty of common conjugal life on the part of the spouses, excludes the presumption of origin of the child from the mother's husband if the child was born at least 300 days from the separation decision, it becomes necessary to decide in respect of parental authority and contacts with the child, as well as about alimony for the child and respectively for the other spouse, or about the common apartment of the spouses. The court decides whether and which of the spouses can be ascribed guilt for the disintegration of marriage, except for proceedings in the non-litigious mode, the latter resulting in a no-fault separation. The obligation of mutual aid between the spouses maintains despite separation, but the duty to cooperate for the interest of the family becomes extinguished. A very important consequence of the separation judgment is the termination of statutory community between the spouses and the emergence of the compulsory regime of property separation. Finally, the result of both separation and divorce is the exclusion of the separated spouse from the range of statutory heirs of the other spouse.

243. Separation can be lifted by a court at any time at the concordant request of the spouses. Taking on common conjugal life once again does not yet decide about the expiry of separation, which in every case must be lifted by judicial decision of the court which adjudicated separation. Provisions of both the FGC and the PCPC allow to alleviate the results of separation in such cases and suspend, for instance, the initiated eviction of one of the spouses from the common matrimonial home. On the contrary, the result of lifting separation is not an automatic revocation of constituent decisions comprised in the separation judgment. The court has to decide anew about parental authority over the spouses' child. The situation of the child requires considerable caution on the part of the court and delivery of a resolution which best suits the interest of the child. As far as the property relationships between the spouses are concerned, expiry of separation results in the expiry of the compulsory regime of property separation, unless the spouses wish to remain bound by this regime, which is a relatively frequent case. This depends however on the intention of the spouses and their financial position.

Chapter 3. Relations Between Parents and Children

§1. Mother and Father of the Child

I. Maternity, Its Determination and Denial

244. Changes introduced by the Act of 6 November 2008 amending the FGC as well as certain other statutes,[84] had serious consequences which reached the very core of certain institutions regulated in the Code. This concerns in particular questions related to the child's origin, which makes an additional element of adjusting Polish family law to international conventional law, the EU legislation and Strasbourg judicature. The changes reflect as well serious problems which arise along with the development of medical sciences in the field of assisted procreation,[85] which in turn is connected with severe demographic disturbances resulting from the decrease in birth rate and changes in civilization presented in the introductory part of this article.

245. When it comes to maternity, this phenomenon had not been previously regulated in a statute. The Roman dictum *mater semper certa est* was taken for granted as a valid principle in Polish society. At the same time, both judicature and doctrinal writings noted that this principle was not always correct. Doubts which emerged in the course of determining the maternity of a particular child seemed to contradict the Roman dictum. The doubts resulted from various causes which can be divided into certain groups:

(1) Organizational grounds: these consist of the substitution of children born in hospital by medical personnel – typically by accident, or deliberately by two mothers, the first having just lost the baby she was carrying at birth and the second who has just given birth to a healthy baby that she does not wish to keep, where after discharge from the maternity facility, that child is transferred to the first mother. A situation may also occur where a pregnant woman who does not wish to have the baby she is carrying, uses the documents of another woman at the time of birth and that other woman is subsequently registered as the mother of the newborn child. In such ways, adoption procedures can be evaded. Practices such as this can in part be blamed on adoption procedures that are seen by many prospective adopters as being overly complicated, take far too long to accomplish and offer no guarantee of success.

(2) Surrogacy grounds: the rapid development of medical sciences in recent years, especially in the field of medically assisted procreation, has led to the emergence of so-called surrogate motherhood, in turn giving rise to highly complicated legal questions concerning the origin of the child.[86]

84. Journal of Statutes 2008, no. 220, item 1431.

85. R. Hubbart, A. Jaegger & W. Stanford, *Nasze ciala, nasze życie* (Gdańsk, 2008), 403–404.

86. M. Nesterowicz, *Prawo medyczne* (Toruń: TNOiK, 2007), 258 et seq.; Piasecki, 'Article 61^9 Commentary', in K. Piasecki (ed.), *Kodeks*, 623–628.

246. As far as the first group is concerned, and the possibility of inadvertent substitution of a child, it would be neither complicated nor difficult to prove that a given woman whose child had been substituted or replaced is not the mother of the particular child if the father is known and the biological evidence generally used in the proceedings regarding the establishment of paternity is allowed. However, this requires early discovery of the substitution, which more often than not comes to light until long after the child's birth. The mother might learn of the child and initiate legal proceedings which lead to the repudiation of motherhood recorded in the civil status records and the subsequent judicial ascertainment of motherhood of another woman, namely the biological mother of the child.

247. The second group is even more complicated. The notion of surrogate motherhood can cover various states of affairs. First of all, it may refer to a situation in which a woman who can conceive and complete pregnancy is clinically impregnated and delivers the child for another woman, or man, to raise.[87] Unquestionably, in such circumstances, the surrogate mother is the genetic mother (since the egg cell is hers) and the biological mother (because she completes the pregnancy and delivers the child). Still, such cases are rare in practice. Most frequently surrogate motherhood is the case where an embryo created from an oocyte of a woman and a spermatozoon from her husband (the donors) is transferred to the uterus of another woman (the surrogate) who incurs the obligation to complete the pregnancy, deliver the child and pass it over to the donors who will then raise it as their own offspring.[88]

248. At the same time, for many years it has been emphasized in scholarly writings that establishing who the mother is remains an absolutely fundamental question that must be decided in order to determine the child's origin. In the case of failure in its determination, it becomes impossible to establish who the father is. Since in Polish law paternity most frequently follows from the presumption that the child comes from the mother's husband, maternity must be determined in advance if we are to establish who her husband is or was at the time of delivery. The presumption upholds as well if the child is born within 300 days from termination or annulment of marriage or the adjudication of separation. If there are no grounds for this presumption, the fatherhood of a child may be determined by acknowledgement of paternity by the child's father, which must be confirmed by the mother of the child within the period specified in Article 73 §1 FGC, which serves to confirm that motherhood must be established in advance. Moreover, the man who claims to be the biological father of the child may prove this only based on the fact of having had sexual intercourse with the child's mother in the conceptive period. If he fails to demonstrate who the mother is, he cannot successfully claim paternity. The third method of determination of the child's paternity is its judicial ascertainment, based on the presumption expressed in Article 85 §1 FGC. This provision stipulates that

87. M. Safjan, 'Prawne problemy zastępczego macierzyństwa', in W. Lang (ed.) *Prawne problemy ludzkiej prokreacji* (Toruń: TNOiK, 2000), 292.
88. *Ibid.*, 293, and Nesterowicz, *Prawo medyczne*, 257, *see also*, P.F. Silva-Riuz, 'Macierzyństwo zastępcze', *RPEiS*, no. 7–8 (1991): 123.

the father of the child is the man who had sexual intercourse with the child's mother in the so-called conceptive period (i.e., not earlier than the 300th day and not later than the 181st day before the day the child was born). Thus, the determination of maternity is of primary importance.

249. After the above-mentioned amendment of the FGC, the statute still fails to regulate questions of surrogate motherhood. Nevertheless, Article 61^{9} FGC establishes the principle that the woman who delivered the baby is considered the child's mother. In light of such a solution, it becomes disputable whether discussion over the admissibility of surrogate motherhood is justified or even sensible since it has become impossible to enforce the woman legally recognized as the mother to surrender the child to another woman who cannot be considered as the mother under current legal provisions.[89]

250. The stance taken by the legislator in this regard results in the first place from Article 2 of the European Convention on The Legal Status of Children Born Out of Wedlock of 15 October 1975.[90] This provision stipulates that the origin of a child born out of a wedlock shall be determined solely on the basis of the child's birth, which in turn follows from the certificate of birth of the child.[91] Such principle is applicable in most EU Member States. As a result, it was also included in Polish legislation. Unfortunately, the rule does not eliminate doubts that may emerge as to maternity in a specific situation.

251. Should uncertainty arise as to the motherhood of a child, the woman who claims to be the mother has to prove that she delivered the child. However, this may be as simple as it seems if it transpires that the documentation concerning the child's delivery is itself a source of doubt, or if another party proves that specific events took place, such as forgery of the birth certificate, or that the child had been taken unlawfully. Clearly, it cannot be taken for granted that the documentation alone provides absolute confirmation of an event, namely the delivery of a particular child by a particular woman. Moreover, it seems that the thesis about the sufficiency of the genetic link between a given woman and the child is flawed. In a situation where a woman delivers a baby after being implanted with an embryo derived from the gametes coming from another woman and her husband, under the discussed provision, the only person who can be recognized as the mother is the surrogate mother because she is the one who has given birth to the child.

252. This type of interpretation is triggered by serious biological considerations. One could summarize these in a single question: should the genetic heritage be decisive for the child, or are the conditions which take place in a woman's organism during pregnancy, her biological conditions and the way of life, diet, intellectual and emotional development, etc., be more important?

---

89. K. Gromek, *Kodeks*, 697–702.
90. Journal of Statutes 1999, no. 79, item 888.
91. Piasecki, 'Article 61^{9} Commentary', in K. Piasecki (ed.), *Kodeks*, 627–628.

253. In light of investigations in modern perinatology, it turns out that the conditions of prenatal life exert a serious influence on the formation of the foetus and genetic preconditions are important for the further development of the child. It would be impossible to neglect the specific phenomenon of emergence of a strong emotional bond between the woman who is pregnant and delivers the child and the baby she gave birth to. This connection becomes especially intensified in the period of birth, feeding the child and the necessity to satisfy its biological and emotional needs.[92] As shown in practice, the emotional link is the cause of frequent cases of refusal to pass the baby over to the genetic parents by the surrogate mother.

254. It seems that the provision which stipulates that the mother is the woman who gave birth to the child should result in a decline of interest in surrogate motherhood since the norm questions the possibility of achieving the purpose of the contract for surrogate motherhood on the part of the genetic parents, that is the reception of a child being their genetic offspring. In the case of refusal to pass over the baby on the part of the surrogate mother, there are no grounds to evaluate her behaviour negatively since the law regards her as the mother and as the mother, the woman undergoes constitutional protection following, for instance, from Articles 47 and 71 §2 CRP.

255. While discussing these issues, it should be added that the current legal situation does not completely exclude the possibility of achieving the final goal of surrogate motherhood. Currently, contracts for surrogate motherhood are treated by courts as juridical acts contrary to law and the principles of social coexistence. There is always a possibility that the woman who delivered the baby should decide that she does not intend to raise it and agrees to her child's adoption. It might happen on such occasions that the adopting parties would be the genetic parents of the child. In the same way, the effect of the agreement could be produced, the genetic parents obtaining the child in a situation where the genetic mother was unable to complete the pregnancy and give birth to the child personally. In no way, however, can any agreement prior to the child's birth by the surrogate mother provide for her obligation to give consent to adoption.

256. In the first place, this would be contrary to the fundamental principles on which the construction of adoption is based in the FGC, which does not provide for contractual grounds for adoption. In Polish law, adoption can take place only as a result of a court decision (Articles 114-114^2 FGC and following ones).[93] Moreover, pursuant to Article 119^2 FGC, the consent to adoption cannot be expressed earlier than six weeks after the child's birth. One should agree with H. Ciepla[94] that this period is justified not only in light of the European Convention on Adoption but

92. R. Bokiniec, *Podstawy neonatologii* (Warszawa, 2008); F. Gomella, M.D. Cunningham & F.G. Eyal, *Neonatologia* (Katowice, 1993).
93. Cf. B. Walaszek, *Przysposobienie w polskim prawie rodzinnym oraz w prawie międzynarodowym prywatnym i procesowym* (Warszawa, 1966); J. Panowicz-Lipska, 'Przysposobienie (Zagadnienia wybrane)', in *Rodzina w świetle prawa i polityki społecznej*, ed. T. Smyczyński (Poznań UAM, 1990), 59; H. Haak, *Przysposobienie. Komentarz* (Toruń: TNOiK, 1996), Gromek, *Kodeks*, 932.
94. Ciepła, 'Article 119^2 Commentary', in K. Piasecki (ed.), *Kodeks*, 877.

above all, it is to prevent premature consent of the parents, especially the child's mother, to adoption. Additionally, if such consent had been given before the expiry of the six-week period, it would not be valid, and the expiry of the discussed period would not result in the validation of such an ineffective consent.

257. As can be derived from the provisions discussed above, the correct establishment of the child's origin sometimes requires the determination or repudiation of maternity. Both remedies may be employed only after the child's birth. The repudiation of motherhood may be necessary in situations where a woman who did not give birth to the child has been recorded as the mother in the civil status record.

258. The subjects entitled to initiate proceedings regarding the repudiation of motherhood are only persons with personal interest, not economic interest (e.g., heirs). In every case, the action can be brought before the court by a public prosecutor. The persons involved include the child, the woman who did not deliver the child but has been registered in the birth certificate as the mother, the woman who actually gave birth to the child, the husband of the woman registered in the birth certificate as a mother, the man who acknowledged paternity based on the belief that the woman registered as a mother is the actual mother, finally the man who has been judicially confirmed as the father as a result of having sexual intercourse with the woman registered as the mother within her conceptive period.

259. A judgment of the court delivered in such a case is of declaratory character, which means that it does not yield effects in the sense of creating a new legal relationship. The judgment is effective *ex tunc* and constitutes grounds for a respective entry in the certificate of birth. Moreover, a binding judgment repudiating motherhood automatically extinguishes any judicial decision on the establishment of paternity, as well as paternity which follows from the presumption of the marital origin of the child.

II. Paternity

260. The legal means of determining the child's paternity provided in the FGC comprise an exhaustive catalogue, even though one can encounter the opinion within doctrinal writings that it is impossible to exclude the establishment of paternity on the basis of Article 189 PCPC, which provides that the claimant may demand judicial determination whether a given right or legal relationship exists or not, whenever the claimant has a legal interest in deciding the case.

261. The legal means of determining paternity provided for in the FGC are the presumption that the mother's husband is the father, the acknowledgement of paternity (previously called the acknowledgement of the child), and finally, the judicial establishment of paternity. Since the civil status of a child is indivisible, the determination of paternity cannot take place until the previous determination has been extinguished. For example, the child, even though born within the marital bond, does not enjoy the presumption of the origin from the mother's husband if another man acknowledged the child's paternity in the period before the child's delivery. In consequence, where the biological father has not acknowledged paternity before the child's birth, the subsequent acknowledgement of paternity on his part is going to be possible only after the effective rebuttal of the paternity of the mother's husband.

262. The current formulation of provisions pertaining to both the determination and the denial of paternity, is an expression of the recent advent of accurate scientific testing, in particular DNA testing, which nowadays allows not only to exclude paternity but also to positively establish that a particular man is the father of the child. However, such evidence is not exclusive in the processes leading to the determination or denial of the origin of a child. It still remains necessary to prove the existence of conditions which a particular provision of law treats as the basis of certain presumptions which serve the same purposes. Also, it is necessary to remember that while the use of the latest scientific techniques to gather forensic evidence reduces the risk of error to the nth degree, the process is not totally infallible and, albeit rarely, mistakes can still occur(substitution of analysis results, error in the sampling of particular substance for analysis, improper implementation of procedures or the lack of due care in the examination itself).[95]

A. *Presumption of the Marital Origin of the Child*

263. Legal regulation concerning the determination of paternity on the basis of the presumption of the child's origin from the husband of the mother is contained in Article 62 FGC and makes an expression of the principle deriving from Roman law that *pater est quem nuptiae demonstrant*. The rule in question envisages that where the child was born in the course of matrimony, or before the lapse of 300 days from its termination or annulment, it is to be presumed that the child originates from the mother's husband. However, if the child was born within this period, but after the mother's conclusion of another marriage, it is to be presumed that the current husband is the father. The latter presumption will not apply if the child was born as a consequence of a medically assisted procedure to which the original husband agreed. In consequence, it is meaningless whether or not the spouses remained in common conjugal life at this time, or whether the man knows about the birth of the child by his wife, and whether he was entered as the child's father in the certificate of birth, or another man has been entered therein.[96] This presumption has been excluded only in the situation where the spouses remain in separation resulting from

95. M. Safjan, 'Prawne problemy', 292; M. Safjan, *Prawo wobec ingerencji w naturę ludzkiej prokreacji* (Warszawa, 1990); Nesterowicz, *Prawo medyczne*, 257; M. Fras & D. Abłażewicz, 'Reżim prawny macierzyństwa zastępczego na tle porównawczym', *Problemy Współczesnego Prawa Międzynarodowego, Europejskiego i Porównawczego*, vol. VI (2007): 31 et seq.; J. Holocher & M. Soniewicka, 'Analiza prawna umowy o zastępcze macierzyństwo', *Prawo i Medycyna* 3 (2009): 43 et seq.; Gromek, *Kodeks*, 710–713.

96. Supreme Court decision issued on 10 Apr. 1969, II CR 59/69, OSNCP 1970/4/62.

a respective judicial decision. It should be assumed that since the basis for adjudicating separation was the complete disintegration of conjugal life, which covers among other things sexual intercourse, the child cannot originate from the separated spouse.

264. Naturally, the above mechanisms of determining paternity are only based on legal presumptions, and paternity as such can be determined differently in a situation where the presumptions are rebutted as a result of a claim for the denial of matrimonial paternity. It must be emphasized, however, that effective denial of paternity as a result of judicial proceedings leading to the determination of the child's origin, is the only admissible way of rebutting said presumptions. Therefore, this cannot take place in the course of some other judicial process, for example, divorce or separation proceedings. Proceedings leading to the determination of paternity and the evidence allowable therein have been simplified as a result of the 2008 amendment of the FGC, which proved possible only as a consequence of advances in the area of DNA testing. Such scientific achievements allow determining with a very high degree of probability whether a given child originates or not from a particular man. The diversified premises of denying paternity, as provided in the FGC, have been replaced with only one, namely the demonstration that the mother's husband is not the father of the child, which may now be undertaken with more certainty as a result of allowing the scientific results from a specialist testing laboratory to be accepted as evidence. It is worth mentioning that evidence of this kind is currently in wide use and testing is readily accessible as far as cost is concerned. Bearing in mind the situation presented above, and the fact that the evidence produced might (although very rarely) prove misleading, one cannot definitively claim that it is so certain that it cannot undergo further examination on the part of the court, or that it should eliminate all other forms of evidence. The evaluation of the court cannot meaningfully address the technical aspects of DNA expertise, but it can question issues such as the selection of material subject to analysis, suspicion of its replacement or improper collection. Such circumstances may give rise to the court ordering a second test to be conducted by a different laboratory, subsequently adjudicating on grounds of the court's evaluation as to which of the two tests is correct. Proceedings leading to the denial of paternity may be instantiated by the following parties, who must act within the prescribed preclusive periods:

(1) Mother's husband – this is not the most precise term, since it refers to a man who was the mother's husband at the time of the child's birth or before the lapse of the 300-day period from the dissolution or annulment of marriage, even though he might no longer be the mother's husband when he brings the respective action before the court. The term which precludes the action is a one-year period from the moment he learnt about the birth of the child by his wife, but no later than the day on which the child attains the age of majority (Article 63 FGC). The Code provides also for a special situation if the entitled party within the prescribed period suffered from mental sickness or mental disorders which resulted in his full incapacitation. On such occasions, the guardian appointed for this spouse may within one year from the moment of his or

her appointment or the moment the guardian learnt about the birth of the child bring the respective action for denial of matrimonial paternity. If the guardian fails to institute the proceedings and the incapacitation becomes lifted, the respective spouse may bring the action before the court within one year from the termination of incapacitation. A certain novelty has been included in the present formulation of Article 68 FGC which envisages that the denial of paternity shall not be admissible if the child was born as a result of a medically assisted procedure to which the mother's husband consented. This rule seems superfluous in our view since the courts assumed that the judicial proceedings instituted by the entitled person in the situation of consent to artificial insemination expressed in the course of the procedure violate the principles of social coexistence, which produces effects envisaged in Article 5 PCC, which remains legally binding also in respect to family relationships.

(2) The mother of the child may also bring an action for denial of her husband's paternity within a period of one year from the date she learned that the child did not come from him, but no later than the day on which the child attains the age of majority (Article 69 §1 FGC).

(3) Originally, the child after attaining the age of majority could have instituted the respective proceedings within a period of three years. This provision was found unconstitutional in a 2018 judgment of the Polish Constitutional Tribunal[97] insofar as it prescribed the time limit to institute proceedings, regardless of when the child who attained majority learned about not being the child of the mother's husband. It was held that determining when the prescribed time limit has elapsed without taking into account the moment, the relevant information was acquired by the child who attained the age of majority, violates Article 30 in connection with Articles 47 and 31 section 3 CRP. An amendment of this provision has since come into effect and currently, the child who has attained the age of majority may institute the respective proceedings within a year of learning about circumstances justifying the denial of paternity. If the child has learned about these circumstances before attaining the age of majority, the one-year period starts running when that age is attained (Article 70 §1 FGC).

265. Pursuant to Article 86 FGC, an action for establishing or contradicting paternity and for establishing the ineffectiveness of the acknowledgement of a child can also be brought by the public prosecutor, if it is required by the interest of the child or the protection of public interest. The prosecutor is not bound by any time limitations in this regard. However, if the child died before attaining the age of majority, the public prosecutor may still bring an action for denial of paternity and the ineffectiveness of the acknowledgement provided such action is initiated by the date the child would have attained that age. If the child had died after attaining the age of majority, it is not admissible for the prosecutor to bring an action for denial of paternity and establishing the ineffectiveness of the acknowledgement.

97. Judgment of 16 May 2018, SK 18/17.

266. The judgment delivered in the proceedings for the denial of marital paternity is, according to the majority of academics, of declaratory character, since it does not give rise to any new legal relationship of the child, it only ascertains that there is not and never has been a parental relationship between the child and the mother's husband. This signifies that the parental authority of the affected man over the child expires with retrospective effect, so does the right to inherit from one another, and the alimony obligation of that person in relation to the child. Moreover, the child gains the right to the mother's surname which she had at the time of the child's birth.

B. Acknowledgement of Paternity

267. The acknowledgement of paternity is one of the two means of determining paternity which does not stem from the presumption of matrimonial origin. Before the recent amendment of the FGC, this procedure was referred to as 'the acknowledgement of the child'.

268. The change introduced in the amended statute is not a simple change in wording. As its consequence, the man who recognizes paternity confirms that the child originated from him, and not merely accepts that the child should benefit from the status of being his child. The need for such amendment was triggered by the fact that the essential issue is to determine paternity according to the genetic truth referred to in Article 454^1§2 PCPC which, in the original wording of the rule, was not altogether clear. Moreover, the amendment followed from the necessity to adjust Poland's legislation to accommodate the European Convention on the Legal Status of Children Born Out of Wedlock (ratified by Poland in 1999), which envisaged that the origin of the child may be determined by means of voluntary acknowledgement by the biological father.

269. In light of the above, it is clear that currently, only the biological father may acknowledge his paternity by making a declaration of intent comprising an endorsement, or rather an ascertainment, of his relationship of paternity in respect to the child. Such declaration is made before Registrar of a BMDRO, a guardianship court or a Polish consul abroad, as well as before any other of the officials referred to in Article 74 §1 FGC.

270. Singularly, the declaration constitutes neither a juridical act nor proper acknowledgement. The legal character of acknowledgement cannot at the time being be considered as contractual, since the consent of the child's mother in the present legal order was replaced by her endorsement, i.e., confirmation, that the man acknowledges the child is the father. Moreover, the consent of the statutory representative of a father who lacks in full the capacity to perform juridical acts but who has already attained the age of 16 years, was replaced by a declaration of acknowledgement before a guardianship court. As a consequence, the declaration is a family law act which produces important effects not only between the acknowledging party and the child but towards everyone. When it comes to the premises of validity, it constitutes a family law juridical act.

271. Another crucial modification is that the act of acknowledgement does not require the mother's consent, although her confirmation is still mandatory. In practice, and contrary to the interest of the child, the mother's consent was frequently not given, which led to the introduction of the child's father having the capacity to sue in proceedings leading to the judicial ascertainment of paternity. The current solution seems better. It allows determining the paternity of the child in a case where there are no grounds for determination by other means (presumption of origin from the mother's husband and judicial ascertainment of paternity). Here, It is crucial to underscore that the premise of admissibility of acknowledgement of paternity is the fact that paternity has not yet been determined in any other way, neither by judicial ascertainment of paternity nor by the presumption of origin from the mother's husband.

272. The previous judicature of the Supreme Court in this respect preserved its validity. In its light, acknowledgement of paternity cannot take place as long as paternity following from the presumption of the child's origin from the mother's husband has not been rebutted. On the contrary, where paternity has been acknowledged before the birth of a child already conceived and the mother enters into marriage before delivery of the child, pursuant to Article 75 §2 FGC, the presumption of marital origin of the child shall not apply since the origin of the child has already been ascertained by way of acknowledgement.

273. A new provision contained in Article 75^1 FGC[98] concerns the acknowledgement of paternity of a child born as a result of a medically assisted procreation procedure. Acknowledgement of paternity usually takes place after the birth of the child. However, it may also take place before the transfer to the woman's organism of the reproductive cells of an anonymous donor or an embryo created from the reproductive cells of an anonymous donor or from embryo donation. Here, the man declares to the Registrar of a BMDRO that he will be the father of a child who will be born following a medically assisted procreation procedure using these cells or that embryo, and the woman must confirm at the same time or within three months of the man's declaration, that the man will father the child. The acknowledgement of paternity becomes effective at the time of the child's birth. Both the acknowledgement and confirmation are effective only if the child is born no later than two years from the day when these statements were made. If the child is born after the mother has entered into a marriage with a man different to the man who acknowledged paternity before the medically assisted procedure, the new husband will not be presumed to be the father of the child.

274. The second prerequisite refers only to a child that has been conceived but as yet not born or to a minor child. Consequently, it would be impossible to

98. Journal of Statutes 2015, item 1087, became binding on 1 Nov. 2015.

acknowledge the paternity of a child who has attained the age of majority and a child who had died, unless death occurred before the child came of age (Articles 75 and 76 FGC). The man may make the declaration acknowledgement within the term of one year from the moment he learnt of the child's death, but no later than the day on which the child would have otherwise attained the age of majority (Article 76 §2 FGC). Acknowledgement may regard only a child whose maternity has been determined. In the same way, it is impossible to acknowledge the paternity of a child originating from unknown parents, or a child whose maternity following from the birth certificate has been denied. One cannot as well acknowledge paternity of a child who has become adopted in absolute terms, that is as adjudicated on the basis of anonymous consent of the parents to such adoption, because this type of adoption cannot be dissolved. However, acknowledgement can take place if the child was fully adopted but in a way that is wholly or partially dissoluble.

275. As far as the requirements pertaining to the man who acknowledges paternity are concerned, it is accepted that the declaration of acknowledgement may be made only by a person who has sufficient understanding as to the sense and effects of the acknowledgement of paternity. It is required that the acknowledging party be at least 16 of age and that there are no grounds for his full incapacitation. Consequently, this cannot be a person suffering from mental sickness or mental deficiency, or a person affected by mental disorders derived from alcoholism or drug addiction which affect the person to such an extent that he is no longer capable of controlling his conduct. However, admitting the possibility of acknowledgement by a minor over 16 years of age follows as well from Article 453^1 PCPC which provides that in actions for determination or denial of paternity the mother and father of the child have the right of action also where they have limited capacity to perform juridical acts if they fulfil the requirement of having attained the age of 16.

276. When it comes to the legal effects produced by acknowledgement of paternity, such act leads primarily to the ascertainment of civil status of the child to whom the acknowledgement relates, namely establishment of his or her origin from the person acknowledging paternity. Such determination is of a declaratory character since it only serves to confirm what is already the case biologically, thus enabling that existing personal relationship to be demonstrated. The acknowledgement produces *ex tunc* effects, which means from the moment of the child's birth. Its consequences are effective *erga omnes*.

277. In the area of personal relations, acknowledgement brings about the following special effects:

(1) The child bears the name chosen concordantly by the parents in the declarations made together with the statements on acknowledgement and endorsement of acknowledgement. As a result, the child may, according to their will, bear the surname of either parent, or surname being a combination of the mother and father's surnames.
(2) The father enjoys *ex lege* parental authority. In our opinion, since the acknowledgement produces *ex tunc* legal effects, and is of declaratory character only,

it should be accepted that also in this respect one may speak of the retrospective effect of recognition. Especially in a situation where before the acknowledgement the father exercised custody over the child and made certain acts in the interest of the child because he was conscious of his paternity, there are no grounds to assume that the acts were ineffective since made before the acknowledgement of paternity.

278. In the sphere of property relations acknowledgement of the child is highly significant, because:

(1) the mutual right of inheritance arises, following from family relations;
(2) there exists the duty of alimony between the father and the child, as a result of which a person who supported the child without any legal title before the acknowledgement of paternity may claim reimbursement of the costs of that support from the child's father.

279. Acceptance of the concept of acknowledgement different from the previous model also triggers legal consequences concerning the possible ineffectiveness of acknowledgement, in respect to which certain minor modifications have been introduced.

280. This takes place as a result of ascertainment of the ineffectiveness of paternity acknowledgement by the court. A child who has attained the age of majority may request the ascertainment of the ineffectiveness of paternity recognition within one year from the date on which he or she found out that the man who acknowledged paternity was not the father. If the child learned of this before attaining the age of majority, the one-year period starts to run from the date that age is reached. In relation to the period prescribed to raise such a claim, it has been added to Article 81 §3 FGC, that the rules of Articles 64 and 65 FGC (which refer to prolongation of the term to bring an action for the denial of marital patrimony due to specified circumstances) shall apply accordingly. Unquestionably, in the proceedings leading to the determination of ineffectiveness of the acknowledgement of paternity, the child should clearly indicate that the man acknowledging paternity was not, or could not be their father, or that some person other than the man who acknowledged paternity is the actual father.

281. The man who has acknowledged his paternity may bring an action for ascertaining its ineffectiveness within one year from the date on which he found out that the child is not his descendant. If the acknowledgement was made before the child was born, the period does not begin to run until the date of the child's birth. However, if paternity was acknowledged on the basis of Article 75^1 FGC, ascertaining its ineffectiveness is admissible only if the child was not born as a result of a planned medically assisted procreation procedure (Article 81^1 FGC). Since the law provides for the possibility to acknowledge paternity exclusively in the case where the man making the acknowledgement is the biological father of the child, in our opinion, this man, as well as the child's mother, may raise the claim for ascertaining the ineffectiveness of paternity acknowledgement only when it becomes apparent that the acknowledging party is not the biological father, regardless of whether or not the declaration of acknowledgement was made in conditions that qualify as a defective manifestation of intention. This follows as well, as has been correctly assumed in the doctrine, from the equal position of all persons having a direct interest in such proceedings, that is the child, the father and the mother.[99]

C. Judicial Determination of Paternity

282. As far as judicial determination of paternity is concerned, the recent amendment did not introduce any crucial modifications. The introduction in Article 84 FGC (as a result of an earlier amendment to the Code) of the capacity for the presumed father to sue, was triggered by the fact that the child's mother frequently declined to confirm paternity acknowledgement even though the father was willing to acknowledge it. There are, of course, situations in which the mother might consider refusal to be justified in the best interest of the child, for example, where she believes the man making the acknowledgement is not acting in the child's interest but rather his own, including for financial gain. However, this does not serve to excuse refusal. Under the current legal mechanism, the mother does not express her consent to the acknowledgement of paternity. Pursuant to Article 73 §1 FGC, she is required to confirm either simultaneously or within the period of three months from the date of the man's declaration that he is the father of the child. If the mother refuses to confirm the man's declaration because she believes that he is not the father of the child, this may raise sufficient doubt as to the child's origin to cause the Registrar of the BMDRO to refuse to accept the declaration of paternity recognition (Article 73 §3 FGC), but this is not always the case. It would be difficult to consider such a refusal as justified if its sole motivation was the mother's opposition concerning the determination of paternity of the child and acceptance of her exclusive parental rights. In consequence, we are of the opinion that the capacity to sue on the part of the father of the child has been justly preserved when it comes to the judicial determination of paternity. This provides him with the possibility to define the family status of the child as a result of judicial proceedings and with his own status as the child's father being thoroughly examined within the proceedings where the paternity is to be ascertained or excluded.

283. The Judicial determination of paternity takes place in litigation mode if there is a dispute as to the fatherhood of the child. The capacity to sue is vested in such cases in the persons who have a direct legal interest in the determination of the child's origin. These parties are:

99. Piasecki, 'Article 78 and 79 Commentary', in K. Piasecki (ed.), *Kodeks*, 686–687; W. Stojanowska, 'Europejska Konwencja o statusie prawnym dziecka pozamałżeńskiego a stan prawny obowiązujacy w Polsce', in M. Safjan (ed.), *Standardy prawne Rady Europy, Teksty i Komentarze* (Warszawa, 1994), 65, S. Kalus, 'Zmiany w kodeksie rodzinnym i opiekuńczym dotyczące problematyki pochodzenia dziecka', in J. Mazurkiewicz (ed.), *Kodeks rodzinny i opiekuńczy po nowelizacji* (Wrocław: Wydawnictwo Uniwersytetu Wrocławskiego, 2010), 33–43.

(1) the child who may sue independently after coming of full age or the mother may sue on behalf of a minor child;
(2) the child's mother on her own behalf or on behalf of the child, regardless of whether or not she enjoys parental authority. Moreover, as a result of an amendment to the PCPC in such cases both the mother and father of the child shall have the procedural capacity to sue also when they have limited legal capacity to perform juridical acts if they have attained the age of 16 years (Article 453^1 PCPC);
(3) the child's father. Before the recent amendment to the FGC, there was no capacity to sue provided for the presumed father of the child in this respect, justifying this with the fact that he may acknowledge the child. The lack of cooperation from mothers who would refuse their consent regarding the acknowledgement of paternity led to awarding fathers the power to sue. As far as the father's capacity to sue is concerned, this also applies to minor fathers after attaining the age of 16 years, and where the father has not attained the age of 16 years, his guardian may raise the claim on his behalf with the consent of guardianship court;
(4) the public prosecutor. He has the capacity to sue independent of the permission of the child's mother, or the child itself, even where the child is a major child, as long as the initiation of the proceedings is justified by the interest of the child and public interest.

284. Judicial determination of paternity is based on the presumption that the father of the child is the man who had sexual intercourse with the child's mother not earlier than on the 300th and not later than on the 181st day preceding the child's birth (Article 85 §1 FGC). The foregoing is deemed to represent the mean maximum and minimum gestation periods in which a foetus can develop in the womb and the resultant child be capable of survival at birth. The time scale is a product of scientific research and is subject to change as knowledge in the field widens.

285. Proving that sexual intercourse did or did not occur within the period stated in para 283 above is of vital importance. As indicated in the doctrine and judicature, the admission of other evidence for the origin of the child is precluded without this key ascertainment. The defendant may claim that he had no sexual relationship with the child's mother at all, or that he did not have sexual intercourse with her during a conceptive period. Only if this can be proven, can the man proceed to introduce it as evidence that he might not be the father of the child even though he was involved in an intimate relationship with the mother.

286. In the proceedings on judicial ascertainment of paternity, the court hears evidence from the respective witnesses involved, the parties to the case and professional witnesses were called and reviews evidence of scientific evidence submitted, in particular biological evidence. Such evidence may include the expertise of an assessor who matches the date of sexual intercourse and the level of the child's development at the moment of its birth, blood type examination, DNA analysis, anthropological or dactyloscopic investigations. Different legal systems attach varying degrees of significance to these examinations, but in Polish law, the most trusted evidence is DNA analysis and blood type comparison; however, the latter is only deemed certain when it comes to the exclusion of paternity.

287. An interesting rule stems from Article 85 §2 FGC. It provides that if the mother had intercourse in the fertile period with another man, this can form the basis for rebutting the presumption referred to in §1 of this provision, but only in a situation where the paternity of the other man appears more probable. This constitutes the so-called *exceptio plurium concumbentium* defence. However, the opinion of the doctrine seems correct in that the legal and evidential status of the defendant is not particularly easy here, mainly because he is encumbered with the burden of proof. Moreover, it is not sufficient for him to simply demonstrate that the child's mother had intercourse in the fertile period with another man. He must point to that particular man and show that his paternity is more probable.

288. The above-mentioned defence would require the participation of the other man with whom the mother had intercourse in the court proceedings as a party (not merely a witness). Moreover, the court would have to execute subjective conversion of the action in the form of Article 194 PCPC, which might not be feasible. Another problem is triggered by the fact that in conditions of significant sexual laxity among some young women, an extramarital relationship involving just one man is not always going to be the case. Consequently, establishing whether there was more than one man involved and then ascertaining which of them is the most probable father might prove impossible. That and the potential costs involved is the reason why this particular means of defence is rarely used.

289. This rule was well justified in the period when the FGC was first enacted, namely in 1964. Medical science at the time lacked the possibilities to prove that a given child actually originated from a specific man, only that there existed a lesser or greater probability that the child was not his. The most frequently used evidence at the time was blood type. It provided proof which could exclude paternity to a significant degree of probability, but that was all. It could not prove paternity. Therefore, it seems that amendment of the discussed provision is desirable. However, its abrogation cannot be excluded either.

290. As in the case of other judgments pertaining to the child's origin, the judgment referring to judicial ascertainment of paternity is also of declaratory character, since it is a mere ascertainment of the biological origin of the child. Nonetheless, it produces *ex tunc* effects, thus with retrospective force from the moment of delivery of the child and, where the child is to be the heir of the determined father, from the day of conception. This judgment brings about results in the area of the child's civil status since it determines that the child remains in family relations with the determined father. As a consequence, in the respective judgment determining paternity, the court shall give a surname to the child pursuant to Article 89 §§1 and 2 FGC.

291. When it comes to parental authority over a child whose paternity has been determined, such authority is vested in both parents, unless the court, taking into account the interest of the child, suspends, restricts or completely revokes parental authority in respect to one or both of the parents. If the parents of the child are factually separated, the court may, or rather should, determine the way of exercising parental authority. This follows expressly from Article 107 §§1 and 2 FGC. This provision envisages decisions analogical in respect to the ones discussed in the case of component decisions of a divorce judgment. The court leaves the parental authority unrestricted to both parents. This solution is employed if the parents present a written agreement concerning the performance of parental paternity and contacts with the child. If there is no such agreement, the court, taking into account the child's right to be raised by both parents, decides on parental authority. In particular, the court may vest the exercise of parental authority in one of the parents, restricting at the same time parental authority of the other to particular rights, obligations in relation to the child. Upon a unanimous request of the parents, the court also decides about contacts with the child.

292. The recent amendment to the FGC in this area provides for the possibility of settlement between the parents as to the exercise of parental authority, and where the court recognizes that the settlement is in conformity with the interest of the child and that it is justified to expect that the parents are going to cooperate on the issues concerning the child, the court is going to endorse the settlement. By taking such a decision, the court examines if the principle that siblings should be brought up together has been taken into account unless the interest of the child necessitates an alternative solution.

293. Proceedings on the judicial determination of paternity are additionally connected with the need to decide in respect of the alimony for the child since the fact of consanguinity between the child and his or her father gives rise to the alimony obligation. Even though there is no family relation between the child's mother and father, the FGC envisages the possibility for the child's mother to raise the claim for contribution to the fulfilment of her needs corresponding to her three-month maintenance in the period of birth. However, the court may award alimony to her for a longer time if important reasons support such a solution, e.g., where the needs of the mother are enhanced by her health condition, loss of job or other means of independent maintenance.

294. These problems are regulated within the FGC in Article 141, which deals with compensation issues. This article provides for the duty to reimburse the mother's expenses incurred in connection with pregnancy and delivery, such as treatment costs, additional nutrition, transport to health care centres, purchase of proper items necessary in the birth period, loss of entitlements to avail of medical services covered from social insurance, etc. The rights of the child's mother in this respect strengthen her grounds for the claim that the child's father should pay a certain sum in advance to cover the costs of her maintenance in the period of pregnancy and the costs of the child's maintenance for the period of three months following its birth. These claims can be secured under Article 754 PCPC; however, in such a case the child's mother is obliged to bring an action before the court for judicial determination of paternity within the period of three months from the child's delivery.

D. Artificial Methods of Procreation

295. Contemporary parenthood is not particularly easy, not only because it is difficult to support the family on economic grounds, but also because more and more people put off the decision to have children until a later age, once a high level of professional education and employment assuring the maintenance of a family with children has been achieved. This gives rise to many women's problems with the conception of the child. Another common problem of contemporary families is infertility, which can stem from various causes. This leads to the application of different means of in vitro fertilization, and artificial insemination (homological, heterological and mixed insemination).[100] A fairly recent Act of 25 June 2015 on the treatment of infertility regulates the basic issues concerning medical procedures, including handling embryos, connected with treating infertility.[101]

296. Naturally, these issues are difficult and raise many doubts, not only moral but also legal ones. There is no doubt as to the motherhood of a child born as a result of supported procreation. In light of recent amendments to the FGC, the mother of the child is the woman who delivers the baby, regardless of the donors of the genetic material. If the woman is married, bearing in mind that the question of having children is one of the crucial matters of the family, the mother should consult this question with her husband, who should give consent to such procedure. Where he declines to consent, most obviously, despite the presumption of the child's origin from the mother's husband, where the child is born during the marriage, the paternity of this man can be denied. If the consent was properly given and the mother's husband was willing to deny his paternity, before the amendment of the FGC it was assumed that such denial is inadmissible as an abuse of his subjective right (Article 5 PCC). Currently, the problem is decided independently in Article 68 FGC, in accordance to which the denial of paternity shall not be admissible where the child was conceived as a consequence of a medical procedure to which the mother's husband agreed.[102]

297. The issues of supported procreation are additionally covered by general principles of law concerning health care institutions, the patient's consent to a medical procedure and liability for the damage resulting from medical procedures.[103] Moreover, in Poland provisions of the European Biomedical Convention (Convention for the Protection of Human Rights and Dignity of the Human Being with regard to the Application of Biology and Medicine) of 1997 are observed. So is the Recommendation of the Council of Europe regarding *inter alia* protection of

100. Smyczyński, *Prawo*, 230–231, Nesterowicz, *Prawo medyczne*, 254 et seq.
101. Consolidated version: Journal of Statutes 2017, item 865.
102. B. Walaszek, 'Inseminatio artificialis', *Palestra*, no. 5 (1960): 28; B. Walaszek, O niektórych aspektach prawnych inseminatio artificialis', *RPEiS*, no. 1 (1969): 55; Z. Radwański, 'Stanowisko prawne dziecka w nastepstwie sztucznego unasiennienia matki', *Studia Iuridica Sielesiana* 5 (1979): 171; K. Krzekotowska, 'Sytuacja prawna dziecka urodzonego wskutek sztucznego zapłodnienia i implantacji embrionu', *Nowe Prawo*, no. 5–6 (1982): 98; M. Safjan, *Prawo wobec ingerencji w naturę ludzkiej prokreacji* (Warszawa, 1990).
103. Kalus, 'Liability', 47.

embryos and restriction of genetic intervention. These documents undoubtedly set certain restrictions on scientific research and medical practice in this respect.[104]

§2. Legal Position of the Child (General Questions)

I. Name and Surname of a Child

298. The child's name is an element of the civil status, or strictly speaking family status. Bearing this in mind, the surname of a child points to its origin and place in the family. Provisions of the FGC envisage that the naming of the child is correlated with the determination of the child's paternity. When it comes to the name of the child who benefits from the presumption of origin from the mother's husband, in pursuance with Article 88 §1 FGC, the child usually bears the surname of both spouses. Where the spouses have different surnames, the child bears the name indicated in their concordant declarations made simultaneously about the surnames of the spouses after the formation of marriage. This can be the name of both or one of the spouses, or a name derived from combining surnames of the mother and father. Such declaration can be modified by the parents when the birth certificate of their first child is drafted.

299. If the paternity of the child is determined as a result of acknowledgement, the child bears the name indicated in the concordant declarations of the child's parents, made simultaneously with the declarations necessary for the child's acknowledgement. Also, in this case, this can be the surname of the father or mother or a combination of these two. In the lack of the respective declarations, the child shall bear the name derived from the combination of the parents' surnames. If the paternity of the child follows from judicial ascertainment of paternity, the court decides as well in the question of the surname of the child; however, if the child has reached the age of 13, a change of his or her name requires the child's consent. If the paternity of the child has not been determined at all, the child shall bear its mother's surname, and if it remains unknown who the parents of the child are, which is the case, for instance, as regards abandoned children, the surname of such child is chosen by the guardianship court.[105]

300. Children coming from the same parents bear the same surname. Article 90 FGC envisages as well that where the mother of the minor child enters into marriage with a man who was not the father of her child, the spouses can make concordant declarations before the Registrar of a BMDRO that the child is going to bear the same name as their common children. Nonetheless, it is not admissible to give this surname to the child where he or she bears the surname of his or her father or the name created by combining the names of the father and mother. The same rules apply where the actual father of the child enters into marriage with a woman who is not the child's mother. Because of the provisions on combining surnames, Article

104. Nesterowicz, *Prawo medyczne*, 268.

105. Ciepła, 'Article 88 Commentary', in K. Piasecki (ed.), *Kodeks*, 712 et seq.

90[1] FGC does not allow that the name deriving from the combination of the father and mother's surnames should have more than two parts.

301. When it comes to the first name of the child, it is only an element of its personal status. It is not a manifestation of any family relationship. This name is chosen by the child's parents who make the respective declaration concerning the selection of the name by the preparation of the child's certificate of birth. It follows from Article 59 CSRL that the Registrar refuses to administer such declaration if the parents choose more than two names if they intend to give the child a ridiculing name or a name which does not allow to differentiate the child's sex. The only female name that can be chosen for a boy is Mary, but it is predominantly used as a second name. There might arise a situation in which by the preparation of the child's certificate of birth the parents fail to make the choice of its name(s). On such occasions, the Registrar enters into the birth certificate a name regularly used in the country, noting this fact in the births, marriages and deaths register.

II. Duty of Support and Respect

302. Among general provisions on the relationships between the parents and children, Article 87 FGC prescribes the duty of mutual respect and support. The duty is not restricted in any respect or differentiated depending on whether the children are minor or not, since the obligation is not attached to paternal authority. It is very significant, especially in the situation where the parents are in old age and their efforts in order to bring up and educate the child, as well as assure proper chances in life, may be practically compensated with the child's care for the parents. The second provision pertaining to this area of legal relationships is Article 91 FGC which envisages in the first place the duty of a child who earns money by his or her own work and lives by the parents to contribute to the maintenance of the family, and, additionally, the obligation to help in the common household on the part of the child who remains supported by the parents and lives with them. Observance of these obligations gives rise to partner relations within the family and prepares the child for independent life and fulfilment of family duties.[106]

III. Parental Authority and Its Modifications

303. 'Parental authority' is a term which has been a source of many disputes in the doctrine of Polish family law. It is emphasized in the first place that the name does not correspond to contemporary social conditions, in which the parents, and especially the father, no longer enjoy unrestrained rights to the child. The child does not make an object of competence of the parents. Quite conversely, the child is a subject whose interest constitutes the essential premise delimitating the content of the parents' authority. It is often suggested to replace the term with the notion of 'parental responsibility' which sounds much calmer and allows to shift attention to

106. *Ibid.*, 725–727.

the person under parental care, and not the perspective of the entitled parents. In the legislation of the Council of Europe, the notion of authority has been replaced by 'parental responsibility', which phrase is nowadays in broad use. The amendment of the FGC of 2008 did not change the statutory term, but significantly modified the legal character of this institution. In particular, the changes were necessitated by the following pieces of international law:

(1) Convention on the Rights of the Child of 20 November 1989.[107]
(2) European Convention on the Exercise of Children's Rights of 25 January 1996.[108]
(3) European Convention on Recognition and Enforcement of Decisions Concerning Custody of Children and on Restoration of Custody of Children of 20 May 1980.[109]
(4) Recommendation of the Council of Europe No. R(84) 4 of 1984 on parental responsibilities.

304. The above pieces of legislation give rise to the following principles; both of the parents exercise control over the child, bring up the child and remain responsible for him or her. Their rights and obligations towards the child precede competencies of any other persons, institutions, public authorities. The rights and obligations of the parents in relation to the child are equal. By exercising parental authority, they should be guided by the interest of the child and commonly make decisions regarding the child. The court is in the position to decide about their relationship towards the child in the case of dissolution of marriage by divorce or separation. The parents are also obliged to inform one another about the exercise of their parental rights and obligations, especially the ones pertaining to important issues of the child.

305. The parties of the relation of parental authority are parents and children. Pursuant to Article 93§1 FGC, parental authority is vested in both parents and emerges *ex lege* at the moment of delivery of the child, and if at this time they could not enjoy the authority, they gain it automatically when the reason for which their authority was excluded becomes nullified. In Polish doctrine, it has been proposed that parental authority emerges already at the moment of the child's conception; however, this view has not become widely accepted.[110]

306. The above principle fails in the case where both parents do not enjoy full capacity to perform juridical acts because of their minority or incapacitation. Moreover, parental authority cannot emerge if the particular family law relationship has

107. Journal of Statutes 1989, no. 220, item 526, with subsequent amendments.
108. Journal of Statutes 2000, no. 107, item 1128.
109. Journal of Statutes 1996, no. 31, item 134.
110. J. Gajda and the criticism of his opinion by Ciepła, 'Article 92 Commentary', in K. Piasecki (ed.), *Kodeks*, 729.

not been established, that is where paternity or maternity has not yet been determined.[111] In such instances, the court must appoint guardianship for the child, since the child cannot function without the statutory representative.

307. The scope of parental authority is composed of personal care of the child, control over his or her property and the child's representation.

308. Personal care of the child denotes concern about his or her upbringing, satisfaction of the child's fundamental life needs, overall development or physical integrity. It follows from Article 96 FGC that personal care consists of concern of the parents for the physical and emotional development of the child, his or her preparation to life in society, right and obligation of the child's upbringing and control of the child's conduct. The total of these activities affects not only the child's development but also its legal situation. If the parents are to bring up the child correctly, they should determine the residence of the child in such a way as to assure themselves of the impact on the upbringing and guidance of the child. Where the parents make a decision concerning a longer stay of the child away from the parental home, this decision falls under the category of important questions of the family and even though it is sometimes necessary bearing in mind the interest of the child (stay in a medical institution, an educational trip abroad), the decision should be made together by both parents. In Polish conditions, another crucial question is the parents' decision to use the assistance of their parents in the process of upbringing of the grandchildren. This should not, however, entail a permanent shifting of care for the child to the grandparents, and release of the parents from the duty of personal care over children and their property.[112] On the contrary, it is indicated in the literature and judicature that the parents' concern for proper formation of the child's personality should also imply their care for enabling the child's contact with relatives, especially grandparents, who can often exert a positive impact on the child, remain strongly attached emotionally to the child and form proper patterns of cooperation in a multigenerational family.[113] Other decisions which affect the legal situation of the child are, for instance, the decision of the parents as to the termination of the child's labour contract, consent to the child's adoption, consent to a medical procedure and decision concerning abortion of pregnancy of a minor daughter.

309. An element which has pointed thus far to the weaker position of the child towards his or her parents was the child's duty of obedience in relation to the parents envisaged in Article 95 §2 FGC. As a result of a recent amendment to the FGC, this duty has become significantly restricted. While it has still been preserved as such, the same provision sets out currently that in questions where the child can make decisions independently and manifest declarations of intent, that is once the child already enjoys partial capacity to perform juridical acts, in questions that do not require the consent of the statutory representative the child should only take into account the opinion of the parents, given in the child's best interest, but does not

111. Haak, *Władza*, 36, Smyczyński, *Prawo*, 256–257.
112. Supreme Court judgment issued on 21 Nov. 1952, C 1814/52, OSN 1953/3/item 92.
113. Supreme Court resolution issued on 14 Jun. 1988, III CZP 42/88, OSN 1989/156.

need to comply with it. Moreover, the legislator has taken into consideration postulates frequently raised in the doctrine to include in the provisions on parental authority the principle which before followed only from the rules regarding guardianship. This consists in the introduction of §4 into Article 95 FGC which stipulates that 'the parents, before making a decision in an important question concerning the child, or the child's property, should hear the child's opinion, as long as his or her intellectual development, health condition and degree of maturity allow this, and allow on a best-effort basis the child's reasonable wishes'.

310. Article 95 §3 FGC sets limits to the exercise of parental authority, which are the interest of the child and the social interest. The child is prepared to live in society, and the upbringing activity of the parents should (in accordance with Article 96 §1 FGC) lead to the child's preparation for work to the benefit of the society, adequately to the child's skills. As a result of the amendment, this provision now stipulates that even the parents who do not exercise parental authority on the grounds of the lack of full capacity to perform juridical acts should not feel released from the care of the child, since they are to participate in the current personal care over the child and the child's upbringing unless the guardianship court should decide otherwise with a view to the child's interest.

311. The exercise of the duty of personal care comprises emotional formation, that is instilling moral principles and principles of social coexistence into the child, forming the child's character, conscientious attitude, diligence and sense of duty, the habit of respect for somebody else's property, including public property and preparation for professional work. The duty of care covers as well physical upbringing, attention to health and life of the child, his or her physical fitness, sports, immunization of the child and proper treatment.[114]

312. Due preparation of the child for future professional work may encompass university education if the skills of the child, his or her ambition and persistence prove sufficient not only to start and continue studies but also to successfully accomplish them. The alimony obligation brought up-to-date by the inclusion of university studies may cease as a result of the lack of positive results in university education.[115]

313. For another thing, one cannot exclude from the scope of the discussed duty the parents' care of proper support of the child, in particular due nutrition, clothes, accommodation and educational equipment or medical aid, which is not tantamount to the alimony obligation, since the latter consists in the provision to the benefit of the child of the means of maintenance and upbringing. Article 96 FGC imposes additionally on the parents the duty of care for the physical and emotional development of the child, and in pursuance of Article 133 §1 FGC, parents are obliged to

114. Ciepła, 'Article 96 Commentary', in K. Piasecki (ed.), *Kodeks*, 741–745, and Smyczyński, *Prawo*, 260–261.
115. Supreme Court judgment issued on 12 Feb. 1998, I CKN 499/97, LEX no. 50545.

alimony renditions for the child who is unable to support himself or herself independently, also in a situation where the child suffers from deprivation. In light of the discussed rules, it should be accepted that the parent is to share even small incomes with the child.[116] They should also claim alimony owed to the child if the alimony is to be paid by persons other than parents.[117]

314. Care over the child's property encompasses as well a number of activities among which one can enumerate factual acts, juridical acts and procedural acts made before courts and other state authorities. It must be remembered that the child can be in possession of his or her own property, even of considerable size, which usually derives from donations made to the child's benefit or from inheritance. As a part of care over property, the parents exercise management of these assets. The scope of management is delimitated in Article 101 FGC. This provision prescribes that both parents shall exercise management over the property, which means that both parents should manage the property with due diligence.

315. This means that both parents are entitled to exercise management and are expected to show average diligence generally required in transactions of a given type.[118] Alternatively, unlike in the case of acts of management of the spouses' assets, a recent amendment does not correlate the need for consent to the particular type of act and a special list of acts requiring consent. The respective provision divides such acts into two categories: *acts of ordinary management*, whose conclusion on the part of the parents is entirely free, unrestricted by judicial control, and *acts exceeding ordinary management*, which cannot be concluded without the consent of the guardianship court, and in relation to which the parents may not give consent when concluded by the child. The legal consequence of a juridical act exceeding the ordinary management is the absolute invalidity of the act. Validation of the act is not admissible.[119]

316. According to the doctrine and judicature, these acts comprise, for instance, payable acquisition by the child of an asset of considerable value, acceptance of donation of an asset, for example, an immovable property which necessitates significant and indispensable expenditures, acceptance or rejection of inheritance in the case of a risk that the patrimony is encumbered with debts, conclusion of a settlement in the proceedings on the division of inheritance, renouncing compensatory claims in relation to the person responsible for inflicting damage, withdrawal of

116. Supreme Court decision issued on 6 Jan. 2000, I CKN 1077/99. LEX no. 51637 and on 14 Nov. 1997, III CKN 217/97, *Prokuratura i Prawo*, no. 9 (1998): 28.
117. K. Jagielski, 'Istota i treść wladzy rodzicielskiej', *Studia Cywilistyczne* III (1963): 150; Supreme Court decision issued on 14 Nov. 1997, III CKN 217/97, *Prokuratura i Prawo*, no. 9 (1998): 28.
118. Due diligence of Art. 355 PCC.
119. Supreme Court resolution issued on 24 Jun. 1961, I CO 16/61, OSNCP 1963/9/187, which has retained validity under the current legislation.

action brought to enforce family status rights, etc.[120] The test which delimitates acts exceeding ordinary management is the natural weight of the concluded act, its results in the sphere of the minor's property, the value of the object of transaction and the broadly understood interest of the child and the protection of his or her prospects in life. The consequence of the lack of permission of the guardianship court provided for in Article 101 §3 FGC is the invalidity of the concluded transaction.[121]

317. Permission awarded by the court should name the act to which the court gives consent, at least its type, after proper evaluation of the respective act from the point of view of its concordance with law, expedience in the economic sense, as well as the interest of the child, which exempts meritorious control of this aspect on the part of other authorities.[122] However, the award of judicial permission does not signify that the parents become obliged to conclude the respective transaction.

318. As has been already mentioned, most often the property of the child is established as a result of donation or inheritance. The testator or donor might not have sufficient trust in the parents as to their management of the property. As a result, the testator is in a position to appoint a trustee for this type of management or, where he or she fails to do so, he or she may apply to the court for the appointment of a judicial trustee.

319. Article 103 FGC defines as well the destination of the pure income from the child's property, which means income reduced by the costs of property maintenance. It has been assumed that the law should not privilege in this respect only the child who has the property. Consequently, this pure income should be used to support and bring up the child who owns the property and his or her siblings, since the standard of living of all children raised together should be equal, which is referred to as 'family solidarity'.[123] If there is any surplus left, it can be used for other justified needs of the family as a whole (e.g., purchase of items for the common household, vacation trip).

320. The third element of parental authority is the representation of the child. The parents are statutory representatives of the child who either has no capacity to perform juridical acts or enjoys partial capacity to perform juridical acts. This denotes that a juridical act made by them on behalf of the child produces legal effects directly for the represented child. Obviously, this representation following from statutory provisions covers juridical acts, acts in judicial and administrative proceedings. These can cover different areas: juridical acts concerning the child's

120. Supreme Court decision issued on: 9 Sep. 1997, I CKU 13/97, *Prokuratura i Prawo*, no. 3 (1998): 29; 5 Mar. 1962, 4 CR 578/61, OSNCP 1963/6/127; 1 Aug. 1966, II CR 279/66, OSNPG 1966, Nos 11–12, pos. 58.

121. Resolution of the full Civil Chamber of the Supreme Court of 30 Apr. 1977, III CZP 73/76 -OSNCP 1978/2/19; 16 Nov. 1982, I CR 234/82, LEX no. 8486.

122. For example, a notary –Supreme Court resolution issued on 29 May 1990, III CZP 29/90, OSNC 1990/12/150.

123. Jagielski, 'Istota i treść', 141.

property, or disposing of particular items belonging to the child's property (alienation of ownership of immovable property, its lease, alienation of inheritance); they may also refer to personal care of the child (consent to a surgery or treatment, raising compensatory or alimony claims on the child's behalf).

321. Since the conclusion of acts mentioned above may be connected with a danger to the child's interests if they collide with the parents' interest, the interest of the siblings of the child whose property is managed, provisions of law envisage situations in which the representation of the child by its parents becomes excluded. In accordance with Article 98 §2 FGC none of the parents may represent the child as regards:

(1) transactions between the children remaining under their parental authority;
(2) juridical acts concluded between the child and one of the child's parents, or the parent's spouse, unless this juridical act produces gratuitous benefits to the child (e.g., donation uncharged with order), or regards means of maintenance and upbringing owed to the child from the other parent (alimony).

322. Where neither of the parents is capable of representing the child who remains under parental authority, the child is represented by a curator appointed by the guardianship court (Article 99 FGC). In the situations indicated in Articles 98 §§2 and 3 FGC, the court hearing the case is obliged to resort to the guardianship court and request the appointment of a curator for the party who lacks the capacity to sue.[124] As a rule, there should be as many curators as there are children to be represented. In the non-litigious mode, the exclusion of the parents' representation is to be evaluated *ad casum* and order such exclusion wherever there arises a possibility of even the slightest, or even only theoretical, conflict of interest.[125] The legislator has also specified who may be appointed as a curator for a child. First, this may be an attorney or a legal counsel who exhibits expertise in dealing with such cases, or cases materially similar to the one to be handled, or who has completed training concerning the principles of representing a child or regarding the rights and needs of a child (Article 99^1 §1 FGC). In less complicated cases, particularly when the court has prescribed in detail the content of the juridical act to be performed, the curator appointed to represent the child may be any person with a completed university legal degree and exhibiting a knowledge of the child's needs. If there are particular circumstances, the person appointed to be a curator may not be required to have a completed university legal degree (Article 99^1 §2 FGC). The above, however, does not apply if the curator is to represent the child in penal proceedings. In such cases, the appointed curator must always be an attorney or legal counsel, pursuant to Article 99^1 §1 FGC. Duties of the child's curator, concerning providing information to or gathering it from parents or other institutions, as well as informing the child about the proceedings are regulated in Article 99^2 FGC.

124. Supreme Court decision of 4 Oct. 1966, II CZ 117/66, OSNCP 1967/2/40.
125. Supreme Court decision of 9 Sep. 1997, I CKU 13/97, *Prawo i Prokuratura*, no. 3 (1998): 29.

323. Once the management over the child's property terminates, the parents in accordance with Article 105 FGC ought to hand over the managed property to the child or the child's statutory representative. At the request of the child or the child's statutory representative submitted before the lapse of one year from the termination of management, the parents are obliged to present the management account. However, this document does not include an account of the incomes from the child's property, which could be spent on purposes indicated in Article 103 FGC. Where the parents inflicted damage to the child as a consequence of their undue management or dissipation of the child's assets, they become liable for the damage caused to the child on the ground of Articles 471 PCC and following ones since it constitutes an instance of liability for defective performance of an obligation imposed on the parents by law. Such a solution is crucial to the child because the burden of proof that the damage was caused as a result of circumstances for which they cannot be held responsible rests on the parents.

IV. Judicial Intervention in the Exercise of Parental Authority by Its Restriction, Suspension or Deprivation

324. In the period when parental authority is exercised by the parents, there may arise situations where, in spite of the principle of integrity of family life envisaged in the CRP, the necessity of judicial intervention in the exercise of parental authority emerges. Moreover, whenever such a situation is the case, the doctrine of family law and judicature does not hesitate to defend such interventions if they are aimed at the protection of the child's interest in the possibly most appropriate manner, adequately to the degree and causes of threat to the interest of the child, as well as the possibility to remove the threat.

325. It should be remembered that threats to the material and personal interests of the child may be the result of miscellaneous circumstances, not just the defective performance of parental authority. One should reject the opinion that the threat to the interest of the child must be connected with undue exercise of parental authority.[126] Especially in large municipal areas, the child is exposed to the very harmful impact of various environments – the child's peers, criminals, and sometimes even within the family or neighbourhood serious problems emerge. On the contrary, we do agree with the thesis that restriction of parental authority does not function as a means of repression in relation to the parents. Rather, it is a means of protecting the endangered interest of the child. Its purpose is to protect the child and at the same time provide assistance to the parents who, for a number of possible reasons, have difficulty in bringing up the child and properly exercising parental authority. Family bonds between the parent and the child are usually based on the affection of love, which in principle makes a sufficient guarantee of the proper exercise of authority. This presumption became the foundation for the concept accepted in Polish law that the parents, unlike guardians, do not undergo supervision of the guardianship court

126. Ciepła, 'Article 109 Commentary', in K. Piasecki (ed.), *Kodeks*, 792.

ex lege. However, if it turns out that the interest of the child so dictates, the court is in a position to order such supervision.[127]

326. One should agree with the statement that in light of the diversity of causes of demoralization or defective socialization, provisions of law should allow for the application of various means leading to the removal of threats to the child's interest on the part of guardianship courts. These courts may adjudicate both certain measures which discipline the parents and submit them to judicial control over their conduct, order their cooperation with auxiliary bodies of the court, social aid institutions, or institutions providing various types of assistance to children. The measures can be both temporary or permanent. Judicature points to the fact that for the enforcement of Article 109 FGC the type of possible defect in the exercise of parental authority does not matter, as long as the defect is the source of threat to the child's interest, whether material or personal. In any case, the threat should be serious, since the intervention of the court in a minor case could do more harm than good.[128]

327. Once the child's well-being is threatened, Article 109 FGC provides for the possibility of delivery of various orders on the part of the court. These orders are not exhaustively enumerated, but their goal is to remove the relevant threat in a manner proportionate to its character. Jurisdiction of Polish courts depicts that this provision correlates the restriction of parental authority only to the prerequisite of threat to the child's interest. Judicial intervention on this ground is not dependent on whether the danger to the interest of the child has been caused by the faulty conduct of the parents. This measure was not meant to be repressive in character. The aim of restricting paternal authority is not only for the protection of the child but also for the provision of help to the parents in order to assure proper exercise of this authority. The discussed provision gives rise to the directive of the prophylactic character of judicial rulings, which orders intervention in the sphere of parental authority once the threat to the interest of the child has emerged, in order to bar the negative results of the defective or incompetent exercise of this authority.[129]

328. These orders comprise in particular:

(1) obliging the parents and the minor to particular conduct, for example, to submit the minor to particular medical procedures, enable the child's artistic activity, or participate in a particular sport, file a motion for the prosecution of a perpetrator of a crime detrimental to the child, refer the parents to proper institutions or specialists dealing with family treatment, counselling or providing other necessary help to the family, and at the same time determine the manner of control of the performance of the respective orders;

---

127. Supreme Court decision issued on 28 Apr. 2000, II CKN 452/00, LEX no. 52548.
128. Supreme Court decision issued on 5 Mar. 1947, II C 1043/46, OSN 1947/59 with a gloss by J. Ignatowicz.
129. Supreme Court decision issued on 13 Sep. 2000, II CKN 1141/00, LEX no. 51069.

(2) determining what acts cannot be concluded by the parents without judicial permission, for instance, the change of profile of the child's education;
(3) submitting the exercise of parental authority to permanent supervision of a judicial trustee. These curators perform an important activity of an educational, socializing and prophylactic character prescribed by the guardianship court. They make community interviews which give the court a possibility to obtain much information crucial for evaluation of the child's situation, first of all about the functioning of the child's family;
(4) referring the minor to an organization or institution established to conduct vocational training or other institution exercising partial care of children;
(5) placing the minor in a foster family or a care and education institution.

329. Obviously, the last type of order intervenes the most in the situation holding between the parents and the children, because it is connected with the disintegration of the previous family bonds. Unfortunately, such a solution is sometimes necessary. It is justified by the fact that sometimes there arises the need to help a family, which help is to remove the family's inefficiency only to finally restore the child to his or her natural family. Consequently, after a recent amendment to the FGC, §4 has been added to Article 109. This rule envisages that in the case of placement of the child in a care and education institution or foster family, the court shall inform the proper unit of social aid which provides relevant help to the family of the child and submits reports concerning the situation of the family, and provide assistance to the court in a period determined by the court. Social aid institutions cooperate as well with judicial trustees. The court may correlate in this manner restriction of parental authority with the submission of parental authority to the supervision of a judicial trustee, as shown above.

330. The issues of providing support for families experiencing problems with raising children as well as concerning foster families are regulated in the Act of 9 June 2011 on the support for the family and the system of foster care.[130] Foster care may take the form of a foster family or institutional foster care. Foster families may be either comprised of persons who are relatives of the child needing care or ones who are not in any way related to the child. There are quite extensive requirements concerning all instances of performing foster care, but their goal is to secure the proper choice of persons for such an important social function as foster care of children.

331. If a foster family has been appointed for a minor without the deprivation of paternal authority of his or her natural parents, that is in the case of the application of this measure as a restriction of parental authority, the parents retain the power of deciding on important questions concerning the child. The child is still represented in judicial proceedings by the natural parents, and not the parents of the foster family in which the child has been placed.[131] Moreover, Article 112^1 FGC provides that

130. Consolidated version: Journal of Statutes 2020, item 821, with subsequent amendments.
131. Judgment of the Voivodeship Administrative Court in Gdańsk issued on 13 Dec. 2007, III SA/Gd 369/07, LEX no. 460741.

the obligation and entitlement to exercise current care of the child placed in a foster family or care and education institution, the child's upbringing and representation in such cases, in particular as regards claims for alimony renditions, are entrusted in the foster family or care and education institution. The remaining obligations and entitlements following from parental authority are vested in the natural parents of the child.

332. In order to establish foundations for the proper exercise of this vital function, it is extremely significant to make the right selection of persons as foster parents for the situation of a particular child. At this point, such circumstances are indicated in the doctrine as decisive for the selection as the fact whether the child remains in the relationship of consanguinity or affinity with the foster parents if they exert proper impact on the child and may improve his or her situation, preparation of the candidates to the fulfilment of the functions of a foster family, sufficient age difference between the members of the foster family and the child, degree of development and fitness of the child, requirements in the area of prophylactic and educational, or socializing, aid, possibilities to fulfil the child's needs and finally the directive following from international conventions and pertaining to non-separation of siblings.

333. A further means of intervention of the court in the exercise of parental authority is its suspension. Article 110 FGC empowers the court to such a decision only in the case where a temporary hindrance occurs in the exercise of the authority by one or both parents. Obviously, in such a case, the court is not obliged to adjudicate this measure, since the hindrance may be so short-lived that it is unnecessary to suspend parental authority, especially in the case where the temporary lack of care on the part of the parents can be compensated with the aid of foster family, and the interest of the child does not require any stricter reaction. In the case where the court decides that the cause of suspension of parental authority ceases to exist, the suspension is lifted by the court. Expiry of the hindrance does not yet lift the suspension *ex lege.*

334. The most severe intervention in the exercise of parental authority is its deprivation in relation to natural parents. This does not mean, however, that the court should order more lenient measures in the first rank, and only where these measures prove ineffective, resort to this solution. Sometimes the prerequisites of deprivation of parental authority affect the child with such intensity that it can be more harmful to the child to wait if other measures could prove sufficient. On certain occasions, the life and health of the child are at stake.

335. These premises have been formulated in Article 111 FGC. The first prerequisite is the non-performance of parental authority by the parents because of a permanent hindrance. By permanent hindrance disabling the exercise of parental authority one should understand such an arrangement of conditions which excludes performance of the authority by the parents in such sense that the duration of such condition cannot be reasonably predicted, or – at least – that the problematic arrangement of conditions is going to maintain for a long period of time.[132] Consequently, this is the type of hindrance which according to all reasonable predictions is not going to expire at all or at least not before the child's coming to full age. As examples, the literature frequently quotes instances of migration of one of the parents abroad where all contacts with the child are discontinued, long-term imprisonment of a parent, stay in a secure hospital because of an incurable sickness.

336. The second condition which justifies the application of this measurement is the abuse of parental authority. Abuse of authority is the case when the parents overuse alcohol, undertake criminal activities and evade alimony renditions in respect to the child. In principle, this is the sufficient cause of deprivation of parental authority on the basis of Article 111 §1 FGC,[133] even though on many occasions the ground for the enforcement of the discussed provision is the excessive punishment of the child, with resort to corporal penalties, sexual harassment of the child, forcing the child to hard labour or prostitution, to the commitment of crimes independently or together with adults, making the child drink alcohol or do drugs, finally its upbringing in the atmosphere of hostility towards the other parent or the other parent's family. In judicature, it is frequently accepted that the deprivation of the minor of his or her natural family environment and direct care of the mother, as well as the possibility of staying together with his or her siblings, forcing the child to stay against the child's will in a foreign country, constitutes an abuse of parental authority on the part of the father which justifies sufficiently deprivation of the father of parental authority.[134]

337. The third condition which can justify the deprivation of parental authority is gross negligence of parental responsibilities towards the child. This could take place most frequently where the parents because of the alcohol or drug addiction, immaturity or promiscuous way of life and persistent negligence of the alimony obligation do not care about the maintenance of the child, starve the child, do not assure proper clothing and lock the child up for a longer period in the house without providing chances for nutrition or care. Obviously, the court may deprive on these grounds either one of the spouses where such conduct is observed only in respect to this particular parent of the child, or both of them, even on different factual grounds. The same sanction towards the parents of the child can be enforced by the court where the efforts to assist the family by use of means provided in Article 109 FGC did not succeed, in a situation where the minor was previously placed in a foster family or care and education institution, especially in a situation in which the parents are permanently disinterested in the lot of the child.

338. The decision on deprivation of parental authority produces very far-reaching legal effects of the loss of the total of rights and responsibilities comprising the authority, which leads to the necessity of establishing guardianship over the

132. Supreme Court decision issued on 2 Jun. 2000, II CKN 960/00, LEX no. 51976.
133. Supreme Court decision issued on 12 Jan. 2000, III CKN 834/99, LEX no. 51565.
134. Supreme Court decision issued on 14 Oct. 1970, III CRN 181/70, OSNCP 1971/6/107 and on 1 Oct. 1998, I CKN 834/98, OSNC 1999/72.

child and appointment of a guardian. Nevertheless, the child's parents do not forfeit these rights and obligations which are vested in them on the ground of the family relation holding between them and the child. They can still invoke the civil status of the child who originates from them, and they retain the right to alimony from the child unless the court should state that their alimony claim makes a violation of the principles of social coexistence. The parents inherit from the child unless the court acknowledges them as unworthy of the succession. They even retain the right to personal contact with the child as long as the court does not exclude this entitlement by ordering a ban on personal contact with the child. Where the cause of the parents' deprivation of authority expires, just as in the above example, parental authority does not become validated automatically. Moreover, the court may restore the deprived power but is not obliged to do so.

Chapter 4. Adoption

339. In contemporary Polish law, adoption means the establishment between the adopter and the adoptee of a family law relationship which imitates relations between a natural parent and a child.[135] It is an act of formal character, whose conclusion depends on the fulfilment of premises required by the provisions of law.[136]

340. The function of adoption is to create a family environment for the minor child and to ensure care and fulfilment of everyday needs to cater for the child's natural immaturity and incapability. There also appears the question of whether one may accept that adoption should also address the need of satisfying the natural maternal or paternal instinct present in adults who for various reasons could not have their own offspring. Provisions of the FGC, in particular Article 114 §1, envisage that only the first of these functions is taken into consideration by the legislator, which could lead to the conclusion that the only reason for adoption should be the interest of the child. This seems confirmed in light of Article 125 §1 FGC which provides for inadmissibility of dissolution of adoption where the interest of the adopted party could suffer from such dissolution.[137] On the contrary, judicature assumes that the premise does not exclude additional consideration of the consequences of dissolution of adoption from the perspective of other persons.[138]

341. In contemporary conditions, where the institution of an orphanage is relatively rare, adoption bears an important function in the area of assuring an environment which imitates a natural family to children rejected by their parents, neglected by them, or placed in care institutions, as well as children coming from broken families in which one of the former spouses has already entered into a new matrimony. In such instances, adoption allows for the emergence of the so-called reconstructed family. Adoption is not contractual in character, as it becomes established exclusively by way of a judicial decision, and not a juridical act, however, its nature is non-pecuniary. Adoption realizes the postulate to safeguard the interest of the child, and since, in accordance with the principle following from Articles 121 §4 and 124 §1 sentence 2 FGC, the effects of adoption always extend to the descendants of the adopting party, one can distinguish the principle of equal treatment of natural and adopted children. Among the fundamental principles on which adoption is based, one can also enumerate the principle of limited dissolvability of adoption, secrecy of adoption and finally state supervision over adoption.

---

135. Smyczyński, *Prawo*, 300.
136. Winiarz, *Prawo*, 231–232.
137. Supreme Court decision issued on 15 Sep. 1951, C 715/51, OSN 1953/11/37.
138. Supreme Court decision issued on 7 Dec. 1965, ICR 309/65, OSNCP 1966/7-8/132.

§1. Premises of Adoption

342. Among the premises of adoption, one can enumerate both premises which must be fulfilled on the part of the adopter and the adopted child and the so-called common premises.

343. The first group includes the manifestation of intent to adopt the child in the form of the adopter's request for the judicial adjudication of adoption, which follows from Article 117§1 FGC providing for the capacity to bring such action before the court. One should agree that the request as such contains the consent of the petitioner for adoption.

344. Where the adopter is married, it is obvious that the *consent* of his or her spouse shall be necessary for adoption (Article 116 FGC).[139] Consent of the other spouse is not required only where he or she does not enjoy the capacity to perform juridical acts, that is where the other spouse is a fully incapacitated person, or where communication with the other spouse is impossible or barred by hardships difficult to surmount. By the notion of such impediment, one should understand an objective obstacle whose duration is impossible to predict, or where it seems obvious that the impediment is durable. For example, this may refer to a situation where the other spouse went abroad and his or her location remains unknown, or where the spouse suffers from a serious illness which disables successful communication. As to the form of consent, the FGC does not envisage any special requirements. Consequently, the consent may be given orally to the protocol before the court or expressed in writing with a signature endorsed by a notary.[140]

345. Moreover, since the adopter is to fulfil the same function as the child's parent, he or she must enjoy *full capacity to perform juridical acts* (Article 114^1§1 FGC and respectively Article 94 FGC). Provisions of FGC relating to adoption do not envisage that certain personal qualities or qualifications of the adopting party should be a condition of adoption. However, it seems clear that, if such qualities are required of a person who is to play the role of the minor's guardian, they should be also taken into consideration in relation to a person who is to be treated as a father or mother of the adopted child. This follows indirectly from Article 586 §4 PCPC which sets out that before delivering the decision in an adoption case the court should hear the opinion of an adoption and guardianship centre or opinion of another specialist institution. The object of investigation by these units is to establish whether the adopter is a person of high ethical standing and if he or she gives the guarantees of creating a suitable family environment for the adopted child.

346. The premises concerning the *adopted person* are predominantly: his or her *minority*, at the latest on the date of submitting the motion for adoption (Article 114 §2 FGC). This premise follows from the purpose of adoption, which is to ensure for

139. Smyczyński, *Prawo*, 307–309; Ciepła, 'Article 116 Commentary', in K. Piasecki (ed.), *Kodeks*, 854.
140. Article 96 of the Law of Notaries Act 1991 (LNA).

the child conditions of upbringing and development imitating family bonds as closely as possible. The second premise in this group is the *interest of the adopted*. This criterion is regarded as decisive. Its significance finds manifestation in judicature, which has formed certain well-grounded hints concerning the evaluation of whether in the particular case adoption is going to satisfy this interest (decision of the Supreme Court quoted above of 15 September 1951). The judicature demonstrates that the evaluation of the discussed premise should be performed by the court deciding the case not only bearing in mind the prospective improvement of the child's material situation, but above all the questions whether the upbringing of the child by the adopter shall better prepare the child better to work to the benefit of the society, according to the child's needs, capacities, and whether the change of environment shall not influence negatively the emotional bonds between the child and the child's natural family. Precedence of arguments relating to personal bonds over material premises was professed by the Supreme Court also in other decisions.[141]

347. When it comes to *prerequisites referring to both parties*, one should emphasize that in order for the relations between the parties to adoption to closely reflect family relations, Article 114^1§2 FGC provides that the age difference between the parties should be 'appropriate', which means such as normally is the case between parents and children. However, the Code does not delimitate the age difference precisely. This means not only that the difference should not be too small, which could lead to the establishment of emotional bonds between the adopter and adoptee closer to relations between persons of the opposite sex, but also not too considerable. Where the adopter is much older than the adoptee, it should be examined whether he or she, bearing in mind his or her age and health condition, is going to be capable of fulfilling the obligations connected with upbringing and guidance of the child, its education and preparation for life in the society until the child becomes independent.[142]

348. The second of the premises in this group is the consent of the child's parents to adoption. The consent is not required where the parents have been deprived of parental authority if the parents are unknown, or where communication with them is impossible or impeded by hardships difficult to surmount (Article 119 §1 FGC). These circumstances must relate to both parents of the child; however, in relation to each the reasons may differ. Moreover, the court may also adjudicate adoption in the absence of parental if the circumstances justify such action, e.g., where the parents' capacity to perform juridical acts is limited and the refusal of consent is in obvious contradiction with the child's interest (Article 119 §2 FGC).

141. Decision issued on 30 Sep. 1952, C.1513/52, OSN 1954/1/5; resolution issued on 9 Jun. 1976 r. III CZP 46/75, OSNCP 1976/9/184, decision issued on 13 Feb. 1980, III CRN 181/79, OSNCP 1980/10/193.

142. Supreme Court decision of 13 Feb. 1980, III CRN 181/79 OSNCP 1980/10/193.

349. Parental consent always refers to the particular proceedings and a concrete candidate for the adopting party, when it concerns full or partial adoption. Each consent of this type may be given no sooner than six weeks after the child's birth *(tempus deliberandi)* since this kind of decision must be well thought through. The parents' consent is their personal act, which does not follow from the right of the child's representation or exercise of parental authority, although it is undoubtedly linked to this authority. Consent cannot be given by proxy. Refusal to grant consent should not stem from the egoistic motivation of the parents and should not be detrimental to the child. If this is found to be the case, the court may deprive the parents of parental authority, and their consent to adoption shall not then be required.[143]

350. As far as the special type of adoption is concerned, namely absolute adoption, which is indissoluble, the natural parents may give consent to adoption without naming the adopter (the so-called blank consent). Such consent is given before a guardianship court before the initiation of adoption proceedings and regardless of such pending cases. Parents who have given such consent lose parental authority and the right to have contact with the child. They may withdraw their consent, but only before the adoption proceedings have been instigated (Article 119^1 §1 FGC). Rules on adoption without the parents' indication of the adoptive parents are to be applied mutatis mutandis in cases when one of the natural parents issues the mentioned blank consent and the consent of the other parent is not required pursuant to Article 119 FGC and Article 119^1 §2 FGC. However, this does not apply to situations in which the consent of the other parent cannot be obtained due to the fact that communication with him or her is impossible or impeded by circumstances difficult to surmount. Finally, provisions on adoption on the basis of a blank consent are to be applied mutatis mutandis when the parents are unknown or have passed away and the court in its decision on adoption decides on this type of adoption (Article 119^1 §3 FGC).

351. Provisions pertaining to foreign adoption envisage one more prerequisite, in particular, Article 114^2§1 FGC. This norm provides that such adoption, in the result of which is that the child has to change his or her place of residence and move to another country, may be adjudicated only where it is possible to assure that the adopted child is to be provided with a proper replacement family environment. More on this type of adoption follows in §3.

§2. Types of Adoption and Its Legal Effects

352. The essence of adoption is the establishment of a new family law relationship between the adopter and adoptee of the type which normally exists between parents and their child. However, the FGC provides for three types of adoption which differently shape the relationships between the adopted child and relatives of the adopter. This allows to account not only for the needs of the adopted but also

143. Ciepła, 'Article 119 Commentary', in K. Piasecki (ed.), *Kodeks*, 868.

the family situation of the adopter and exerts immense influence on the scope of entry of the adopted child into that family of the adopting party. Currently, after the amendment of the FGC of 1975[144] three types of adoption are distinguished, namely:

(1) full adoption;
(2) partial adoption;
(3) absolute adoption (full indissoluble adoption).

I. Full and Partial Adoption

353. Initially, FGC knew only two kinds of adoption, that is full adoption (as a rule) and partial adoption (less frequent). The amendment of the FGC in 1975 introduced the third kind of adoption. As a result of adjudicating adoption, there arises a relationship between a parent and child, and not just between the adopter and adoptee. Also between the child and relatives of the adopter, there emerge such bonds as between natural relatives. The manifestation of this bond is that the child inherits from the adopter's relatives, and, in turn, these relatives inherit from the child. The same result concerns the alimony obligation. The family connections between the child and his or her natural relatives become discontinued, just as between the child and its natural parents. Nonetheless, it should be emphasized that the results of adoption shall extend to descendants of the adopted, who gain the legal status of the adopter's descendants. There is, however, a single aspect in which the connections mentioned above are not extinguished. This concerns the situation in which one of the spouses adopts the child of the other spouse with the intent to give him or her full family and imitate the relationship of natural origin. In such instances, affinity with natural relatives of the child remains preserved (Article 121^1§1 FGC).

354. The practice of the BMDRO demonstrates that after the last amendment of the CSRL, in the case of full adoption, especially where this is the adoption of a child by the mother's husband, a new certificate of birth is generally prepared in order to imitate the family relation to a fuller extent.[145]

355. An interesting development in these types of adoption is the introduction in 2015 of the possibility for parents to nominate the future adopting party as opposed to giving up the child for adoption and having an adoption centre select the child's future parents. This possibility should in practice apply to situations in which, e.g., an only parent is terminally ill and would like the child to be adopted by a relative or by another person that is known and trusted. The provision had to be framed in a manner which excludes any potential for 'selling' children. This could happen if the natural parent(s) (often young, teenage girls), particularly of

144. Journal of Statutes 1975, no. 45, item 234.
145. E. Holewińska -Łapińska, 'Przysposobienie po nowelizacji', *Monitor Prawniczy*, no. 12 (1995): 362.

newborn children, would be allowed to nominate strangers as the chosen adoptive parents, which in practice might serve to stimulate illegal and undisclosed payments that the nominated adoptive parents would be willing to make in order to adopt a newborn child without going through normal adoption centre procedures. Consequently, the legislator provides that the parents may indicate, in front of a court, the person by whom the child is to be adopted. However, that person must be a blood relative of one of the parents and must, in front of the same court, confirm that they will adopt the child. The person indicated by the parent of the child may also be a non-parent spouse (Article 119^{1a} FGC).

356. The establishment of a parental relationship between the adopter and adoptee does not result, however, in the complete loss of the previous civil status with regard to the child's origin. As a result, it is possible, despite the adoption, to determine paternity or motherhood of the adopted, as well as denial of his or her marital paternity, or annulment of the acknowledgement of paternity. This is the case because adoption of this type is still dissoluble in nature, and the child's return to the civil status and origin from before the adjudication of adoption cannot be entirely excluded.[146]

II. Absolute Adoption

357. This type of adoption takes place when the child's parents have given consent to adoption without nominating the adopting party. In pursuance of Article 119^1§2 FGC, provisions on adoption on the basis of anonymous consent shall apply appropriately where one of the natural parents gave such consent and the consent of the other is not necessary for adoption, for example, where the other parent has been deprived of parental authority.[147]

358. This type of adoption has been introduced in the FGC to ensure the anonymity of adoption. This was a consequence of numerous cases in which the child's questions about being adopted frequently led to the crisis in the adoption. The fundamental feature of this adoption is its anonymousness and indissolubility. In order to safeguard the anonymous character, a new certificate of the child's birth is prepared on the basis of Article 71 of the CSRL, in which the adoptive parents are included as the parents, and the previous certificate of birth becomes confidential, although this confidentiality is not of absolute character. The old certificate of birth is made available to the court whenever necessary or to the adoptee but only after she/he has attained the age of majority (Article 73 CSRL). In this manner, the

146. Supreme Court decision issued on 28 Mar. 1960, 2 CR 16/60, OSN 1961/2/37, on 21 Feb. 1973, III CRN 332/72, OSNCP 1973, on 20 Mar. 1976, III CZP 77/75, OSNCP, 1976/9/185.

147. Haak, *Przysposobienie*, 82.

secrecy of adoption, which may be beneficial to the child, is protected but simultaneously the child is not prevented from discovering his/her biological origin should such need or desire arise.[148]

359. However, since this relationship is indissoluble, it becomes no longer possible within this type of adoption to petition for any sort of determination of the child's natural origin. The adopted cannot preserve his or her previous surname from before the adoption since the essence of the discussed relationship is an expunction of the natural origin of the adopted child. The child shall inherit from the adoptive parents as though he or she were their offspring. The child shall also inherit from the adoptive parent's relatives but not from his or her natural relatives.

360. Since this kind of adoption produces such far-reaching consequences, it should not be adjudicated in situations where it remains unknown whether between the adopting and adopted party an intense emotional bond is going to emerge, which must be the case if the adoption is to be successful for both parties. As a result, the FGC amendment of 1995[149] introduced a crucial change in the form of a certain trial period, and at the same time the possibility of direct contact between the adoptee and adoptive parents prior to the adjudication of adoption. This is a relatively new solution, but one correctly allowing to make sure as to the adoption of a particular child and preventing life tragedies which may derive from premature adoption. Pursuant to Article 120^1 §1 FGC before adjudicating adoption the court may prescribe a period of personal contact between the prospective adoptive parent and the child as well as indicate the manner of exercising these visitation rights. Provisions on foster families are to be applied *mutatis mutandis*, with the exception that the cost of such visitations encumbers the prospective adoptive parent (Article 120^1 §1 FGC). The adjudicated visitation rights include a range of possibilities beginning from visitation at the adoption centre, taking the child out to events, taking the child home for weekends/holidays, and finally taking the child home for more substantial periods of time (weeks or months) while the adoption proceedings are pending.[150] In the case of national adoptions, the described trial period in which visitation rights are awarded is optional and not mandatory.

361. In the case of international adoption, the above-mentioned trial period is obligatory. It enables a better acquaintance between the parties, showing the potential adoptive parent whether the decision to adopt a particular child is correct. In the case of older children, it also facilitates a more conscious decision of the child as to whether he or she should agree to the adoption. Also, the court gains the opportunity to verify whether the prospective adoptive parent is the correct person, whether his or her personal qualifications allow for the positive decision, what the prognosis is as to the relations between the parties in future. It seems correct for the legislator

148. M. Wilejczyk, 'Znajomość czy nieznajomość pochodzenia genetycznego rzeczywistym dobrem osoby urodzonej w wyniku procedury medycznie wspomaganej prokreacji. Uwagi na marginesie ustawy o leczeniu niepłodności', *Przegląd Sądowy* no. 11-12 (2017), 73–74.
149. Journal of Statutes 1995, no. 83, item 417.
150. See E. Holewińska-Łapińska, 'Przysposobienie', in T. Smyczyński (ed.), *System Prawa Prywatnego. Tom 12. Prawo rodzinne i opiekuńcze,* (Warszawa: C.H. Beck – PAN, 2011), 596–599.

to have adopted for the purposes of personal contacts between the parties in the pre-adoption period the construction of the foster family, with the sole reservation that no entitlements to benefits for the child's maintenance should emerge on the part of the prospective adopter (Article 120^1§2 FGC). Moreover, one should wholeheartedly agree with the legislator that within the discussed period, the court should supervise the contacts of the prospective adoptive parents with the child, by engaging for this purpose adoption and guardianship centres (Article 120^1§4 FGC).

§3. Foreign Adoption and Its Functions

362. Experiences gained by Polish courts with regard to international adoption and statements of the doctrine in this respect from before the 1995 FGC amendment led to the express regulation of this type of adoption in the FGC.[151] Academics contended that the lack of supervision over such adoptions usually leads to the violation of the child's interest, illegal organization of foreign adoptions, with no possibility to stop such practices once the child has been taken abroad.[152]

363. One might wonder whether the statement of the Supreme Court is accurate that, even though in light of Article 114^2§1 FGC foreign adoption should be regarded as *ultima ratio*, the superior interest of the child and the possibility of full and harmonious development might require in a particular case that the principle of precedence of national adoption be rejected.[153] It was, however, accepted as a result of the amendment, pursuant to Article 114^2§1 FGC, that if the result of adoption shall be a change of residence of the child and his or her relocation abroad, this may happen where only in this way a proper replacement family environment can be ensured to the child.

364. These regulations were additionally motivated by the need to implement international conventions ratified by Poland, in particular, the Convention on Adoption of Children concluded in Strasburg and ratified by Poland in 1996.[154] The legal character of the norms of this Convention was disputable, whether they are direct or indirect, the latter only obliging the legislator to transpose into the national order. The Supreme Court took the stance that the norms are directly binding in a Resolution of the panel of seven judges of 12 June 1992.[155] Introduction of rules conforming with the Convention has ended the discussion. In consequence, we should take a look at the regulation introduced in Article 114^2 FGC, pertaining to the possibility of foreign adoption.

365. These provisions demonstrate in a clear manner that the stance of the doctrine is correct that foreign adoption should be admissible where it is the only way

151. L. Gardocki, 'Organizowanie adopcji a handel dziećmi', *Palestra*, no. 11 (1994): 44–46.
152. Supreme Court resolution issued on 29 Nov. 1995, I KZP 33/95, OSNKW 1996/1-2/3 with a gloss by M. Filar.
153. Supreme Court decision issued on 5 Jul. 2006, IV CSK 127/06, LEX no. 232819.
154. Journal of Statutes 1999, no. 99, item 1157.
155. III CZP 48/92, OSNCP 1992/10/179.

to assure a proper family environment for the child. It is crucial, at the same time, that international adoption should not stray to the detriment of the child from national standards in the area of adoption, both relating to the legal situation of the adopted and conditions of his or her life.

366. As far as issues of the conflict of laws are concerned, which must be taken into consideration in the instances of foreign adoption, the relationship of adoption, in accordance with Article 57 §1 of the PIL, is regulated by the national law of the adopting party. However, the procedure cannot be completed without observance of the national law (thus indicated by the connecting factor of nationality) of the adopted child in questions of the adopted party's consent to adoption, consent of the statutory representative, permission of the respective state authority, as well as restrictions of adoption resulting from the change of domicile to residence in a foreign country.[156] In consequence, it is necessary to determine the content of the respective law since it might have negative consequences in the area of recognition of the Polish court's decision abroad.[157]

367. In practice, the most frequent cause of foreign adoption recently seems the specific needs of the child who requires medical treatment with methods not admitted in Poland, or inaccessible because of excessive costs. Other grounds occur relatively rarely since the standards of living and civic freedoms in Poland nowadays correspond in full to the EU standards.

§4. Dissolution of Adoption

368. Since adoption is established by judicial decision, the expiry of the adoption relationship may be influenced by such factors as:

(a) defective adoption proceedings, procedural defects which may result in the abolishment of the decision by means of effective appeal or cassation, or resumption of proceedings;
(b) ineffectiveness of adoption following from the ascertainment of non-existence of adoption in the mode of Article 189 PCPC;
(c) dissolution of adoption in the mode of Article 125 FGC.

369. The last mode occurs at the request of the adopting or adopted party. It requires the demonstration of two premises: that important reasons for the dissolution occur, and that the dissolution shall not be detrimental to the child's interest.

156. M. Pazdan, *Prawo prywatne międzynarodowe*, (Warszawa: Wolters Kluwer, 2017), 321–322.
157. J. Ciszewski, 'Praktyka sądów w sprawach o przysposobienie obywateli polskich przez cudzoziemców i osoby zamieszkałe za granicą', *Problemy Wymiaru Sprawiedliwości*, no. 13 (1977): 80 et seq.; B. Gnela, 'Przysposobienie obywateli polskich przez cudzoziemców w świetle orzecznictwa SN', *Palestra*, no. 10 (1988): 6–21; J. Panpwicz – Lipska, 'Przysposobienie dziecka', in *Konwencja o prawach dziecka. Wybrane zagadnienia prawne i socjalne*, ed. T. Smyczyński (Poznań: UAM, 1994), 208.

370. Among 'important reasons' the judicature and doctrine enumerate frequently the non-existence between the adopting and adopted persons of such close bonds that generally exist in a natural family. The lack of such bonds and the irreversibility of their decomposition, the emergence of hostility between the parties, physical violence, close relations of the adopted child with aggressive peer environment, thefts to the detriment of the adoptive parents, etc., are usually indicated as important reasons. Moreover, important reasons may also relate to the child's interest or well-being where a matrimonial impediment to marriage emerges between the parties of adoption, and the mentioned impediment may be removed by the dissolution of the relationship of adoption, or where the child is factually brought up in its natural family in the conditions of normal emotional bonds with the parents.[158]

371. The legal effects of judicial dissolution of adoption are substantial and manifold. Among these, one can enumerate:

(a) the expiry of the civil status acquired by adoption and the return to the status from before adoption;
(b) parental authority over the child expires on the part of the adopting party, and the natural parents' parental authority is revived;
(c) the rights to inherit from one another by intestate succession expire, and the ones from before the adoption are reactivated;
(d) the mutual alimony obligation expires, although the court may preserve it according to the circumstances of the case.[159]

§5. Secrecy of Adoption

372. Secrecy of adoption is a personal interest protected by the European Convention on Human Rights, the Covenant on Civil and Political Rights and the Charter of Fundamental Rights. Although it is not included in Article 23 PCC, the list contained therein is not exhaustive, there are no doubts that the catalogue of this provision is far from complete. The problem of respect towards the secrecy of adoption found its manifestation in Polish reservations concerning the ratification process of the Convention on Adoption.

373. The significance of this problem can be demonstrated by the fact that absolute adoption, protecting the secrecy of adoption in full, was introduced in the Code only in 1975 and followed from the needs of practice. It is also true that the person adopted on the basis of blank consent of the parents, once the adoption decision becomes binding and the new birth certificate is prepared in which the adopting parents are included, forfeits the possibility to claim the determination of his or her natural origin on the basis of Article 124^1 FGC. As a result, it should be acclaimed that Article 73 §3 of the CSRL envisages the right of scrutiny on the part of the

158. Ciepła, 'Article 125 Commentary', in K. Piasecki (ed.), *Kodeks*, 906–907.
159. Smyczyński, *Prawo*, 321–323.

adopted once he or she reaches the age of majority into the previous certificate of birth, which allows the adopted to learn about the identity of his or her natural parents.

374. It is also noteworthy that the violation of the secrecy of adoption is meaningful not only to the adopted party but also to the parents. The Strasbourg Court took a negative stance on the absolute character of the adopted person's right to learn of his or her biological parents in the judgment *Odievre v. France* of 13 February 2003, No. 42326/98. As a result, opinions on this question seem divided. One could, obviously, by invoking legislative solutions accepted in other countries, advocate the superiority of systems enabling full openness in the area of adoption secrecy, praise institutions encountered in other states, for example, open adoption; however, one cannot neglect the special conditions of secrecy protection stemming from the local circumstances of a given country.

375. One should agree with the opinion expressed in the Polish doctrine that, while recognizing the existence and importance of the adopted person's right to learn about his or her natural origin, the court should examine very carefully petitions for disclosure of this origin. The court should also make use, while making the decision, of all measures accessible to the court, in particular the report of a judicial trustee about the last place of residence of the child's biological parents and the opinion they enjoy in this environment.[160]

160. Holewińska-Łapińska, 'Przysposobienie', in T. Smyczyński (ed.), *System Prawa Prywatnego. Tom 12.*, 673–678, M. Safjan, *Prawo wobec ingerencji w naturze ludzkiej prokreacji* (Warszawa, 1990), 292.

Chapter 5. Guardianship and Curatorship

376. The concept of guardianship is not unanimously understood in the literature. In the civil law sense, it signifies an institution which serves the purpose of protecting personal and property interests of minors who do not remain for various reasons under parental authority, as well as fully incapacitated persons. These parties clearly require not only personal care and control over their property, but also representation, both in everyday life and in relation to more important factual and juridical acts concerning the dependents, made before public authorities, including courts of law.

377. In spite of many similarities, there are certain differences between the two types of guardianship. These differences concern guardianship's very essential functions. It has been emphasized that guardianship over a minor person makes a substitution of parental authority, of which the dependent is entirely deprived, whereas guardianship over a fully incapacitated person should come in place of reasonable actions of the incapacitated individual.[161] The aim of guardianship over a child is to create a substitute for parental authority and the child's proper upbringing, whereas the aim of guardianship over the incapacitated is the concern for fulfilment of his or her life needs and correct treatment.[162]

378. It has also been indicated in the doctrine that the relations of guardianship can have a complex character and bear features of civil law, public law and family law relationships.[163] It is incorrect and unjustified to put emphasis in regard to these relationships on material, property-related aspects, which are especially manifest in the special approach to the problems of the dependent's representation.[164] Rather than that, it is more justified to stress the upbringing function of guardianship and put essential emphasis on personal care over the dependent.[165] This allocation of significance should directly affect the interpretation of statutory solutions concerning guardianship, their application, requirements pertaining to the person of guardian, evaluation of this person's correctness in the exercise of his or her duties, etc.

§1. Basic Principles of Guardianship

379. The statutory regulation of guardianship has been based on certain principles, the catalogue of which is viewed differently within the doctrine. In our opinion, the principles can be formulated in the following manner:

- the principle of protection of the interest of the dependent;

161. Kalus, *Opieka*, 75.
162. J. Ignatowicz, 'Opieka', in J. Piątowski (ed.), *System prawa rodzinnego i opiekuńczego*,(Wrocław-,Warszawa, Kraków, Gdańsk, Łódź: PAN Ossolineum, 1985), 1096 et seq.
163. Winiarz, *Prawo rodzinne* (Warszawa: PWN, 1983), 288.
164. S Kalus, *Opieka*, 82.
165. Zieliński, *Opieka*, 3.

- the principle of universality of guardianship and official character of guardianship court activities;
- the principle of judicial supervision over guardianship; and
- the principle of the limited gratuitous character of guardianship.

380. The first of these principles is an extension of the fundamental principle of Polish family law, namely the principle of protection of the child's interest, but in the case of guardianship, it is broader, as it concerns additionally the person fully incapacitated. The principle makes a criterion of selection of the guardian, evaluation of performance of his or her duties and restrictions in representation of the dependent.[166] The principle's significance is even broader than in the case of the remaining principles since the interest of the child constitutes the source of these remaining principles.

381. The second of the principles entails that for each minor person who, for various reasons does not undergo parental authority, as well as for every fully incapacitated person, guardianship should be established at once, whenever the situation occurs which raises the necessity to appoint a guardian. The guardianship court which acquires information about the need to establish guardianship and appoint a guardian should initiate respective proceedings ex officio, regardless of whether or not there is any factual care over the person who is to be submitted to guardianship.[167]

382. The principle of judicial supervision over guardianship, accepted in Polish law, bears crucial significance from the point of view of the protection of interests of the person submitted to guardianship. It assures professional and independent control both over the person entrusted with the function of guardian and the manner in which he or she is going to carry out the resulting responsibilities. The shape of this principle has been affected by certain experiences following from the multiplicity of legal systems in force on the Polish territories before the unification, which lead to the conclusion that neither guardianship functions on the part of administrative authorities, nor family law councils lead to due protection of the interests of the persons submitted to guardianship. As a result, the supervisory function has been vested in independent courts.[168] This supervision entails both the power of operating control of the activity of the appointed guardian and the entitlement to issue binding orders and suggestions to this guardian.

383. The last of the listed principles is the principle of gratuitous character of guardianship, which luckily has been modified as a result of the recent amendment of the FGC, in the direction of guardianship attaining a payable character, even if only a partial one. The old solution was often justified by reference to morality and

166. Kalus, *Opieka*, 90–93.
167. J. Marciniak: *Treść i sprawowanie opieki nad małoletnim* (Warszawa, 1975), 21; Kalus, *Opieka*, 92.
168. Kalus, *Opieka*, 94; Marciniak, *Treść*, 22–23.

the fact that since the CRP provides for the obligation of protecting the young generation, the exercise of guardianship over a person who needs such care makes it a constitutional duty of every citizen. This is, however, a very poor argument, especially in a situation where guardianship does not concern a child but also a fully incapacitated person. It would also be difficult to reasonably argue that a minor's guardian should not require remuneration in a situation in which nobody questions the need for providing financial means to foster parents. When it comes to incapacitated persons, it is worth mentioning that they often require constant care, twenty-four hours a day, while very often serious problems arise with the acquisition of alimony renditions to the benefit of the incapacitated. As a result, it should be accepted that remunerating guardianship would definitely be justified from the point of view of the interest of the dependent.[169]

§2. GUARDIANSHIP

I. Establishment of Guardianship and Appointment of the Guardian

384. Article 94 §3 FGC envisages that in a situation where neither of the parents remains entrusted with parental authority or the parents are unknown, the court establishes guardianship for the child. This entails that such circumstances must apply to both parents of the child, even if the grounds for the non-existence of this authority should differ in relation to each of the parents.

385. Parental authority is not vested in the parents where:

(a) they have died;
(b) they do not enjoy full capacity to perform juridical acts as a result of minority or incapacitation;
(c) they have been deprived of parental authority by the court;
(d) their parental authority has been suspended;
(e) the punitive measure provided for in Article 51 PPC has been adjudicated in relation to the parents, that is, deprivation of parental and guardianship rights; such decision is made by the guardianship court in the case of commitment of a crime to the detriment of a minor or with joint participation of a minor;
(f) the court declined to award the authority to the child's father in the judgment ascertaining paternity, and the child's mother does not enjoy parental authority likewise.

386. As has been pointed out above, the legal grounds for the establishment of guardianship and appointment of the guardian emerge whenever a physical person has become fully incapacitated. As far as partial incapacitation is concerned, there is also the principle of necessity of assuring legal assistance to the incapacitated, manifested in the appointment of a curator whose scope of activity is narrower than

169. Kalus, *Opieka*, 98–99.

the guardian's, since the capacity to perform juridical acts, even if partial, remains vested in the dependent. The crucial problem, oftentimes raised in Polish legal literature is that the court should not wait until the need to act on behalf of the incapacitated person in a particular case, but establish guardianship or curatorship directly after the court's intervention in the legal situation of a natural person.

387. The proceedings leading to the establishment of guardianship and appointment of the guardian fall within Polish procedural law under the category of non-litigation mode and has been regulated in Articles 568–578 PCPC. In this proceeding, one can differentiate two stages, namely: decision instituting the system of care over the minor or incapacitated person and the appointment of a particular person as the guardian. Most frequently, in the proceeding on the establishment of guardianship also, this particular person is appointed as guardian. Separation of these two proceedings becomes apparent only in the case of change of the guardian when there is no need to institute guardianship, but only to appoint the new guardian.

388. The proceedings are initiated not at request but ex officio. In accordance with Article 570 PCPC, the guardianship court may initiate the proceedings ex officio if it acquires information that there is legal ground to do so. In the literature, it is emphasized that the principle of official activity of the court, which does not wait for a respective motion of the entitled party, follows from the purpose of guardianship proceedings, which is the overall protection of persons who require legal care, both personal and property-related.

389. The PCPC sets out the obligation for every citizen who knows about an event which gives rise to the initiation of such proceedings to inform guardianship court about the event (Article 572 §1 PCPC). In this manner, the court receives an impulse to initiate the discussed proceeding. In particular, in pursuance of Article 572 §2 PCPC, the burden of duty rests on the BMDRO, courts, public prosecutors, notaries, court executive officers, self-governmental authorities and administration, Police authorities, schools, social workers, organizations and institutions dealing with taking care of children and mentally sick persons.

390. The guardianship court, by initiating the proceeding ex officio issues an order which is served to the participants to this proceeding. The court informs the participants about the initiation of the proceedings ex officio, defines its type and instructs them about the possibility to file evidence motions. Territorial jurisdiction of the guardianship court follows from Article 569 §1 PCPC, according to which the exclusively competent court shall be the guardianship court of the place of residence of the person whom the proceeding is to concern, and in the lack of residence – the guardianship court of the place of the person's location. Where this basis is missing too, the competent court shall be the district court of the capital city of Warsaw.

391. One of the crucial problems from the procedural perspective seems the question of participation of the minor or incapacitated person in the guardianship proceeding. The procedural situation of such parties differs according to whether or not they enjoy even partial capacity to perform juridical acts. If such person enjoys such capacity, in accordance with Article 573 §1 PCPC, the person enjoys as well the capacity to make procedural acts in the proceeding pertaining to himself or herself. However, where, as a result of not having reached the proper age, or as a consequence of full incapacitation, the person does not enjoy this capacity, he or she cannot as well independently make a procedural act in the guardianship proceeding.

392. Special significance regarding the correctness of decisions made by the guardianship court can be attached to the direct contact of the court with the person whom the proceedings concern.[170] As a result, the principle of oral character and the duty to hear the participants becomes vital. The guardianship court may order personal attendance of the person submitted to guardianship, and order his or her compulsory appearance in the court; also the factual caretaker can be obliged under penalty of fine to bring the dependent to the courtroom (Article 574 §2 PCPC), obviously as long as this person is capable of appearance and communication with the court.

393. The proceeding on the establishment of guardianship is concluded by the appointment of the guardian who should subsequently take up his or her responsibilities shortly, that is make a respective oath without unnecessary delay. Only at that moment can the guardian act on behalf of the dependent.

II. Appointment of the Guardian

394. If the child remains in a foster family, when the need to appoint guardianship emerges, the court in pursuance of Article 149 §4 shall entrust the guardianship to the foster parents. Further problems concern the qualifications required of the person whom the court may appoint as guardian. These questions have been regulated in Articles 148 FGC and following ones. These rules envisage in the first place who cannot be appointed as guardian. The negative prerequisites concern: persons without a full capacity to perform juridical acts, persons deprived of public rights, deprived of parental authority or sentenced for a crime against sexual freedom or decency, or for intentional offence with the use of force towards another person or a crime committed to the detriment of a minor, or in joint commitment with a minor, finally a person in relation to whom the ban has been adjudicated on activities connected with upbringing, treatment, education of minors, guardianship over them or the duty to refrain from staying in particular environments or places, ban on contacts with particular persons or prohibition to leave a particular location without judicial consent. Undoubtedly, such a person would not make a proper guardian for a minor or a fully incapacitated person. Among punitive measures which decide about the inadmissibility of such person as a guardian, Article 148 §1 FGC lists deprivation of public rights. The court may adjudicate this measure while sentencing to prison for a period not shorter than three years for the crime committed as a result

170. Kalus, *Opieka*, 111.

of motivation deserving particular condemnation. Most obviously, the interest of the minor requires that such a person should not be appointed as the minor's guardian.

395. This relatively casuistic enumeration of limitations concerning the appointment of particular persons as guardians is complemented by the general rule that the curator must not be the person who is suspected of potential non-compliance with the guardian's responsibilities. This is not merely about the disqualification of a given person because of his or her negative qualities. By the determination of occurrence of this premise, one should take into consideration not only the qualities of the candidate for guardian mentioned above but also certain criteria deriving from the purpose of guardianship, the responsibilities and tasks of the guardian. The court should examine certain conditions which contribute to the decision whether or not in the particular case one may expect that the given person is going to perform diligently his or her responsibilities as a guardian.

396. These are circumstances such as moral attitude, health condition and personal features of the candidate for guardian, but also personal features and property affairs of the minor, previous relations between the prospective guardian and the minor, or the general attitude of the guardian (willing or unwilling) towards the function.[171] Seniors, candidates suffering from illnesses, or disabled ones in principle are not going to make good guardians, especially in a situation where the minor is an especially vital child, who causes serious upbringing difficulties. Most frequently, also persons seriously engaged professionally are evaluated negatively from the point of view of qualifications to become a guardian, especially where their job is connected with frequent and durable business travels.[172] As far as guardianship over an incapacitated person is concerned, the court should consider the guardian's capabilities of coping with a mentally sick person, capability of understanding and interpreting the dependent's conduct.

397. Also, the personal features of the minor or mentally sick person have real significance to the question of selection of the guardian. These qualities decide whether the candidate for guardian can comply with his or her responsibilities. In particular, this refers to the condition whether the dependent is a person easy to guide, submitting without greater difficulties to the educational impact of the guardian, if the minor evades the school obligation (absenteeism), runs away from the place of residence or remains connected with criminal environment. Also, property-related issues of the minor are of primary importance. Very often a conflict of property interests of the guardian and the person submitted to guardianship follows from co-inheritance. There may also arise a situation in which the incapacitated person has certain assets and permanent pension, and the candidate for guardian does not. Oftentimes property-related issues exclude the possibility of appointment of a particular person.

171. Kalus, *Opieka*, 115; Kalus, 'Article 148 Commentary', in K. Piasecki (ed.), *Kodeks*, 1020–1021.
172. Kalus, 'Article 148 Commentary', in K. Piasecki (ed.), *Kodeks*, 1021.

398. Similarly, previous relations between the dependent and the candidate for guardian may exert vital influence on the evaluation of whether he or she is the suitable person. Where this relationship has been characterized by friendliness, where the minor knows the candidate for guardian well, for instance, as a result of a good long-term neighbourhood or doing sports under the candidate's supervision and remains on friendly terms with this candidate, or the candidate was in friendly relations with the minor's parents – such conditions make good prospects in case of appointment of the candidate as the minor's guardian. Conversely, where the relation is unfriendly or even hostile, the candidate should not be taken into consideration while appointing the guardian.

399. The attitude of the candidate towards the possibility of appointment is another factor crucial in the selection of guardians. Where it is negative in advance, there are usually no reasons to assume that such guardianship might be exercised duly.[173]

400. Provisions of the FGC envisage rules of precedence in embracing guardianship by certain persons. It should be, however, emphasized that they do not bind the court absolutely since they are in the first place dependent on whether the interest of the dependent does not interfere. When it comes to the guardian for a minor, priority lies in the first rank to the persons indicated by the father *or mother*, unless they have been deprived of parental authority. Most frequently, the parents have the best knowledge about the person who is most probable to comply with the responsibilities of a guardian. One should agree with the opinion that the possibility of indicating the guardian refers not only to natural but also to adoptive parents.[174]

401. Also, the case law of the ECtHR favours recognition of the parents will in this respect. The judicature of the Court demonstrates that the assumption of guardianship on the part of public authorities, including persons entrusted with that guardianship by public authorities, cannot entail the end to natural family relationships. The child's parents usually have the best knowledge about these relatives.[175] However, such indication shall not be taken into consideration in a situation where the parents have been deprived of parental authority and whereby a court decision, they were deprived of parental or guardianship rights, as well as in relation to the father whom the court has not awarded parental authority in the judgment ascertaining paternity.

402. If the candidate for guardian has not been indicated in such a manner, he or she should be selected from among the relatives or other persons close to the minor,

173. Kalus, *Opieka*, 115 and the literature quoted therein.
174. Kalus, 'Article 149 Commentary', in K. Piasecki (ed.), *Kodeks*, 1025 et seq.
175. Decisions in cases: *Margareta and Roger Andersson v. Sweden* of 25 Feb. 1992, A.226, Report of the European Commission of Human Rights of 3 Oct. 1990, complaint 12963/87, *Klass et al. v. Germany* of 6 Sep. 1978, *Olsson v. Sweden* of 22 Jun. 1988, *Eriksson v. Sweden* and *Kruslin v. France* of 24 Apr. 1990 – European, 736, 737. That is why the best solution is where the parents point to the person of guardian.

or to the minor's parents. In the lack of candidates to embrace the function indicated in such a manner, the guardianship court should resort to the appointment of a candidate for guardian to the bodies enumerated in the statute mentioned in Article 149 §3 FGC. This does not mean that the court shall be bound by such appointment, because also these candidates are examined from the point of view of their qualifications to embrace guardianship, and it might be the case that the court shall appoint yet another person as the guardian.

403. When it comes to a person fully incapacitated, the primacy in the indication of the prospective guardian belongs to the spouse of the incapacitated, and in the lack of such spouse his or her father or mother. When it comes to the spouse of the affected person, the primacy should be approached with caution, and we agree with the statement that in order to take the spouse's opinion into account it is necessary to determine if he or she has not initiated divorce or separation proceedings, or does not intend to do so, for in such instances the interest of the incapacitated person might become endangered. If these persons are missing too, because the incapacitated person is unmarried, and the parents have died, the guardian should be sought among other persons. Frequently, such guardians are employees of the medical institution where the incapacitated person stays, who act under the court's supervision.[176]

404. The amendment of the FGC of 1975 decided the problem which previously remained controversial, namely admissibility of vesting guardianship in spouses.[177] Essentially, if guardianship over a minor is to substitute parental care, it is well justified to entrust guardianship to spouses who specifically 'imitate' natural parents. However, this provision signifies that it would be inadmissible to entrust guardianship to two persons living in an informal relationship or persons who formed a marriage but only a church one. This regulation stands in opposition with the tendency present in certain EU Member States to admit in this situation relationships established as a result of sex change or civil partnerships, which is however a solution not accepted in the majority of the EU Member States.[178] On the contrary, there are no legal impediments to entrust guardianship to spouses who remain in separation. In our opinion, however, vesting common guardianship in such persons could stand in opposition with the interest of the child. There holds no common conjugal life between such persons and no property community; the marriage exists only formally. Entrusting guardianship commonly to both spouses is recommended generally where the child is brought up in a foster family or the so-called family orphanage.[179] The FGC provides for the possibility of appointing a single guardian for a number of dependent persons. The rules of the code entail even the need to appoint one guardian for siblings, when possible.

---

176. Kalus, 'Article 176 Commentary', in K. Piasecki (ed.), *Kodeks*, 1083–1084.
177. Kalus, *Opieka*, 122–123; Kalus, 'Article 146 Commentary', in K. Piasecki (ed.), *Kodeks*, 1017.
178. Report *X.Y.Z. v. Great Britain* 27 Jun. 1995.
179. Smyczyński, *Prawo*, 366.

III. Content of Guardianship: Personal Care and Care of the Property of the Dependent

405. The responsibilities of the guardian comprise care over the person of the child or the incapacitated person, care of his or her property and statutory representation. The guardian undoubtedly is an organ of guardianship, but not an organ of the guardianship court. As a result, even though the court bears supervisory functions over guardianship, there is no element of hierarchical subordination between the court and the guardian.

406. Pursuant to Article 155 §1 FGC, the guardian takes care of the person and property of the dependent, in which the guardian is supervised on a permanent basis by the guardianship court. Provisions on parental authority apply appropriately to the exercise of parental authority. This does not however define the content of guardianship, since in accordance with Article 159 the guardian is not in the position to represent the dependent only in the case of juridical acts exhaustively enumerated in the discussed provision. If this is the case, the content of guardianship comprises as well representation of the minor.[180]

407. Since the content of guardian's care is analogical to parental authority, provisions on parental authority shall also apply to the exercise of guardianship with certain insignificant reservations following from special rules of the FGC. This means that there are certain differences between the two. The legislator seems to believe that, since the parents are linked to the child by blood relations, this makes a certain guarantee of due exercise of their authority, and the scope of parental authority can be broader, while its exercise should be left, as far as possible, to the parents' discretion. Since the guardian might be a person completely unrelated by the bonds of consanguinity with the dependent, the scope of the guardian's care must be narrower than in the case of parents. The guardian's care is also permanently supervised by the guardianship court.

408. Not all principles pertaining to the exercise of parental authority on the part of the parents may be applied to the guardian's care. In particular, the doctrine emphasizes that the fact of the parents being the closest relatives to the child entails certain personal rights entrusted to them, which are to protect the 'own' interest of the parents.[181] The situation of guardian is different. The guardian enjoys broad entitlements, but these are only the technical measure enabling his or her proper exercise of guardianship not in his or her own interest, but exclusively in the interest of the person submitted to guardianship.

409. An element which naturally differentiates guardianship and parental authority is the scope of care exercised by the guardian. While the parents exercise personal care over their child, the guardian undergoes in this respect constant

180. Kalus, 'Article 155 Commentary', in K. Piasecki (ed.), *Kodeks*, 1038; Marciniak, *Treść*, 42.
181. Kalus, 'Article 155 Commentary', in K. Piasecki (ed.), *Kodeks*, 1033; J. Ignatowicz, 'Opieka', in J. Piątowski (ed.), *System*, 1154.

supervision of the guardianship court, since he or she is obliged to obtain permission of the court to make all major acts in the sphere of the respective type of care.[182]

410. The differences between the legal situation of the guardian and parents' concerns as well the duty of alimony towards the minor. While the alimony obligation to the benefit of the child encumbers the parents if the child is unable to support himself or herself independently, regardless of whether or not the parents enjoy parental authority, the guardian is not encumbered with alimony obligation at all, unless the guardian is a relative of the child, and accordingly is obliged to alimony as a party belonging to the catalogue of persons mentioned in Article 128 FGC.[183] The usual sources of the child's income, according to the literature, are as follows:

- alimony obligation of the parents or more distant relatives;
- incomes from the assets of the dependent;
- means coming from social funds or social aid.

411. Care of the child submitted to guardianship encompasses the following elements: upbringing of the child, guidance of the minor, concern for the acquisition of means of maintenance and upbringing for the child and the child's representation.[184] When it comes to care of a fully incapacitated person, its basic elements are concern for the proper treatment of the dependent and assurance to the dependent of decent conditions of existence, as well as representation of the dependent substituting his or her reasonable actions.[185] The guardian undergoes constant, permanent control of the guardianship court, and with the view to the interest of the dependent, the guardian is more strictly limited in the exercise of his or her powers as compared to parents. This follows from the fact that the rule of Article 156 FGC provides that the guardian is obliged to obtain permission of the court in all major questions which concern the person and property of the dependent. It is argued that the notion of major affairs can be derived from their significance to the dependent. By this concept, one could understand such questions which have a decisive meaning for proper development or health condition of the dependent, or for his or her preparation to life in the society. Among these, the literature and judicature enumerate determination of the child's location, which is particularly crucial if release abroad of a child of Polish nationality is considered,[186] choice of the minor's profile of education or selection of his or her profession, consent to a medical procedure regarding the minor, especially where the procedure is especially complicated and connected with particular risk to life and health of the child, and the opinion of physicians as to the procedure's purposefulness is doubtful, bringing an action for determination of the child's origin, conclusion of a settlement of behalf of the

182. *Ibid.*
183. Kalus, 'Article 155 Commentary', in K. Piasecki (ed.), *Kodeks*, 1037; Marciniak: *Treść*, 61; A. Oleszko, *Roszczenia alimentacyjne. Zagadnienia ogólne* (Warszawa, 1984), 12.
184. Marciniak, *Treść*, 46.
185. Kalus, 'Opieka nad ubezwłasnowolnionym całkowicie', in K. Piasecki (ed.), *Komentarz*, 1080.
186. Supreme Court decision issued on 7 Oct. 1998, I CKN 745/98, Lex Polonica no. 390908.

dependent,[187] consent to the adoption of the minor, consent to the acceptance, rejection of inheritance or renunciation of succession and filing a motion for a change of surname of the person submitted to guardianship.

412. When it comes to acts within the scope of care over the property of the dependent, it seems that one can associate these with acts exceeding ordinary management of the child's assets. These are acts which result in a considerable decrease in the substance of the child's property or entail inevitable risk of such detriment. The court takes into account whether the considered act is destined to protect the rights of the dependent and broadly understood material interests of the child, if the act is profitable and purposeful for the dependent, if it corresponds to the concept of proper management with which it should be concordant.[188] Such acts may consist in: acquisition, alienation and encumbrance of immovable property, property rights, acquisition or encumbrance of ownership right to housing society premises, establishment, lease and sale of an enterprise, taking a credit and granting a loan, incurring bill and check obligations, granting warranties and acquisition of others' debts, etc.[189] Also drawing valuables, securities and documents from the court deposit, or cash from the bank account of the dependent are acts which require judicial consent.

413. Proceedings concerning the award of such permission take place on the basis of Article 593 PCPC, and the permission is granted by the court at the request of the guardian if the court deems that the interest of the child justifies the conclusion of the act. The court should include in its ruling all essential elements of the act *(essentialia negotii)*, and non-essential clauses *(naturalia negotii)* only where the court considers it necessary taking into consideration the situation of the dependent. Under no circumstances may this be a blank permission without the specification of the act and the conditions of the act's conclusion.[190] As far as representation of the dependent is concerned, the guardian suffers identical restrictions on the ground of Article 159 §1 FGC as the child's parents on the basis of Article 98 §1 FGC.

IV. Judicial Supervision over the Exercise of Guardianship

414. The supervision of the guardianship court over the exercise of guardianship has a very important character and its diligent performance on the part of the court makes a guarantee of the correct functioning of guardianship, which means the exercise in which the interest of the child or incapacitated person is observed and which leads to proper upbringing and formation of the child, and to fulfilment of basic life interests of the fully incapacitated person.

187. Supreme Court resolution issued on 24 Jun. 1061, I CO 16/61, OSNCP 1963/9/187.
188. Kalus, 'Article 156 Commentary', in K. Piasecki (ed.), *Kodeks*, 1044.
189. Supreme Court decision issued on 5 Mar. 1962, 4 CR 578/61, OSNCP 1963/6/127 and on 23 Jul. 1998, III CKU, 34/98, unpublished.
190. Zieliński, *Sądownictwo*, 221.

415. Supervision on the part of the guardianship court may have a permanent or periodic character, specific and general one.[191]

416. Permanent supervision concerns standing control of the guardian's activity and issuing to the guardian instructions and orders on the part of the court. Its purpose is not to allow emergence of irregularities in the exercise of guardianship and prevention of such irregularities already at the stage of particular guardianship acts of the guardian. Such supervision operates on a permanent basis, regardless of how the guardian carries out his or her responsibilities. This differs guardianship from parental authority, which undergoes judicial supervision only sporadically, in the situations where the FGC provides for the parents' obligation to obtain permission for the conclusion of acts exceeding the scope of ordinary management over the child's property.[192]

417. Periodic supervision, on the contrary, is realized by an analysis of periodic reports and accounts from management of the dependent's assets submitted to the guardianship court in pursuance of Articles 166 and 167 FGC in the terms appointed by the court, not more seldom, however, than once a year. Frequency of the reports derives from circumstances of a particular case, such as the recent appointment of the guardian, which results in the lack of his or her experience in the performance of guardianship responsibilities, particular upbringing difficulties which arise on the part of the minor submitted to guardianship, his or her poor health condition, difficulties in submission to the proper treatment on the part of the incapacitated, her particularly poor mental condition requiring particular involvement on the part of the guardian, etc.

418. Undoubtedly, it is impossible to enumerate exhaustively all the data that should be included in the report of the guardian, because this depends on the particular situation and particular relationship of guardianship. These data should be sufficiently detailed to enable the court to acquire extensive information about all issues crucial for the person submitted to guardianship, and the manner of performing care on the part of the guardian, to the extent which makes possible the evaluation of the guardian's activity and application of measures necessary to ensure the proper course of guardianship. In procedural literature, it is emphasized that the guardianship court should counteract reports made in a too general, routine way which does not include the circumstances of a particular case.

419. The analysis of the guardian's report made by the court should not, on its part, be limited to mere examination of the report's content, especially where the court has doubts as to the reliability and truth of the analysed report. On such occasions, the court not only may but also should make use of the assistance of a judicial trustee and check whether the data revealed in the guardian's report correspond

191. Such classification was proposed by A. Józefowicz, 'Szczególny i ogólny nadzór sądu opiekuńczego', *Nowe Prawo*, no. 11 (1968): 1670; Kalus, 'Article 155 Commentary', in K. Piasecki (ed.), *Kodeks*, 1040.

192. Kalus, 'Article 155 Commentary', in K. Piasecki (ed.), *Kodeks*, 1040–1041.

to the actual state of affairs. The consequence of examination of the guardian's report by the court may be the issuance of recommendations and orders to the guardian or delivery of respective rulings concerning major affairs whose resolution seems necessary in light of the guardian's report. When it comes to the recommendations and orders, these may concern the manner of conduct in respect to the dependent, fulfilment of the dependent's needs, his or her submission to proper medical examinations or procedures, contacts and cooperation of the guardian with the school, use of assistance of the dependent in the guardian's household, etc.[193]

420. When it comes to accounts from the management over the dependent's assets, the court examines these meritoriously, in light of principles of accountancy, and orders their correction or completion if needed, decides whether and to what extent it should endorse the accounts (Article 167 §1 FGC). In such conditions, the regulation of §2 of the discussed provision has been harshly criticized in the doctrine. The questioned rule stipulates that the endorsement of account by the court does not exclude the guardian's liability for damage inflicted by his or her undue exercise of management over the property of the dependent.[194]

421. Apart from the measures depicted above, supervision of the guardianship court is realized by way of still different means, among which the following can be distinguished:

(1) duty to learn about current activity of the guardian, giving the guardian recommendations and instructions;
(2) duty to issue orders to the guardian, correcting the manner of exercising his or her responsibilities in the mode of Article 168 FGC;
(3) duty to examine periodic reports of the guardian, to analyse and endorse accounts from management of the dependent's property;
(4) requesting the guardian for explanations in all questions related to care, and submission of necessary documents which enable the court's evaluation of the guardianship;
(5) ordering that the minor should appear in court personally or ordering compulsory appearance in the mode of Article 574 PCPC;
(6) issuing respective orders where the guardian carries out his or her responsibilities defectively;
(7) meting out fines to the guardian in the case of the guardian's non-compliance with the orders of the court;
(8) discharging the guardian of his or her duties if he or she commits acts and omissions which violate the interest of the dependent.[195]

---

193. *Ibid.*, 1080.
194. *Ibid.*, 1082.
195. Kalus, *Opieka*, 175, where an analysis of the courts' enforcement of these measures on the basis of empirical research is presented; Marciniak: *Treść*, 137; Kalus, 'Article 165 Commentary', in K. Piasecki (ed.), *Kodeks*, 1063–1064.

V. Termination of the Relationship of Guardianship

422. Termination of guardianship ex officio takes place when the cause of its establishment becomes nullified. In the case of a minor, this happens once the minor comes to full age, or where parental authority becomes restored. As far as a fully incapacitated person is concerned, guardianship terminates when the incapacitation becomes lifted, or replaced with only partial incapacitation.

423. As mentioned above, the full age is acquired in accordance with Article 10 PCC at the moment when the person reaches the age of 18, or as a consequence of matrimony, even one which in pursuance of Article 10 FGC, as a result of the age impediment, could be annulled by the court. When it comes to restoration of paternal authority, this may happen by a respective judicial decision either restoring this authority or lifting its suspension.

424. The termination of guardianship entails the necessity to undertake certain measures envisaged in Articles 171–174 FGC. These include the duty of further management over the dependent's property if, at the time of termination of guardianship, there exists an impediment to instantaneous seizure of management by the person previously submitted to guardianship, or that person's statutory representative (where guardianship does not terminate, but only the present guardian becomes released of his or her duties) or his or her heirs; the guardian's duty to submit the final account from management of the dependent's property within the period of three months from the termination of guardianship unless the court should release the guardian of this obligation; finally the duty to promptly, that is without unnecessary delay, hand over the managed property to the dependent or the dependent's statutory representative (in the case of release of the contemporary guardian).[196]

§3. CURATORSHIP

I. Differences Between Guardianship and Curatorship

425. Curatorship is a legal institution aimed at supporting natural and juristic persons who for various factual or legal reasons cannot independently conduct their affairs. Such definition has been accepted in the doctrine of both substantive and procedural civil law. This follows from the fact that the purposes of curatorship are convergent with the aims of guardianship. As a consequence, legal regulations of both institutions have been contained in a single piece of legislation, namely in the FGC. The legislator abandoned in this way the previous manner of regulation in which the rules concerning guardianship were located in the Family Code and curatorship was covered by general provisions of civil law.

426. As compared to guardianship, curatorship is characterized by *certain characteristic features*:

196. Kalus, 'Articles 171–174 Commentary', in K. Piasecki (ed.), *Kodeks*, 1076–1079.

- the dominant element is the protection of pecuniary interests; moreover, in many cases of curatorship there is no component of personal care at all, for example, *curator absentis*;
- in general curatorship is temporary in character; it is oftentimes limited to the conclusion of a particular transaction or representation of interests of a party for whom the curator was appointed in a particular proceeding;
- curatorship becomes established, apart from instances listed in statutory provisions, also where, with the view to the public or justified private interest, it proves necessary;
- the question of impulse for its establishment makes another difference between curatorship and guardianship. While guardianship is established by the guardianship court ex officio, curator is appointed ex officio where his or her appointment is to protect individual interest of a given person. The curator shall be appointed at the request of an interested party if the curatorship is to protect individual interest. The public prosecutor may file the motion where protection of public interest or legality is at stake (Article 7 PCPC);
- the bodies competent to establish guardianship and curatorship are different. While guardianship is established only by the guardianship court, curatorship can be established either by the guardianship court or the court which decides in a particular case or sometimes even some other body (notary or administrative authority);
- another difference between the two constructions is the issue of remuneration. A curator, in pursuance of Article 179 FGC, has the right to adequate remuneration and the payable character of this function is a rule. Exception to this rule may only concern the situation where the exercise of curatorship complies with the principles of social cohabitation. The source of covering the expenses for the curator may be property of the person for whom the curator was appointed or property of the party who requested the appointment of curator or finally the State Treasury.

427. There are also the following similarities between guardianship and curatorship:

- social obligation of embracing both the function of guardian and curator;
- reservation of the right of selection of the guardian and curator to the court which adjudicates their appointment;
- the court's obligation to supervise the exercise of both guardianship and curatorship.

II. Forms of Curatorship

428. Since the situations of curatorship are characterized by being variegated, as they stem from various needs and normative grounds, the task of their classification has become extremely difficult. Nevertheless, academics attempt to classify particular types.

429. In particular, one can differentiate curators whose appointment is provided for in various pieces of legislation: the FGC, PCPC or other statutes.[197]

430. However, it seems more sensible to define the types of curators according to their function. This criterion allows for the following classification:

(1) curator for the nasciturus;
(2) curator for a person partially incapacitated;
(3) curator for a mentally sick person;
(4) curator for an absent person;
(5) curator who substitutes the statutory representative;
(6) curator for management of the property;
(7) curator in family status cases;
(8) procedural curator;
(9) curator of a juristic person;
(10) inheritance curator.

431. As can be seen, these are completely different kinds of curatorship, and the premises of establishment of curatorship in particular situations are covered by provisions which envisage the appointment of curators. One can, however, differentiate between certain types of curatorship, for example, the type of durable curatorship of a broad scope of care, which comprises curatorship for a partly incapacitated person, or curatorship for the mentally sick. Another general type is curatorship with a limited range of care, which includes: curatorship for management of the property of a minor deriving from a donation or inheritance where the donor or testator excluded the parent's or guardian's management, curatorship for inheritance non-embraced by heirs, curatorship for the child's property in the instance of restricting parental authority or guardian's care over the property in this respect, curatorship established for judicial proceedings, finally curatorship for a *nasciturus*, and curatorship for an absent person. A specific type of curatorship is the instance of family status cases, whose purpose is to enable denial or proper determination of the child's origin, where a public prosecutor plays a vital role.

197. Kalus, 'Article 178 Commentary', in K. Piasecki (ed.) *Kodeks*, 1087–1093.

Chapter 6. Financial Support among Relatives (Alimony Obligation)

§1. General Questions

432. Regulation of the alimony obligation is contained in Article 128 FGC and following ones, however, these rules are not exhaustive. This follows in the first place from the fact that the discussed obligation has a highly specific character. It can be observed not only in the situations and in relation to the persons set out in the respective provision of the FGC. The FGC stipulates that the duty to provide means of maintenance, and means of upbringing if needed, encumbers lineal relatives and siblings.

433. As far as the object of the obligation is concerned, the resulting claims may be raised only where certain additional circumstances arise, which must be instantiated for the alimony obligation to emerge. In principle, the duty becomes activated only in a situation when the entitled person poverty is in poverty. When this condition expires, the alimony obligation terminates. Should the entitled person suffer from poverty again, he or she may again raise the claim for alimony.[198]

434. When it comes to the subjective aspect, the regulation of Article 128 FGC prescribing that the obligation encumbers lineal relatives and siblings is likewise imprecise. It is justly recognized that the obligation refers as well to the father in relation to an extramarital child (Articles 141–143 FGC), spouses as far as contribution to the fulfilment of needs of the family is concerned (Articles 23 and 27 FGC), a divorced spouse to the benefit of the other spouse (Article 60 FGC), separated spouses (Articles 58 §1, 60, 61, 61^3§1 FGC), the adopting and adopted party, as well as biological descendants of the adopting person (Article 128 FGC). The sources of the alimony duty are, in the first place matrimony, consanguinity and affinity, and adoption.[199]

435. A characteristic feature of the alimony obligation is that it is not only pecuniary in character and it does not solely consist in payment but also (sometimes even preponderantly) in personal care of the obliged party towards the person entitled to alimony, and the satisfaction of this person's needs concerning maintenance and upbringing. This pertains not only to a child but also to a disabled person (Article 135 §2 FGC). Moreover, a characteristic feature of this obligation is its mutual nature, which means that the persons obliged to alimony may as well become entitled to it when they fall into poverty. Another quality of this obligation is its attachment to the person of the entitled and obliged party. The obligation shall last

198. Smyczyński, *Prawo.*, 336–338; T. Domińczyk, 'Article 133 Commentary', in K. Piasecki (ed.) *Kodeks*, 960–962.
199. Domińczyk, 'Article 128 Commentary', in K. Piasecki (ed.) *Kodeks*, 916–917.

as long as these persons live. In the case of death of any party, the alimony obligation expires and does not form a part of the estate left by either the entitled or obliged person. What is more, this obligation is inalienable, impossible to renounce and unaffected by limitation periods.

436. Limitation periods do not affect the alimony duty itself (which follows from Article 117 PCC), but particular alimony instalments can be barred by limitation. Such instalments as periodic renditions are covered by the three-year limitation period. This follows as well expressly from Article 137 FGC. However, the problem is that the needs of the entitled party arise regardless of whether or not the obliged person fulfils his or her obligation, which frequently results in debts on the part of the entitled party in relation to third persons. This issue has been a frequent theme in judicature pertaining to the inclusion of such obligations in the awarded behindhand instalments.[200] As a result of the amendment of the FGC of 2008, Article 137 §2 FGC was added, pursuant to which unsatisfied needs of the entitled party from the time before initiating judicial proceedings for alimony are to be allowed by the court by the adjudication of a respective sum of money.

437. One can only fully agree with the thesis that duty plays a characteristic role in society. The alimony obligation stems from the family bond, and even though the state creates a system of social insurance for the citizens who may acquire certain funds as social benefits in the case of a very difficult situation, like old age, sickness, invalidity, or unplanned motherhood, these means are generally not sufficient. In practice, social benefits may only bear a complementary function in covering particularly essential needs.[201]

§2. Alimony Obligation in Relation to Relatives

I. Premises and Content of the Alimony Obligation

438. Polish doctrine distinguishes between the emergence of alimony obligation, which takes place when a particular family relationship emerges between the parties justifying alimony as such, and the obligation to carry out the claim, to comply with the duty, which becomes activated when certain conditions occur on the part of the entitled person (usually poverty) and on the part of the entitled one (in what order he or she is obliged). These premises have been defined in the FGC in a non-uniform way; they depend on the type of family relationship which institutes them, and differences among particular relatives.[202]

200. Supreme Court resolution issued on 25 Nov. 1968, III CZP 65/68, OSNCP 1969/5/83, *Nowe Prawo*, no. 4 (1970): 602 with a gloss by J. Gwiazdomorski, *Nowe Prawo*, no. 11–12 (1969): 1711; Supreme Court decision issued on 5. 1976, III CRN 88/76, OSNCP 1977/2/33; and on 5 Jul. 1995, III CZP 86/95, *Palestra*, no. 3–4 (1996): 236.

201. Smyczyński, *Prawo*, 346–348.

202. *Ibid.*, 283.

439. If the alimony relationship is bilaterally individualized, its preconditions and content must be influenced by the situation on both sides of this relationship. The legislator spotted this problem, providing in Article 135 §1 FGC that the scope of renditions following from the alimony obligation shall depend on the one hand on the justified needs of the entitled party, and on the other hand, on the earning and property income capacities of the obliged person.

440. Justified needs of the entitled are a diversified category, depending on the circle of persons to which the entitled and the obliged belong. They shall be treated differently where the entitled party claims alimony renditions from his or her close relatives, and differently where the claim refers to more distant ones, especially if their material situation is radically different. The same applies in the situation where the entitled party has lived thus far to a high economic standard and has intense cultural needs connected with his or her level of education and creative activity so far conducted. The scope of obligation depends as well on whether or not the entitled is healthy and able. It is equally important who the entitled person is. Justified needs of a child, which follow from the child's age and level of education, encompass nutrition, clothing, and first of all educational needs connected with the child's skills, twists, and possibilities of gaining the level of education which allows achieving very good conditions of existence and satisfaction with life.[203] The situation of an old person unable to function independently, even in relation to his or her basic needs and activities of everyday life, looks quite different from a completely fit young person.

441. Determination of the needs is also connected with the notion of poverty, which has not been defined in FGC. However, judicature accepts that poverty shall be the case where 'the entitled person cannot fully by his or her own efforts and means satisfy his or her justified needs'.[204] However, there remains the question which springs to mind in connection with alimony claims of certain people who have property, even of considerable size, but the property does not generate any income. Its sale could allow for the fulfilment of needs of the person living in the condition of financial poverty and unable to support himself or herself. Here, we entirely agree with the opinion that such a situation would pose an impediment to award alimony to the claimant.[205] This should be the case since every person should make efforts to fulfil his or her needs from the proceeds of their incomes and property, taking into account the alienation of items of this property, making use of one's own qualifications and capacities. It was a characteristic quality of the period of economic and social transitions in Poland that the source of fulfilment of these needs were incomes from labour. Currently, more frequent generation of income from other payable activity can be observed, as well as income from personal assets,

203. Supreme Court decision of 29 Nov. 1949, Wa.C. 167/49, *Nowe Prawo*, no. 2 (1951): 52.
204. Smyczyński, *Prawo*, 337; T. Smyczyński, 'Pojęcie i metody pomiaru niedostatku, jako przeslanki obowiązku alimentacyjnego', *Państwo i Prawo*, no. 12 (1982): 75; Supreme Court resolution issued on 16 Dec. 1987, III CZP 91/86, OSNCP 1988/4/42.
205. Domińczyk, 'Article 133 Commentary', in K. Piasecki (ed.) *Kodeks*, 961.

earnings from capital investments, management of immovable property, and renditions from insurance and social benefits, pensions of various types.[206]

442. As has been pointed out above, the prerequisites of the alimony obligation in certain cases have to be defined differently. This refers in particular to the alimony obligation of parents in relation to the child, which exists for as long as the child is unable to support himself or herself, regardless of whether or not the child remains in financial poverty (Article 133 § 1 FGC). The parents are obliged to alimony to the benefit of the child if the child does not enjoy incomes from labour or other remuneration, earnings from his or her own property sufficient to satisfy the child's needs. In addition, pursuant to Article 133 § 3 FGC, once the child attains the age of majority, the alimony obligation of parents towards children may expire if the alimony burden is excessively onerous for the parent, or the child is not making efforts to acquire the ability to support oneself.

443. The income which can be acquired by the child may originate from civil law titles (compensation, pension, income from the child's own capital, from his or her chattels and immovable property). These sources are compared to earning capacities of the parents, however, in this type of relationship (parents – child), responsibilities of the parents are treated more strictly and a well-grounded line of judicature depicts that the parents should make greater efforts in order to fulfil the needs of the child, share even very modest financial resources with this child, or even sacrifice the substance of their property if this is necessary to save the child's life and health.[207]

444. Yet different are the prerequisites of alimony obligation of the spouse exclusively guilty of the divorce in relation to the innocent spouse. Article 60 §2 FGC envisages that this obligation becomes activated where the divorce brings about essential deterioration of the material condition of the innocent spouse, even though that spouse is not in a situation of financial poverty. The relevant factor is not the changes which took place in the material position of the innocent spouse within the period between the factual separation of the spouses and divorce, but the comparison of the spouse's financial situation which would be the case had the spouses remained in common conjugal life and the situation emerged as a result of the divorce.[208]

445. A special obligation of the father of the child who is not the mother's husband has been provided in Article 141 FGC. The content of this duty is to contribute to the coverage of expenses connected with pregnancy and giving birth, to the extent which corresponds to the circumstances. The duty includes the necessity to cover the three-month costs of the mother's maintenance in the period of birth. If

206. Smyczyński, *Prawo*, 338–339.
207. Supreme Court resolution issued on 9 Jun. 1976, III CZP 46/75, OSNCP 1976/No.9/pos. 184.
208. Supreme Court decision issued on 7 Jan. 1969, II CR 528/68, OSNCP 1969/10/179 and on 28 Oct. 1980, III CRN 222/80, OSNCP 1981/5/90.

important reasons are at stake, the child's mother may additionally claim the father's participation in the costs of her maintenance for a longer period of time.

446. Where the mother has encountered other necessary expenses as a result of pregnancy and giving birth, or incurred property loss, she may also claim their partial compensation by the father of the child. Undoubtedly, as a result of the pregnancy and confinement there arise various detriments on the part of the child's mother, especially when unmarried. Claims envisaged in the discussed provision are of integral character, and major significance is ascribed to the purpose these claims serve. The vast majority of the doctrine is of the opinion that these claims fall under alimony obligation since their aim is to satisfy the mother's needs in the scope of her maintenance, but there are also authors who deny such character to the discussed claims. Both the duration of the obligation and its scope follow from the 'circumstances of a particular case'. This means that where the mother of the child has no resources, earning capacities or capital incomes, the father of the child should cover the costs of her maintenance in full. If the father of the child is in this situation, the mother should cover the costs in total.

447. Raising these claims becomes possible after the determination of paternity of a man who is not the mother's husband, that is acknowledgement of the child's paternity on his part or its judicial ascertainment. There are no impediments against combining the claim based on the discussed provision with the action for determining the child's paternity.

II. Financial Capacity of the Obliged and Needs of the Entitled

448. On the part of the person obliged to alimony, the legal prerequisites of the emergence of the obligation are sufficient earning capacities or capital incomes. It should be emphasized that the relevant criteria are not the real earnings or pure income from the assets of the obliged, but also incomes he or she has not acquired as a consequence of his or her omissions, but which were possible to generate. If the earnings or incomes of the obliged person are unstable, which is a frequent situation in the conditions of general lack of stabilization in economic relations, the basis of assessment of the alimony obligation shall be usually the average income calculated for longer periods. If the basis is income from a farm or business, again the average income achieved in the conditions of due management, and not the actual income in the situation of omissions or lack of diligence on the part of the obliged party, shall be taken into consideration.

449. In judicature, there are a number of decisions pointing *de casu ad casum* to the possible understandings of the earning and capital income capacities. One can invoke, for instance, rulings delivered in the situations where until recently military service was compulsory, in which courts stated that the impossibility of wage labour caused by the service in the military could be the ground to release the soldier from the alimony obligation only where the soldier had no property capable of generating income. When he had such property, there were no reasons not to award alimony from him.[209] Many decisions depict the situation of incarcerated convicts who cannot gain income for the lack of labour offers for condemned persons, which releases the prisoners from alimony obligation.[210]

450. Currently, it turns out that in the present conditions of economic crisis a vast number of binding decisions adjudicating alimony cannot be enforced, and execution proceedings carried out by court executive officers prove ineffective. Under such circumstances, social benefits play an important role, predominantly those which are aimed at the material support of the family. The benefits are awarded for maintenance of non-working members of the family, because of temporary decrease of income in the family, its loss (especially in the situation of loss of work), and because of the impossibility to obtain alimony from the persons directly obliged.

451. Another kind of benefit is family benefits of the insurance type and social security renditions. The former are to promote personal involvement of the entitled party or an adult family member in order to assure means of maintenance to the family. That is why the court shall take them into account when meting out the amount of alimony instalments and adjudicate alimony of particular value, so as to make this alimony complement the sum necessary to support the needs of the family.

452. Yet different, subsidiary, is the character of renditions from the social aid, which should be returned when the member of family obliged to alimony appears, or renditions from the alimony fund, whose function is to provide current financial means which the entitled party cannot obtain by way of execution of the alimony awarded to him or her. This follows clearly from the amended Article 135 §3 FGC which stipulates that these renditions do not affect the scope of alimony obligation.[211]

III. Subjective Scope and Order of Persons Obliged to Alimony

453. The catalogue of persons entitled and obliged to alimony, as envisaged by the FGC, includes:

(1) *Lineal relatives and siblings*: Lineal relatives, in pursuance of Article 61^7§1 FGC, are persons of which one originates from the other. These are both

209. Supreme Court decision issued on 18 Nov. 1955, II CR 55/55, OSN 1956/2/54 and on 1 Apr. 1957, GR 163/57, *Nowe Prawo*, no. 6 (1958): 124.
210. Supreme Court decision issued on 7 Apr. 1994, I CR 3/94 unpublished and on 15 Oct. 1998, I CKN 860/97, LEX Polonica no. 353788.
211. Smyczyński, *Prawo*, 347.

ascendants, that is, parents, grandparents and great grandparents; and descendants, that is: children, grandchildren and great-grandchildren. All of them are potentially obliged to alimony. Collateral relatives are persons who descend from a common ancestor. Among these relatives, only siblings have been encumbered with alimony obligations. This refers both to natural siblings, originating from both common parents, and half-siblings, originating from the common mother or common father only.

(2) *Persons connected by affinity*: alimony obligation concerns as well certain parties connected by affinity, the stepfather and stepmother in relation to the stepson and stepdaughter, and the other way around. However, in both directions, the obligation is going to be activated where principles of social coexistence justify such alimony. The Supreme Court in the resolution of 1968 stated that the step-parents' obligation should be treated in the same way as the natural parents' duty in relation to their child, but cannot precede the latter, since such condition would contradict the principles of social cohabitation. The child may, however, claim alimony from its stepmother or stepfather in whole or in part where the natural parents are unable to fulfil their alimony obligation in relation to the child, or if the parents' earning and capital income capacities prove insufficient to satisfy the justified needs of the child in the scope of maintenance and upbringing. In any case, such a solution must be supported by principles of social coexistence.

(3) *Spouses*: existence of the obligation between the spouses has frequently been questioned, since the duty to provide means of maintenance derives from a more general obligation to contribute to the needs of the family as a whole, following from Articles 23 and 27 FGC. Nevertheless, this general obligation becomes substantiated in the duty holding strictly between the spouses when it comes to the alimony obligation between the divorced spouses (Article 60 FGC), in the case of separation and annulment of marriage (Article 130 FGC).

(4) *Other persons*: this relates predominantly to the extramarital father obliged in relation to the child's mother in accordance with Article 141 FGC.

(5) *The adopting and adopted party*: since Article 121 FGC envisages that the relationship between the adopting and the adopted person shall be always the same as between the parent and child, regardless of the type of adoption, there shall always be such alimony obligation between these parties as between natural parents and their child. Moreover, in the case of full and absolute adoption, the obligation exists between the adopted child and lineal relatives of the adopting person and his or her siblings. This does not emerge, however, in the case of partial adoption.

IV. Primacy and Persons Obliged in Further Sequence

454. The order of the persons obliged to alimony has been shaped in the FGC taking into consideration the line (lineal/collateral) and degree of consanguinity or affinity according to the rules set out in Article 129 FGC and following ones.

455. In relation to relatives, the sequence is as follows:

- According to the line of consanguinity – the obligation encumbers in the first place lineal relatives without any restrictions, descendants before ascendants, which means that the burden first pertains to children and grandchildren in relation to parents and grandparents. In the second order, the obligation encumbers parents and grandparents in relation to their children and grandchildren. In the lack of lineal relatives, or where lineal relatives are unable to carry out the obligation, the duty refers to collateral relatives, which means siblings.
- According to the degree of consanguinity – first comes the relatives of a closer degree, then more distant ones. In this manner, the alimony obligation of the mother and father precedes the obligation of grandparents and siblings.
- When it comes to the adopted person, the sequence depends predominantly on the type of adoption. In the case of full and absolute adoption, the sequence looks the same as above. In the case of partial adoption, the situation looks different. Here the obligation of the adopted towards his or her natural relatives becomes activated in the last place.
- Between a stepchild and the stepmother or stepfather, the obligation is primarily evaluated from the point of view of its conformity with the principles of social coexistence, but the doctrine is of the opinion that provisions on the alimony obligation of parents in relation to their children should apply appropriately.[212]

456. The general principle is that the alimony obligation of the person obliged in further sequence emerges only in the lack of persons obliged in the previous rank, or where such person exists but is unable to comply with his or her alimony duty, or finally it is impossible or excessively difficult to enforce from that party the means of maintenance in proper time when the entitled person needs the funds (Article 132 FGC). If this obligation should emerge, this means that the person obliged in further rank does not act on behalf of the person obliged in the previous order, but performs only his or her own obligation, as a result of which the obligation of the predecessor expires. The burden of proof of the circumstances envisaged in this article lies in light of Article 6 PCC on the person who claims alimony, although this person may use various pieces of evidence. Sometimes there is a certain division of alimony functions between persons obliged in the primary or further rank by virtue of an agreement, for example, between the child's grandmother and professionally active mother of the child. The grandmother makes efforts to maintain and bring up the child and the mother provides necessary funds. Such cases can be observed very frequently, however, one should generally agree with one of the Supreme Court's decisions in which the Court questioned the correctness of such a division of the alimony obligation between the primarily obliged persons and parties obliged in further sequence.[213]

457. It should be mentioned that pursuant to Article 144^1 FGC, introduced in 2009, the person obliged to alimony payments may decline to fulfil that obligation if the request for alimony is contrary to the principles of social coexistence. This

212. Smyczyński, *Prawo*, 335.
213. Judgment of 24 Jan. 1973, III CRN 378/72, LEX Polonica no. 316346.

right to decline does not apply to alimony payments of parents that their minor children are entitled to. In practice, this provision will concern situations in which parents who had deserted their children and neglected to pay alimony seek them out and demand alimony payments because those parents need funds for living, medical expenses, incurred debts, etc.

458. In view of the significance of alimony decisions, Polish law provides advantages in their enforcement.

- First of all, the court shall ex officio supplement the judgment allowing alimony with immediate execution clause and serve it to the creditor (Article 1082 PCPC).
- Initiation of execution may be requested by the creditor without specifying the manner of enforcement and without pointing to the debtor's assets, which is very crucial since the debtor often conceals his or her property (Article 1081 §1 PCPC).
- Execution can be initiated ex officio by the first instance court which heard the alimony case (Article 1085 PCPC).
- The court executive officer is obliged ex officio to determine the debtor's incomes, his or her property and place of residence (Article 1086 PCPC).
- Alimony claims enjoy the precedence of satisfaction from execution since they are placed at second place among the receivables paid from the amount obtained by execution (Article 1025 PCPC). Even scholarships or benefits generally exempted from execution are affected by enforcement of alimony renditions up to the amount of three-fifths of the total.
- The writ of execution can be submitted directly to the prison warden where it refers to an incarcerated debtor.

459. Unfortunately, it has to be concluded that despite such preferences, the execution of alimony judgments has not been particularly effective.

Part III. Matrimonial Property Law

Chapter 1. Introduction

460. Specific consideration in this chapter must be preceded by certain remarks pertaining to the evolution of legal regulation in the discussed area on the grounds of the FGC. Beyond any doubt, the FGC enacted in 1964 was adjusted to the arrangement of social and economic relations existing at the time of its preparation and legislative process. The first relatively insignificant amendment of provisions regulating property relations was introduced in 1975.[214]

461. The need to introduce far-reaching modifications in this respect definitely emerged after the transition of the Polish environment from the model of planned economy, binding in the period of the so-called real socialism, to the present social and economic regime – social market economy. Amendments introduced by the Act of 17 June 2004[215] were very significant. The legislator preserved the regime of matrimonial community of property as the default statutory type, but abandoned the notion of 'growth in assets'. The term was applied for the purposes of a specific regime of property separation with the division of the growth in assets, but the latter term was conceived in a way completely different than previously.

462. A certain previously missing category of assets was included in the common property of spouses. This refers to means gathered on the account of an open or occupational retirement pension fund of each of the spouses. Moreover, assets belonging to each of the spouses were defined in a different way. In place of separate properties there appeared the notion of personal properties of each of the spouses, which include currently the elements listed exhaustively in Article 33 FGC, as well as things acquired by substitution in relation to all elements of the personal property, not only pertaining to assets acquired in exchange for the property elements acquired before the establishment of common property, or by inheritance or donation, as was the case before the amendment.

463. Moreover, for the sake of avoiding hardships encountered up to the point, personal property of each of the spouses began to incorporate material interests following from joint co-ownership, undergoing separate regulation (partners in a partnership not equipped in legal personality). A serious change, evaluated in different

214. Act of 19 Dec. 1975, Journal of Statutes 1975, no. 45, item 234.
215. Journal of Statutes, no. 162, item 1691.

ways in the doctrine, was a very significant broadening of freedom of each of the spouses to dispense of the common property and restriction of necessary permission of the other spouse to exhaustively enlisted cases in the statute, which is a departure from the previous model in which the entitlements were based on the division between acts of ordinary management and acts exceeding ordinary management of the common property. Also, the responsibility of spouses for obligations incurred by one of them was modified. Finally, a new matrimonial property regime was introduced. The new regime has its equivalent in German law, where it is treated as the statutory default model: regime of property separation with equalization of the growth in assets *(Zugewinngemeinschaft)*.[216]

§1. The Notion and Types of Matrimonial Property Regimes

464. By the notion of matrimonial property regime, the doctrine understands regulation of the legal situation of spouses pertaining to their property, both acquired before entering into marriage and afterwards. When it comes to liability of the spouses for obligations, this question does not constitute a component of the concept of property regime, even if this liability is closely correlated with the type of regime under which the obligation arises. In addition, for a significant period of time, the doctrine has consequently supported the position that debt is not the component of property, but its burden.[217] The possibility to apply within family law the broad concept of property covering also debts and intense connections between matrimonial property law and the law of inheritance, where debts are included in the patrimony (Article 922 §1 PCC) should not be questioned. In particular, pursuant to Article 46 FGC after the termination of the matrimonial community of property the provisions on co-ownership of the inherited estate are to be applied appropriately to the common property of spouses. Similarly, provisions concerning division of inheritance should be applied appropriately to the division of the former common property. Inheritance law knows the broad concept of property which covers also debts.

465. The above arguments justify the postulate of admissibility of application within family law of the broad concept of property, especially in situations connected with the division of the spouses' assets, where the final allocation and adjustment of eventual repayments or additional payments are decided by the balance of the asset and debt side. High amounts of repayments which are the case as a result of the division of the spouses' property, connected in particular with receiving a loan for their common apartment, encourage one to reach for the controversial broad

216. T. Smyczyński, 'Kierunki reformy Kodeksu rodzinnego i opiekuńczego', *Kwartalnik Prawa Prywatnego*, no. 2 (1999): 308; T. Smyczyński, 'Reforma małżeńskiego prawa majątkowego', *Monitor Prawniczy*, no. 18 (2004): 827 et seq.

217. Winiarz, *Prawo*, 98; an opposite opinion is presented by S. Szer, *Prawo*, 100.

concept of property in this respect. Such an approach accounts as well for the existence of the connection particularly difficult to separate between particular debts and particular property interests.[218]

466. Such a choice provides better problem-solving techniques. Problems arise upon the division of the common property, especially after the divorce of spouses. However, it cannot be denied that such a procedure is difficult to reconcile with the prevailing position in doctrinal writings and the need to protect the interests of creditors, for whom it is more beneficial to leave both of the spouses in the position of debtors. Especially after the amendment of the FGC in 2004, the principle of creditor protection seems to dominate over the principle of protection of the interest of the family, and not all civil law scholars seem to accept this primacy.

467. Yet another understanding of the concept of matrimonial property regime was presented by A. Dyoniak, who claimed that a marital property regime concerns only internal property relationships inherent to the family, holding between the spouses, to the exclusion of such relationships which exist between the spouses as a result of the very formation of marriage.[219] In consequence, if we bear in mind the broader scope of matrimonial property relations, one should rather use the term 'the total property situation of the spouses', and the notion of 'matrimonial property regimes' makes only one of its elements.

468. Nonetheless, it should be mentioned as well that in every matrimony, there holds a certain property regime and the regime remains uniform for the particular matrimony according to the principle of uniformity of matrimonial property regime. What is more, in pursuance of the principle of freedom to choose the marital regime, the model depends primarily on the choice of the spouses, except situations of compulsory regimes which are the result of determining the legal situation of the spouses as a consequence of a judicial decision. For another thing, the principle of universality of the default regime results in the situation that, in the lack of choice or certain specific circumstances, the binding regime shall be the model of statutory community of property.

469. Matrimonial property regimes are characterized by certain generic features. They alternatively distinguish only two estates, or also a third one, namely the common property of the spouses described in terms of joint property, without defined shares, undergoing unchanging principles of management. Accordingly, one could divide property regimes into two basic types, namely regimes of community and regimes of property separation.[220]

---

218. M. Nazar, 'Małżeńska wspólność spółdzielczych praw do lokali mieszkalnych', *Kwartalnik Prawa Prywatnego*, no. 2 (2003): 348.
219. A. Dyoniak, *Ustawowy ustrój majątkowy małżeński* (Wrocław [et al]: Ossolineum, 1985), 12.
220. T. Sokołowski, 'Article 31 Commentary', in H. Dolecki, T. Sokołowski (eds), *Kodeks rodzinny i opiekuńczy. Komentarz*, (Warszawa: Wolters Kluwer, 2013), 133.

470. Within the class of community regimes, one can distinguish as separate types: the regime of statutory community of property and contractual types of community, including various sub-types of property systems: extended community and the model of limited community of property. In each of these cases, there exists, in a broader or narrower range, property common to the spouses. Within the class of separation regimes, one can distinguish two types: contractual regimes of separate property (ordinary separation and separation with equalization of the growth in assets) and finally the model of compulsory separation.

471. In light of the presented classification, the compulsory regimes do not form any special category but belong usually to the class of separation models. In addition, the regime which emerges pursuant to the rule of Article 54 §2 sentence 1 FGC (thus community established as a result of lifting separation) is not in its essence a compulsory regime, because there remains the possibility of its modification by means of marriage articles concluded by the spouses. In consequence, one should group this model among community regimes with all consequences of this fact, in particular, the condition that an inherent feature of this model is the possibility of modification according to the parties' intention, hence the lack of compulsory character.

Chapter 2. Default Matrimonial Regime

§1. Statutory Community and Personal Properties of the Spouses

472. The definition of common property of the spouses emerging between them lest they should conclude marriage articles, that is to say, matrimonial settlement is contained in Article 31 FGC, which envisages in §1 that at the moment of formation of matrimony there arises between the spouses' *ex lege* community of property (statutory community) covering assets acquired in the course of marriage by both spouses or one of them (common property). Assets not included in the statutory community belong to personal properties of the respective spouse. Where the acquisition of a right is not a result of a single legal event but makes in a way a process extended over time (e.g., the acquisition of ownership of immovable property subject to a condition or with reservation of a particular period requires the conclusion of two contracts: the obliging one and disposing one), then the immovable property is going to form a part of the common property if the disposing contract is concluded after the entry into marriage, regardless of the fact whether the name of other spouse should be mentioned in the content of the agreement.

473. The quoted provision as well as other rules concerning matrimonial property regimes use quite consequently the term 'items of property'. This does not denote particular objects which exist in the physical world or things but encompasses property interests linked to these objects, such as ownership, other property rights (perpetual usufruct, usufruct, servitudes, property housing society right to a flat, pledge or mortgage) or rights of obligational character (lease, rent, loan for use, leasing, right to compensation). Since the common property of the spouses is usually of special significance to both of them and constitutes the dominant property among all their assets, pursuant to Article 31 §2 FGC gives an exemplary list of the most important components of this estate. The enumeration is not exhaustive but only exemplary, since the provision expressly uses the term 'in particular'. These components are:

(1) collected remuneration for work and incomes from other payable activity of each of the spouses;
(2) incomes from the common property and from personal property of each spouse;
(3) means gathered on the account of an open or occupational retirement pension belonging to each of the spouses.

474. As far as the first component is concerned, one should pay attention to the fact that the remuneration which makes the foundation of personal property for the largest number of citizens, namely salary for work or other type of payable activity constitutes the common property of the spouses only once collected by the respective spouse, most frequently by proper entry on the account of the employee. As long as the remuneration makes only a receivable owed by the employer or contracting party, such receivable does not and may not form a part of the common property even by force of marriage settlement. In any event, it constitutes a component of the personal property of the spouse who works or provides other payable services.

475. Remuneration and income from other payable activities were broadly defined and encompass the remuneration and income (earnings) from any sort of payable operation.[221] These earnings and incomes become components of the common property only once collected, thus receivables to these amounts do not make a part of the common assets, regardless of whether they are already due and payable.

476. Another important element of the common property is income both from the common assets and personal assets of each of the spouses. According to the doctrine of family law, this covers the so-called net income deriving from respective assets in the understanding of tax law, which means after setting off expenses necessary to generate the income and public law payments (taxes). What is more, every benefit stemming from an asset makes for income, even if achieved at the cost of decrease of the asset or its loss. It is also accepted that one of the components of the common property is already the entitlement to gather income from particular assets, and the exercise of this entitlement constitutes a part of management of the common property.[222] Incomes from assets indicated in respective provisions of law are natural profits gathered from the items comprised by the property and civil law profits brought by particular assets. In a similar manner capital incomes (interests or bonuses) enter into the common property even if the capital belongs to one of the spouses.

477. The third of the listed components was introduced into the statute as a result of reform of the retirement pension system and the emergence of pension funds, whose role becomes more and more significant.

478. Among the elements not mentioned expressly in the catalogue but also falling under the category of common property one can enumerate things acquired by means of certain legal events, such as prescription, if the expiry of the period of prescription took place after the entry into marriage, or as a result of expectative vested in both spouses, where the acquisition took place while the matrimony maintained or even after its expiry. The right stemming from a residential lease contract in the case of an apartment leased by one of the spouses during marriage in order to satisfy the housing needs of the family belongs, under Article 680^1 PCC, to the category of common property. A special provision referring to the element of common property because of its significance is Article 34 FGC which stipulates that chattels which make the usual home equipment are covered by the community of property, even if they were acquired as a result of inheritance, testament legacy or donation unless the will of the testator or donor was contrary.

221. Journal of Statutes 2003, no. 119, item 1116, with subsequent amendments.
222. J. Ignatowicz, M. Nazar, *Prawo rodzinne* (Warszawa: Lexis Nexis, 2016), 258–260.

479. Apart from the common property, there exist usually in the regime of statutory community personal properties of each spouse. Before, these used to be called separate properties. Composition of this estate, comprising of assets belonging to each spouse, has been defined in Article 33 FGC.[223] In accordance with Article 33 FGC, the personal property comprises only elements enumerated in this provision, thus the catalogue is closed and exhaustive. Remaining objects not indicated in the discussed article do not enter into the personal property but to the common property of the spouses, and this is the way in which any doubts about particular property components which appear in the doctrine of family law should be solved.

480. Pursuant to this provision (Article 33 FGC), personal property of each spouse comprises the following:

(1) items of property acquired before the emergence of statutory community;
(2) items of property acquired by inheritance, legacy or donation, unless the testator or donor stipulated otherwise;
(3) property interests following from joint ownership on the basis of separate provisions;
(4) items of property which exclusively serve the purpose of satisfying personal needs of one of the spouses;
(5) inalienable interests which are vested only in one person;
(6) items acquired as compensation for personal injury or damage to health, or as atonement for the inflicted harm; this does not concern pension due to an injured spouse on the grounds of partial or complete loss of capacity to wage labour, or because of the increase of his or her needs or decrease in prospects to the future;
(7) receivables pertaining to remuneration for labour or owed for other payable activity of the spouses;
(8) items of property acquired as reward for personal achievements of one of the spouses;
(9) authorship and connected rights, industrial property rights and other intellectual rights;
(10) items of property acquired in exchange for other elements of the personal property unless a special provision stipulates otherwise.

481. Items of property acquired before the emergence of community should not be identified with items acquired before the entry into marriage. In a situation where the spouses by means of matrimonial settlement introduced into their relationship the regime of property separation, then items acquired separately by each of them while the marriage holds between them enter into their respective personal properties. However, if afterwards the spouses decide to introduce by another settlement the model of property community, from that time on the items acquired by them are going to enter the common property, except for elements set out in Article 33 FGC.

223. J. Piątowski, 'Ustrój wspólności ustawowej', in J. Piątowski (ed.), *System*, 359.

On the contrary, items of property or their shares acquired while the spouses remain bound by the regime of property separation are going to enter into their respective personal properties.

482. Very often the spouses acquire certain items of property before entering into marriage. Such a procedure gives rise to the situation in which the items are subject to co-ownership in fractional parts both before and after the matrimonial emergence of property community, and not subject to joint ownership. This denotes that the personal properties of the spouses are going to be broadened by a share expressed in a fraction in the co-ownership of the acquired items.

483. The formulation of Article 33 point 2 FGC has for long raised numerous doubts in the doctrine of family law. The items listed in this provision are subject to testamentary or intestate succession envisaged in the provisions of the PCC (Articles 922 PCC and the following ones).[224] Unfortunately, the statutory regulation is far from being precise, which has been shown in the literature.[225] This follows from a number of reasons: the character of succession and the difference between the situation of an inheritance acquired by only one heir and the succession of a number of persons, the necessity to satisfy inheritance creditors, as well as the obligational nature of legacy in Polish law of succession and position of legacy as a claim. Lastly, the discussed provisions stipulate that particular items of property are to enter the common property if such was the intention of the testator.[226]

484. The same provision envisages the inclusion in a spouse's personal property of items of property acquired by means of donation. As a consequence of performance of this contract in which only one of the spouses is a party, the object of rendition enters into his or her personal property. Exceptionally, if such is the intention of the donor (Article 33 point 2 in fine FGC), the donated item may enrich the common property of the spouses. The situation of donation made only to the personal property of the beneficiary is much simpler; still, in the case of the donor's stipulation that the object of donation should enter the common property of the spouses, there arise, as indicated by the practice of the administration of justice,[227] very serious controversies. In a situation where the donor is one of the parents of one of the spouses and the matrimony functions properly, there are usually no significant dangers. However, if in a marriage there occurs a situation of disintegration of conjugal life, the relations between the donor and one of the beneficiaries undergo serious deterioration, which may give rise to conflicts, especially that Article 898 PCC allows revocation of donation on the grounds of 'gross ingratitude of the beneficiary'.

485. Material rights listed in the following point are in the first order these interests which follow from the relationship of (Civil Code) partnership. This refers in

224. Sokołowski, 'Article 33 Commentary', in H. Dolecki, T. Sokołowski (eds), *Kodeks*, 166–171.
225. Sychowicz, 'Article 33 Commentary', in K. Piasecki (ed.), *Kodeks*, 215–216.
226. S. Breyer, 'Gloss to the Resolution of SN of 7 April 1975', OSP 1976/1/3.
227. Sokołowski, 'Article 33 Commentary', in H. Dolecki, T. Sokołowski (eds), *Kodeks*, 171–175.

the first place to the case where only one of the spouses is a partner in such an undertaking, and where each of the spouses is a partner in another partnership. An important reason for this regulation was to assure to the spouse-partner full freedom in the exercise of entitlements following from his or her participation in a partnership, as well as the need to preserve integrity of the partnership and the rights of other partners. In such a case, the rights connected with the participation in each of the respective partnerships should constitute the personal properties of each of the spouses who act as partners in separate partnerships. This concerns both entitlements of purely financial character: in particular, receivables stemming from the share in gains and receivables to the assets remaining after the dissolution of partnership, as well as the rights to decide about the investment purpose of the gained capital or distribution of the accrued income connected with the share in the partnership. There are, however, no restrictions to the possibility of entry of the income gained from the participation of a spouse in a partnership into the common property of both spouses, since these should be classified as incomes from the spouse's personal property.

486. Certain doubts may arise as well as to the next category of items which enter into the personal property of a spouse, namely items of property which serve the purpose of satisfying only his or her personal needs. Most frequently, it is clear that the things in question are going to be clothes, personal objects, sports equipment suited to the body of the spouse, medical, orthopaedic or rehabilitation equipment. In the literature, one can encounter opinions that along with the growth in affluence of certain families, also a passenger car may be considered an item of exclusively personal use where only one of the spouses uses the car.[228] Beyond a shadow of doubt, if this is a special car adjusted for invalid persons which serves a disabled spouse for the purpose of transport, such a solution seems perfectly correct. However, it seems unjustified to generalize this problem excessively. Yet more complicated seems a situation pertaining to jewellery, especially if we consider that in some legal systems provisions of law expressly exclude such items of property from the personal property of a spouse. Certain authors claim that costly items (jewellery, precious coins, etc.), as long as their value is not too high as compared to the worth of the whole estate of the spouses, should constitute at the moment of their acquisition into the personal property of a spouse. It would be difficult to accept such views. First of all, these days we can no longer make the personal character of jewellery or precious coins dependent on the sex of the spouse, since chains, bracelets or even earrings are not any more worn exclusively by women. As a result, they can be included in the property of a man who uses them.

487. In addition, I cannot agree that it is correct to correlate the evaluation of the possibility to ascribe to a given estate, personal or common, with the criterion of their value compared at the moment of acquisition of the valuables with the worth of the common property of the spouses. It is suggested that it should be determined,

228. Supreme Court resolution issued on 28 Sep. 1979, III CZP 15/79, OSNC 1980/4/ 63.

on the basis of such comparison, if the parties did not attempt to evade statutory provisions on property community by a transfer of value of the jewellery to the personal property of one of the spouses. In my opinion, the most appropriate is the suggestion made by M. Sychowicz,[229] that among the items mentioned in this point one should not include objects whose purpose, type and value demonstrate that in earnest the items make a capital investment or that the purpose of their collection is generation of income. Nevertheless, one should carry out such classifications very cautiously, taking into consideration all relevant circumstances of a given case.

488. Inalienable rights enumerated in point 5 of Article 33 FGC accordingly do not make a uniform category, but these are interests that can be vested only in one person. Jurisprudence and judicature include here plain usufruct,[230] annuity right (Article 912 PCC), housing society tenancy right (Article 9 §5 of the Act on housing societies) and a share in the right of annuity vested in both spouses. Most obviously, this is not an exhaustive list, but one should emphasize that these may be only material rights, and not such rights which can be expressed in money but follow from strictly family relations, for example, the right to alimony. Because of their essence, such inalienable rights form a part of the personal property of a spouse which are strictly connected with the person of the particular spouse (right to remuneration, tied accommodation, certain instances of usufruct, personal servitudes with the exception of the housing easement).[231] The question of the allocation to this category of membership interests in a registered partnership company *(spółka osobowa)* remains disputable, since the articles of partnership may exceptionally admit transferability of these interests. As a consequence, some academics opt for inclusion of these rights to personal property regardless of the measures in exchange for which the interests were acquired.[232]

489. An interesting category is the items of property enumerated in point 6 of the discussed provision. These again do not form a consistent group. This particular point refers to items acquired as compensation for personal injury or damage to health, as well as atonement for the inflicted harm which belongs in part to the personal property of the injured spouse, and in the other part to the common property. In particular, the common property encompasses elements which constitute a certain equivalent of remuneration for labour, acquired as a result of the fact that the injured spouse is completely unable to perform work or unable to perform work to such an extent which would be possible if he or she did not undergo any injury or damage to health. Consequently, if a spouse is a beneficiary of disablement pension or the so-called compensatory benefit because of the enhancement of needs or deterioration of prospects to the future of the injured spouse, these funds are paid in place of wages of the affected spouse, which justifies the treatment of such means as elements of the common property. They can, however, make a component of the

229. Sychowicz, 'Article 33 Commentary', in K. Piasecki (ed.), *Kodeks*, 219.
230. Sychowicz, 'Article 33 Commentary', in K. Piasecki (ed.), *Kodeks*, 220.
231. Supreme Court decision issued on 29 Mar. 1957, 2CR 330/55, OSPiKA 1958/12/301.
232. Sokołowski, 'Article 33 Commentary', in H. Dolecki, T. Sokołowski (eds), *Kodeks*, 175.

common property of the spouses once they are paid. As long as they make receivables, even when already due, they form a part of personal property.[233]

490. When it comes to atonement or in other words compensation for 'physical suffering and moral harm', in our opinion it is owed, quite fairly, to the injured spouse and must form a part of his or her personal property. As far as other compensation is concerned, apart from the above-mentioned pensions, even though the FGC includes them in personal property of a spouse, in our opinion it is not always correct. Most frequently, the costs amounting to the expenses for the treatment of the spouse, his or her additional nutrition, medication, means of replacement restitution (artificial limbs, wheelchairs, etc.) are incurred predominantly from the common property of the spouses, and in consequence, in our opinion, inclusion of compensations in personal property is not entirely justified, even though the law so provides.

491. The next component of personal property of a spouse are receivables regarding remuneration for work or other kind of payable activity. If the collected remuneration falls under the common property, the same cannot be said of their receivables, even if already due and mature. When it comes to a labour relationship, it is a relation between an employer and employee, particularly protected by law and straying from the general model of obligational relationships. As a result, it would be difficult to allow intervention of the spouse of the employee in labour relations. One cannot as well, as already decided by the Supreme Court supported by jurisprudence,[234] treat the receivables as a component of the spouse's assets growth. Likewise, it is inadmissible to extend community by means of marriage settlement to these receivables, especially when they are still not due and mature.[235]

492. By rewards grouped as components of the personal property, judicature understands above all rewards for creative work in the area of fine arts, literature, science, technology, awards won at various competitions, also for achievements which cannot be classified as creative, for instance, saving human life or health, awards for sports achievements, awards at tournaments, quizzes requiring special knowledge of a particular field, etc.[236]

493. The next category of components of personal property mentioned in Article 33 point 9 FGC is rights connected with intangible assets, authorship and associated rights, rights of industrial property and other rights of an originator of financial character. One of such rights shall be in particular the entitlement to demand on the part of the creator the right to remuneration for implementation of a rationalization

233. Ignatowicz, Nazar, *Prawo*, 269–270.
234. J. Piątowski, 'Ustrój wspólności ustawowej', in J. Piątowski (ed.), *System*, 384.
235. Supreme Court resolution issued on 24 Jul. 1997, III CZP 26/97, OSNC 1998/1/3 with an approving gloss by T. Smyczyński.
236. Sychowicz, 'Article 33 Commentary', in K. Piasecki (ed.), *Kodeks*, 223–224.

plan,[237] but this is only an example. Another instance may be the exclusive right of an originator to use his or her work and dispose of it in any area of operation and remuneration for the use of the piece of work in pursuance of Article 17 of Authorship Law. Material interests in industrial property are rights pertaining to inventions, design patents, chip topography, manufacturer's marks, geographic names and rationalization plans, which follows from the Act of 30 June 2000 – Law of Industrial Property.[238] One should agree with M. Sychowicz that in a situation where spouses are co-originators of a piece of work, the authorship right is vested in both of them, which does not mean however that such right is subject to property community. In spite of the presumption of equal shares in the piece of work, one may petition for determination of unequal proportion of their shares by the court which may perform its task on the basis of the actual contribution of each of the spouses to the creation of the piece of work.[239]

494. The last of the constituents of personal property of a spouse are tangible items acquired in exchange for other items of personal property discussed above, which means by way of substitution. The modification introduced by the amendment of the FGC in 2004, since before that time replacement had been envisaged only in relation to the first two types of components of personal property, that is, items acquired before the emergence of common property and assets acquired as a result of inheritance, testamentary legacy and donation. Substitution had also been defined as 'acquisition for funds gained in exchange for items' subject to this replacement. The amendment of the code in 2004 not only broadened the objective scope of replacement but also grasped its character in a slightly different way. Currently, substitution consists of the 'acquisition in exchange for components of the personal property', with the added reservation: 'unless a special provision stipulates otherwise'.[240] In consequence, replacement consists of substitution of a given component of the personal property with another component. In addition, in order to speak of replacement, it is necessary that two premises be fulfilled: for the first thing, that a single event should trigger on the one hand alienation of a particular item from personal property and on the other one the acquisition of the new item must take place at the dispense of a portion of the personal property. Replacement may take place several times in relation to subsequent substitutes.[241]

495. The doctrine of family law distinguishes additionally quantitative and qualitative replacement.[242] The most frequent qualitative replacement consists in the substitution of tangible items alienated from personal property by tangible items acquired in exchange for the former as a result of events independent of the entitled

237. Supreme Court resolution issued on 17 Feb. 1967, III CZP 115/66, OSNCP 1967/6/101; Supreme Court decision issued on 24 Mar. 1975, III CRN 3/75, OSPiKA 1976/9/174 with a gloss by K. Nowicka. Supreme Court judgment issued on 26 Mar. 2002, I PKN 972/2000, OSNP 2004/5/item 81.
238. Consolidated version: Journal of Statutes 2017, item 776 with subsequent amendments.
239. Sychowicz, 'Article 33 Commentary', in K. Piasecki (ed.), *Kodeks*, 224.
240. Sychowicz, 'Article 33 Commentary', in K. Piasecki (ed.), *Kodeks*, 225.
241. Sokołowski, 'Article 33 Commentary', in H. Dolecki, T. Sokołowski (eds), *Kodeks*, 179–181.
242. *Ibid.*

party, juridical acts of the party (e.g., in place of the sold immovable property the estate is enriched by the value gained from its sale), as well as in consequence of a certain process, sequence of events leading to the replacement of one element with the other, new one (in place of an old apartment the parties purchase a new one, better suited to the needs of the family). Both direct replacement – a new item in place of the old one – and indirect replacement – a new item purchased for the funds (money) acquired in exchange for the item subject to replacement.[243] In the case of direct replacement, the new item takes place of the old one and the continuity and character of the old and new elements are preserved (plot of land in exchange for a similar plot of land, a car in place of another car of the corresponding class, etc.). Personal property is enrolled by items purchased for the means acquired in place of the lost or destroyed element. The new objects are of the same character.

496. It should also be remembered that replacement takes place not only where the newly acquired item is covered in whole by the funds belonging to the personal property of a spouse, but also where the means gained as a consequence of alienation of the primary component of the personal property have been mixed with funds which fall under the category of common property. In this manner, the finally acquired item is going to enter into the personal property of a spouse as long as the parties have not stipulated otherwise, but the other spouse may raise certain claims following from expenditures for the personal property of the former spouse from the common property or the latter spouse's personal estate.[244]

497. It is necessary to emphasize that in the amended text of Article 33 FGC objects which serve the purpose of performing a profession or conducting business by one of the spouses have not been mentioned as components of personal property. Notwithstanding, this does not bear greater importance, since such objects, if purchased for the funds falling as well under the category of personal property, as a consequence of substitution, belong as well to this estate, and if they were purchased for the funds stemming from common property, they are enrolled into the common property. In the latter case, Article 36 §3 FGC is of crucial importance. This provision envisages that such components are managed by a spouse who performs the profession independently, and the other spouse may only in the event of temporary hindrance make indispensable operational acts.

§2. Management of the Common Property of the Spouses

498. In the regimes, where common property of the spouses can be distinguished it is necessary to consider how it may be managed by the spouses. The concept of management belongs to the most disputable ones in the literature. In light of the variety of opinions presented by jurisprudence and judicature management is understood as control over financial questions of another person in such a way that

243. Ignatowicz, Nazar, *Prawo*, 272–276.
244. Sokołowski, 'Article 33 Commentary', in H. Dolecki, T. Sokołowski (eds), *Kodeks*, 181–183.

the directly entitled himself or herself would do, which covers both factual dispositions and making proper juridical acts in the name of the represented person and representation of that party (or thing) before public authorities. This denotes the actions of one person in the legal sphere of another one.

499. Since management is regulated by legal provisions, the rules of law entitle the spouses to such activities by means of mandatory norms which cannot be overridden by the will of the parties. The main idea behind the provisions which pertain to this field is such regulation that the management be concordant with the interest of the family. This is why the rules envisage the obligation of the spouses to cooperate in this respect, but at the same time provide for independent exercise of management. Moreover, the discussed provisions take into account the interest of third persons, parties to perform juridical acts made by the spouses in the course of exercising management.

500. The concept of management covers both factual actions necessary to exercise the rights following from co-ownership (factual management) and conclusion of respective juridical acts concerning the common property (legal management), which are aimed at the acquisition of material interests in this co-ownership, disposal of property items enrolled into the estate, disposal of the items, contracting obligations and finally performance of actions leading to the preservation of the common interest (procedural management), including procedural acts both before courts of law and administrative authorities (procedural management).[245]

501. Before the amendment of 2004 FGC provided in Article 36 §2 that acts of management could be divided into acts of ordinary management and acts exceeding the scope of ordinary management, for the performance of which consent of the other spouse was required, expressed in the form necessary for the particular juridical act. The amendment of FGC brought about the modification of the content of this provision. Currently, Article 36 §1 FGC envisages that a spouse may oppose an act of management over the common property intended by the other spouse. Such opposition is however inadmissible if the act pertains to common affairs of ordinary life or is aimed at fulfilment of fundamental needs of the family, or where the act is made as a part of payable activity of the spouse. While it is true that a spouse, pursuant to Article 36 §1 FGC, is obliged to inform the other spouse about the condition of property and the intended acts of management, unfortunately however it is the case that spouses neglect this duty and disable effective opposition on the part of the other spouse. [246]

502. The need to obtain consent of the other spouse is required for the conclusion of particular acts enumerated exhaustively in Article 37 FGC. These are the following:

---

245. Supreme Court resolution of 13 Nov. 1962, III CO 2/62, OSNCP 1063/10/217 with a gloss by S. Szer, OSPiKA 1963/9/238.
246. Smyczyński, *Prawo*, 110–111; Sychowicz, 'Article 36 Commentary', in K. Piasecki (ed.), *Kodeks*, 236–237.

(1) juridical acts leading to alienation, encumbrance, payable acquisition of immovable property or the right of perpetual usufruct of immovable property, and legal acts leading to rendition of the immovable property to third parties for use or gathering profits;
(2) juridical acts leading to alienation, encumbrance, payable acquisition of a right in rem whose object is a building or premises;
(3) juridical acts leading to alienation, encumbrance, payable alienation and lease of a farm or business;
(4) donation from the common property, except minor, customarily accepted donations (gifts).

503. Currently, it bears no significance whether the above acts are to be qualified as acts of ordinary management or exceeding this ordinary management, if they served the purpose of fulfilling the needs of the family or any alternative purposes and if they served for the conduct of business or investment. As long as the particular act belongs to the categories listed in the discussed provision, even though any spouse can make the act independently, consent of the other spouse is required for its validity. The aim of the requirement of consent is to assure protection of the spouses' common property in order to guarantee funds in that estate to the benefit of the family.

504. The consent should mention the type of act it refers to. The consent covers all activities which constitute the act for which the consent was granted. It is going to encompass both a respective offer, negotiations with the other party, conclusion of referendum contract, the contract obliging to transfer ownership or the eventual contract which transfers ownership. The consent should determine as well the object of the intended juridical act to which the consent refers, point to provisions of the future contract which are subjectively important for the spouses and the limits to negotiations of essential elements of the contract, in particular the price. The consent can be expressed before the act is made, or at the moment of its conclusion. Where the consent is given *ex post* once the act already has been made is referred to as 'endorsement'.

505. That is why Article 37 §2 FGC envisages that the validity of contract (but not a unilateral juridical act, since this would be absolutely invalid *ex lege* if made without consent of the other spouse) concluded by one of the spouses independently and referring to one of the acts listed in §1 requires endorsement on the part of the other spouse. Until the moment of grant of the consent, the act made by a spouse is not invalid but should be considered incomplete at *(negotium claudicans).*[247] The endorsement is a unilateral juridical act. Consent is a condition of validity of an independently concluded contract. Similar confirmation is going to be necessary where the contract is concluded by one of the spouses and the other contracting party assigns a period to endorse the act for the other spouse whose consent is required. This other contracting party becomes released after the unsuccessful expiry of the appointed term. One should also pay attention to the fact that consent

247. Sychowicz, 'Article 37 Commentary', in K. Piasecki (ed.), *Kodeks*, 249–251.

given by the other spouse does not make this other spouse a party to the transaction. Only this of the spouses who actually concluded the contract can be considered its party.

506. If a spouse should make independently a juridical act listed in the catalogue of Article 37 §1 FGC without consent of the other spouse, and the action is not endorsed by the other spouse, such act is going to be invalid.

507. However, Article 38 FGC protects the third party acquiring a right on the foot of this juridical act, once the premises are fulfilled which are envisaged by provisions on the protection of a person who in good faith concludes a juridical act with a person unauthorized to dispose of the relevant right. We agree with the opinion that among juridical acts which can fall under this category after the amendment of the FGC there have remained only the transfer of ownership of immovable property or perpetual usufruct, or other right which undergoes entry in the land and mortgage register. However, the release of the third party from the contracted obligation cannot take place, perhaps because of the legislator's omission, because this could only refer to the release from debt exceeding the ordinary management of the common property done without the consent of the other spouse. Currently, since it is not one of the acts expressly listed in Article 37 FGC, such a release does not require consent on the part of the other spouse.

508. Provisions protecting the person acquiring a right entered into the land and mortgage register in good faith from a spouse who acts without the consent of the other spouse would be limited to rules on the principles of public credibility of the land and mortgage register, expressed in Articles 5–9 of LRM.[248] These would apply in a situation where the condition following from the land and mortgage register does not match the true legal status, for instance, because of the fact that the other spouse was not entered into the register as co-owner of the immovable property and the purchaser acted in good faith. This means that the purchaser was unaware of the fact that the content of the land and mortgage register did not correspond to the real legal status and cannot be accused that he or she might have easily learnt about such inconformity. Moreover, the act concluded must be payable, which means that free of charge juridical acts are not protected, because there is no legal interest in the protection of persons who did not incur any expenses in order to acquire the relevant rights.

509. There occur as well exceptional situations in which a spouse independently decides to make an act in respect to which the law requires consent of the other spouse and such consent cannot be obtained even though the needs of the family necessitate the conclusion of the transaction. This is very often the case in connection with labour emigration of one of the spouses and departure from the family in Poland on his or her part whose needs cannot be fulfilled in any other way. Article 39 FGC provides in a situation where the other spouse refuses to give consent or

248. Act of 6 July 1982 on the land registers and mortgages, consolidated version: Journal of Statutes 2018, item 1916, with subsequent amendments.

communication with the other spouse is hindered by obstacles difficult to surmount for the possibility to apply to a court for judicial permission for the conclusion of such transaction, and the court is obliged to award the permission whenever the transaction is justified by the interest of the family.

510. However, whenever important reasons are at play, by which notion the doctrine and judicature understand recklessness of a spouse, his or her incompetent or deliberate actions to the detriment of the family, squander of the common property in order to raise funds for an addiction of a spouse,[249] at the request of the other spouse the court may deprive the former one of the independent management over the common property or order that the conclusion of transactions set out in Article 37 §1 FGC should require judicial permission instead of the other spouse's consent. This should secure the financial and life situation of the family, although such an order may be revoked in the case of a change of circumstances.

511. Proceedings on granting judicial consent in this respect take place in the mode of non-litigation at the request of one of the spouses, although the action may be brought as well by a public prosecutor (Articles 509 PCPC). The ruling takes the form of a decision which may be revoked at any time in case of change of circumstances, or where the cause expires which led to delivery of the decision, or where the spouses jointly resolve the problem otherwise.[250]

249. Sychowicz, 'Article 40 Commentary', in K. Piasecki (ed.), *Kodeks*, 257.
250. Supreme Court Judgment issued on 30 Aug. 1982, III CRN 163/82, *Gazeta Prawna* no. 3 (1983).

Chapter 3. Contractual Property Regimes

512. There are two contractual matrimonial regimes which can be introduced by marriage articles where one can distinguish the common property of the spouses, namely: the regime of extended community and regime of limited community. Apart from that, there are two contractual matrimonial regimes in which there is no common property of the spouses, that is the regime of property separation, also known in the doctrine as ordinary separation, and the regime of separation with the equalization of accrued gains, which was introduced to the FGC as a result of the 2004 amendment.

513. The source of emergence of the above regimes is a matrimonial settlement which, in accordance with Article 47 FGC, makes a contract concluded between the spouses in the form of notarial deed on the basis of which the spouses extend or restrict the statutory community, introduce property separation or property separation with the equalization of growth in assets.[251]

514. The contract may be concluded both before the formation of marriage as well as during the marriage. The contract may be subsequently changed or dissolved, in which case the spouses return to the statutory community regime, unless they stipulated otherwise and selected a different regime. The above is an expression of the principle of autonomy of will of the spouses who are in the position to choose such property regime which suits best their marriage and their economic relations. Freedom of the spouses in this respect undergoes certain restrictions concerning the possibility to expand the community of property. The spouses cannot regulate their property regime by settlement whenever the compulsory regime holds between them. Additionally, the spouses can neither create a property regime not introduced by the legislator (e.g., community which would encompass all the assets in their property – absolute/universal community) nor simultaneously choose a partial extension and a partial narrowing of the community (mixing regimes).[252]

§1. Regime of Extended or Restricted Community of Property

515. The scope of the spouses' liberty as to extending the common property has been confined in Article 49 §1 FGC by the prohibition of its expansion in relation to the items of property which are going to become a spouse's personal property as a result of inheritance or donation, legacy or donation, material interests stemming from joint co-ownership which is regulated by separate provisions, inalienable rights which can be vested only in one person, and receivables relating to compensation for personal injury or deterioration of health, as long as these do not fall under

251. Cf. G. Jędrejek, *Intercyzy. Pojęcie. Treść. Dochodzenie roszczen,* (Warszawa: Lexis Nexis, 2010).

252. Sychowicz, 'Article 47 Commentary', in K. Piasecki (ed.), *Kodeks*, 312 – 313; Smyczyński, *Prawo*, 126–128, criticized by T. Sokołowski, 'Zakres swobody intercyzy w znowelizowanych przepisach kodeksu rodzinnego i opiekuńczego', *RPEiS*, no. 2 (2008): 45.

the statutory community, as well as receivables to atonement for the harm suffered, finally non-mature receivables to remuneration for labour or other payable activity of each spouse. Such regulation makes, on one hand, a realization of the spouses' liberty, and on the other considers basic principles of protection of the freedom of testamentary dispositions, or respect to the will of the donor, whose intention is to transfer the assets to the specific person.

516. As far as the contrary situation is concerned, that is restriction of the community, the freedom of the spouses is not unlimited, since they are free to choose one of the two regimes of property separation.

517. If the spouses choose the regime of ordinary property separation, each of them preserves his or her property acquired before the conclusion of the settlement, and property acquired later, each spouse manages his or her property independently, and the common property does not emerge at all. Obviously, this does not exclude the personal obligation of each of the spouses to contribute to the satisfaction of the needs of the family. The only difference is that this duty is fulfilled materially from the separate personal properties of the spouses. Moreover, it should be emphasized that even despite the introduction of property separation Article 680^1§2 PCC envisages that its establishment does not result in the discontinuance of the community of lease of premises which serve the purpose of fulfilment of the housing needs of the family established by the spouses concluded in the course of matrimony, however, the court may, by applying appropriately provisions on lifting the community of property, lift this community as well at the request of one of the spouses.

§2. Equalization of Accrued Gains

518. The new property regime introduced in the Polish system as a result of the 2004 amendment of the FGC is the regime of property separation with the equalization of accrued gains. This regime has been introduced in order to protect the spouse who is incapable to work for money for various reasons, for instance, because of being overloaded with family duties, poor health conditions, or the loss of prospects for employment in the same field as previously because of scant interest in his or her qualifications on the market. Where the spouse cannot work on such grounds and increase his or her personal property, it seems justified to give him or her the chance to increase this property by means of equalization of the growth in value of the assets of the other spouse in relation to the former one. Obviously, as long as such separation holds there are no differences in the functioning of this regime as compared to ordinary property separation. The differences become manifest only once the separation terminates when the possibility to equalize the growth in assets arises.

519. The spouses' accrued gains are defined in light of Article 51^3§1 FGC as the increase of value of each of these properties after the conclusion of the matrimonial settlement. This provision sets a mandatory rule *(iuris cogentis)*, but in the matters of calculation of the growth, the intent of the parties expressed in their settlement is taken into consideration. In pursuance of Article 51^3§2 FGC, unless the parties have stipulated otherwise, in the calculation of growth items of property should be omitted which have been acquired after the conclusion of settlement, as well as items gained by inheritance, legacy or donation, inalienable rights which can be vested in one person only, items acquired as compensation for personal injury or health deterioration except for disablement pension, compensatory benefit and receivables to remuneration for labour or other payable activity, finally authorship and associated rights, rights of industrial property and other rights of originator, as well as items acquired in substitution for of these rights. However, the value of donations made by one of the spouses becomes added to this amount, with the exception of donations to the benefit of the common descendants of the spouses (children, grandchildren and great-grandchildren) as well as minor and commonly accepted donations to the benefit of other persons, services provided personally by one of the spouses in favour of the property of the other spouse, finally expenditures and costs of upkeep for the property of one of the spouses made by the other one. There is also the binding principle of calculating the accrued gains according to the condition on the moment of termination of property separation, and according to prices from the moment of calculation.

520. Naturally, the growth in value of each of the properties may be a result of the increase of the value of particular items of property enrolling into each of the estates as a result of expenditures incurred directly in order to improve these items, acquire natural benefits from these assets, or civil law advantages. The growth might be as well the acquisition of interests from the amounts deposited on the bank account of a spouse.

521. The equalization of accrued gains takes place after the termination of property separation. The spouse who claims that his or her growth is lesser is in a position to demand from the other spouse to equalize the growths by virtue of contract (agreement). The spouse may also sue the other spouse for a particular sum of money corresponding to the difference between the growths or may request that the court oblige the other spouse to make the respective declaration of intent concerning the transfer of a particular right to the benefit of the claimant, which is to equalize the difference in growths. For important reasons, each of the spouses is authorized to claim mitigation of the obligation to equalize the difference in the growth of assets. Most frequently, such an important reason shall be the reprehensible attitude of the other spouse, which may consist in faulty instances of non-achievement of income, avoiding labour, squander of assets related to the alcohol or drug addiction, other habits, spending the assets on other persons, adultery, etc. The claim for the equalization of growths in assets as a material claim becomes lapsed on the basis of Articles 117–125 PCC. The period of limitation amounts to ten years calculated from the moment of termination of property separation with the equalization of accrued gains, and where the marriage terminated later, from the date of its termination.

522. In the case of death of one of the spouses who remain bound by this regime, the equalization of accrued gains takes place between the living spouse and the heirs of the other spouse. However, the heirs of the deceased spouse may raise the claim of mitigating the duty to equalize the accrued gains only where the testator initiated during his or her life an action for the annulment of marriage, divorce or separation.

Chapter 4. Compulsory Regime of Property Separation

523. The compulsory matrimonial regime emerges under Polish law in the following situations:

(1) adjudication by court at the request of a spouse for important reasons;
(2) adjudication at the request of creditors of one of the spouses;
(3) *ex lege* in the case of incapacitation or announcement of bankruptcy of one of the spouses; and
(4) in the case of adjudicating separation of the spouses.

524. The FGC does not define 'important reasons' for which the court may establish property separation between the spouses; however, they would amount to a threat or violation of crucial material interests of one of the spouses or the whole family.[253] This shall also be the case in situations where the spouses remain in factual separation or extramarital informal relationships, where they suffer from addictions, squander the property, conduct a rackety lifestyle and blatantly mismanage the property.[254] Such demand on the part of the spouse becomes also evaluated from the point of view of principles of social coexistence and the interest of the spouses' creditors.[255]

525. When it comes to allowance of the creditors' claims in this respect, such a decision requires the presence and demonstration of two premises: existence of a receivable confirmed by the writ of execution (enforceable decision endorsed with immediate execution clause – both judicial and administrative) owed by one of the spouses, and substantiation that the payment of this receivable necessitates the separation of the common property holding between the spouses. The latter premise is going to be the case where there are no possibilities of satisfying the creditors from personal property of the debtor spouse, as well as the components of the common property listed in Article 41 §2 FGC, and there are no grounds to seek satisfaction from the common property, for example, as a result of impossibility of obtaining the immediate execution clause against the debtor's spouse.

526. Emergence of property separation may be caused by both full and partial incapacitation of one of the spouses. This effect is produced *ex lege* once the judicial decision on incapacitation becomes binding. The same consequence is brought about by the ruling announcing insolvency of one of the spouses, and where the spouses remained bound by the regime of property community at the moment of announcement of insolvency, the whole common property of the spouses enrols the bankrupt's estate (Article 124 §1 sentence 2 of Insolvency Law). Finally, where the

253. J. St. Piątowski, *Stosunki majątkowe miedzy małżonkami,* (Warszawa: ZPP, 1955), 140, J. Winiarz, *Małżeńskie stosunki majątkowe,* (Warszawa: Wydawnictwo Prawnicze, 1967), 84.
254. Smyczyński, *Prawo*, 142–143; Sychowicz, 'Article 52 Commentary', in K. Piasecki (ed.), *Kodeks*, 340–341.
255. Supreme Court decision issued on 25 Mar. 1958, 2CR 45/56, *Państwo i Prawo*, no. 4–5 (1959): 1072 and on 6 Nov. 1972, III CRN 250/72, *Państwo i Prawo*, no. 10 (1974): 162.

incapacitation becomes lifted, or where the insolvency proceedings are discontinued, completed or abolished, there arises between the spouses the statutory (default) property regime, regardless of the question of what their previous matrimonial property regime had been before the incapacitation or announcement of insolvency.

Chapter 5. The Spouses' Liability Towards Creditors

527. The spouses' liability towards creditors is shaped along certain rules following both from general civil law and from the provisions of the FGC. In the first place, each of the spouses is responsible with his or her personal property for his or her own obligations. Additionally, the spouses are responsible from both the common property and personal properties for obligations incurred jointly. The situation becomes complicated where the obligation is incurred by only one of the spouses, especially if he or she does it without the participation or knowledge of the other spouse, and in the lack of the other spouse's acceptance. This poses a threat to the interest of the non-acting spouse or even a serious danger to financial interests of the family as a whole. This is also not a satisfactory condition for the creditor to whom it does matter whether at all and from which property he or she is going to be satisfied.

528. These problems are covered in the first place in Article 41 §1 FGC which envisages that in a situation where the spouses remain bound by the regime of statutory community and a spouse has incurred an obligation with the consent of the other spouse, the creditor shall be entitled to claim satisfaction not only from personal property of the debtor but also from the common property of the spouses. This does not apply to obligations pertaining to the fulfilment of ordinary needs of the family because liability for these has been regulated in Article 30 FGC. That provision introduces joint and several liability of spouses. Article 41 FGC relates to responsibility for civil law obligations *sensu largo*. Consequently, it shall apply not only to obligations incurred as a result of juridical acts, but also these following from torts, unjustified enrichment, or situations where the source of the obligational relationship are provisions of civil, criminal or administrative law. Article 41 is also applied appropriately to tax obligations following from the Tax Statute 1997.[256]

529. If a spouse contracts the obligation without consent of the other spouse, or where the obligation does not derive from a juridical act (but e.g., from a tort), the creditor may claim satisfaction from the common property of the spouse debtor, from his or her remuneration for labour or income obtained by the debtor from other payable activity, as well as the benefits he or she acquired from authorship and associated rights, rights of industrial property or other interests of an originator (Article 33 point 9 FGC), and where the receivable arose as a result of conducting business, the creditor may become satisfied also from material components of the enterprise. A similar limitation of liability concerns the situation where the credibility arose before the emergence of property community (i.e., before the conclusion of marriage, or where in the course of matrimony the spouses were initially bound by the regime of property separation and then the parties switched to the regime of property community), the creditor may claim satisfaction from personal property of the debtor, and only certain components of the common property, as well as the particular component of personal property mentioned above.

256. Act of 29 Aug. 1997, Journal of Statutes 2005, no. 8, item 60 with subsequent amendments.

530. Pursuant to Article 48 FGC the same principles shall apply appropriately in a situation where there holds between the spouses a regime of property community, namely the regime of extended or limited community.

531. If the creditor claims satisfaction from the common property of the spouses, the creditor should obtain the immediate execution clause from the court against the spouse who is not his or her personal debtor. It follows from the provisions of the PCPC that the binding decision issued against a married person can be supplemented by the immediate execution clause also against the debtor's spouse, limiting the spouse's liability to the assets encompassed by the common property where the debtor demonstrates by means of an official or private document that the receivable ascertained in the enforceable decision derived from a juridical act to which the debtor's spouse gave consent (Article 787 PCPC). If the receivable ascertained in the enforceable decision came into being in connection with the conduct of business, and this fact becomes demonstrated by an official or private document, the court shall supplement the decision with the immediate execution clause against the spouse of the debtor, with the limitation of his or her liability to the enterprise (Article 787^1 PCPC). Where the parties concluded a matrimonial settlement, this fact does not pose an obstacle to the award of the immediate execution clause against the debtor's spouse in pursuance of Articles 787 and 787^1 PCPC and its enforcement on the basis of the writ of execution in relation to items of property which would belong to the common property if the matrimonial settlement had not been concluded. This does not exclude as well legal protection of the spouses by means of anti-execution actions if the marital settlement was effective against the creditor, that is where the creditor knew about such settlement (Article 787^2 PCPC).

Part IV. Law of Succession

Chapter 1. Introduction

532. Succession law is a part of civil law and is regulated in Book 4 (Articles 922–1087) of the PCC. Other statutes may also concern issues relevant to succession. For example, procedural matters connected with succession are contained in PCPC (mainly Articles 627–691) and inheritance tax is regulated in the Inheritance and Donation Tax Act 1983.[257] The right of succession is guaranteed by Article 21 of the CRP, where it is stipulated that the Republic of Poland protects ownership and the right of succession.

533. Succession law deals with the consequences of a physical person's death, namely the devolution of his or her estate to other persons. Provisions of succession law do not, however, deal with the results of dissolving or otherwise ending the existence of a juristic person, as these matters are regulated by separate provisions concerning such persons.

534. The importance of succession law within a legal system cannot be underestimated, as it is very closely connected with the accepted model of proprietary relations (particularly with respect to ownership), which in essence determines the content of the deceased person's estate. The existence of succession law is warranted by the fact that the death of a physical person does not, as a rule, extinguish his or her rights and obligations, which pass on to other persons. Therefore, succession law needs to provide instruments, which will enable heirs to acquire the estate of the deceased. At the same time, the institutions of succession law should favour solutions which guarantee the most efficient exploitation of the deceased person's property.

535. It is necessary to note, that during his or her lifetime, the deceased person creates a number of personal relations, which are connected with him or her exclusively and must expire upon his or her death. Apart from such relations, the deceased also enters into legal relations of a proprietary character. These often satisfy needs which are independent of a person's variable lifespan. If such relations are to realize their objective, the death of the entitled/obliged person should not lead to their termination. Therefore, the law of succession enables the continuation of

257. Act of 28 Jul. 1983, consolidated version: Journal of Statutes 2019, item 1813, with subsequent amendments.

proprietary relations after the death of the entitled/obliged party and creates the possibility to economically utilize the deceased person's assets after his or her death. This eliminates many anxieties about the existence of a proprietary relation after the death of one of the involved parties and strengthens the safety of commerce.

536. Regardless of whether a physical person decides to dispose of his or her estate by means of a will or whether his or her estate devolves according to rules on intestacy, succession law provides him or her with the possibility of somehow prolonging his or her existence in this world. This form of self-fulfilment after death often not only provides comfort to a physical person but also lies in the interest of his or her heirs, as well as the whole society. Consequently, it is important for the institutions of succession law to be constructed in a way, which, on the one hand, stimulate a person's activities and efforts to increase his or her property and, on the other hand, discourage him or her from wasting it. If the above is to be achieved every physical person should be granted extensive freedom of testamentary disposition, but his or her interests should also be protected when, for various reasons, a testament (will) has not been prepared. In the latter case, rules of intestate succession should allow the acquisition of the estate by the relatives of the deceased person according to his or her hypothetical will. In order to achieve this goal, the legislator must take into account a probable point of view of a hypothetical (not an actual) physical person.

537. Succession law is not only strongly connected with proprietary relations but is also closely linked with family law. It is universally acknowledged that provisions of succession law should be aimed at reflecting and strengthening family relationships within a given society. These considerations are taken into account mainly while determining the scope of the liberty of testamentary dispositions (freedom of bequeathing), its possible limitations (*legitim*), the circle of statutory heirs and the order of succession.

538. In the years 2002–2015 Polish succession law was being examined by the PCCCL, in which a working group on succession law was created. The aim of the group was to analyse the provisions of succession law in the context of their validity and prepare a draft of possible amendments. The activities of the PCCCL and the working group of succession law have resulted in amendments concerning intestate heirs (2009), the introduction of *legatum per vindicationem* (2011), an amendment of the principles concerning the heirs' liability for the debts of the estate (2015) as well as in other amendments connected with the entry into force of Regulation No 650/2012 on jurisdiction, applicable law, recognition and enforcement of decisions and acceptance and enforcement of authentic instruments in matters of succession and on the creation of a European Certificate of Succession. The PCCCL which was established in an ordinance of the Council of Ministers in 2002 was dissolved by the new Minister of Justice, after parliamentary elections in 2015 were won by a right-wing party Law and Justice.

§1. BASIC CONCEPTS OF THE LAW OF INHERITANCE

I. Universal Succession

539. Polish succession law is based on the Roman law concept of universal succession. This means that the estate of the deceased person devolves at the time of his or her death to one or more persons (Article 922 PCC). The acquisition of the estate by heirs occurs *ex lege*, at the time of the testator's death, without any additional actions to be taken by the heirs and regardless of whether the persons that are heirs are even aware of this fact.[258] The death of a physical person is the only event required in order for succession to take place, therefore the opening of the succession occurs at the moment of death (Article 924 PCC). All components of the estate are acquired by the heirs upon the opening of the succession (Article 925 PCC) without the need to fulfil any formal or other requirements that would otherwise be necessary in order for an acquisition to occur (e.g., a notarial deed necessary to transfer ownership of real estate).

540. Although the heirs inherit the estate of the deceased instantly, at the time of his or her death, the acquisition is temporary. Each heir, from the day on which he or she learned about his or her title to inherit, has six months to waive the estate. Within that same period, he or she may accept the estate without the limitation of liability for debts (simple acceptance) or with the limitation of liability for debts up to the estate assets' value (acceptance with the benefit of inventory). The lack of acceptance or waiver of the estate within the mentioned period results in a definite acceptance of the estate. Whether that acceptance is a simple one or one with the benefit of inventory depends on the date the opening of the succession took place. If the opening of the succession took place before 18 October 2015, the lack of acceptance or waiver of the estate within the mentioned six-month period brings about a definite, simple acceptance of the estate. In cases of successions opened on or after 18 October 2015, the lack of acceptance or waiver of the estate results in a definite acceptance of the estate with the benefit of the inventory. This new regulation was introduced through an amendment of the PCC[259] and applies to all successions opened on or after the day it came into force (Article 6). Successions opened prior to that date remain governed by PCC rules that were in force before the amendment became binding.

II. The Estate (Inheritance)

541. The estate is the most fundamental notion in Polish succession law as it embodies what is being inherited. Polish law does not provide a *sensu stricto* definition of the estate but merely provides in Article 922 §1 PCC that proprietary rights

258. *See* Supreme Court judgment issued on 26 Oct. 2006, I CSK 178/06, LEX no. 500181.
259. Act of 20 Mar. 2015, Journal of Statutes 2015, item 359, which came into force on 18 Oct. 2015.

and duties of a deceased devolve, at the time of his or her death, to one or several persons. More information is provided in §2 and §3 of the mentioned article, where it is stipulated that:

- the estate does not include the rights and duties strictly connected with the deceased as well as those rights which, at the time of his or her death, devolve to designated persons regardless of whether they are his or her heirs;
- the debts of the estate also include the costs of the deceased person's funeral to the extent in which that funeral complies with the customs prevailing in a given society,[260] the costs of the inheritance proceedings, the duty to satisfy the claims for legitim, the duty to carry out the bequests (legacies) and testamentary burdens, as well as other duties set out in the provisions of this PCC's Book 4.

542. As a consequence of the above, the estate comprises proprietary rights and duties which simultaneously meet all of the following criteria: (A) are derived from civil law relations; (B) are of a proprietary character; (C) are not strictly connected with the deceased; and (D) do not devolve to persons regardless of whether they are the heirs of the deceased or not.

A. *Rights and Duties Derived from Civil Law*

543. Rights and duties which are derived from civil relations should be understood as those rights and duties, which have their source in private, as opposed to public law. They include rights and duties arising not only from civil but also from labour law, however not from tax law, as the latter belongs to the field of public law. It is worth noting, however, that according to Article 97 §1 of the Tax Statute 1997,[261] proprietary rights and duties arising out of tax law pass to the heirs of the deceased. This should not be confused with succession, since tax rights and duties are not, technically speaking, inherited by the heirs, but pass on to them as a result of a direct public law provision.[262] If this provision were to be deleted, the heirs of the deceased could not be held liable for tax obligations. It is also worth mentioning, that the right to claim back a tax overpayment is a civil law claim based on the rules on unjust enrichment and it devolves to heirs as part of the inherited estate. Penalties and other fines are not a part of the estate, because they are not private, but public law instruments.

260. B. Kordasiewicz, 'Glosa do uchwały SN z dnia 22 listopada 1988 r., III CZP 86/88', *Nowe Prawo*, no. 7–9 (1990): 202 et seq.

261. Act of 29 Aug. 1997, consolidated version: Journal of Statutes 2020, item 1325 with subsequent amendments.

262. *See* the judgment of Voievodship Administrative Court in Białystok issued on 6 Feb. 2007, I SA/Bk 446/06 I SA/Bk 446/06; LEX no. 284735.

544. Possession, although in Polish law it is not a right, but is simply a factual state that has been consistently included in the estate both in academic writings as well as in court judgments.[263]

B. Rights and Duties of a Proprietary Character

545. Not all private law rights and duties are of a proprietary character. Personal rights and duties of the spouses, like fidelity, mutual help, cooperation in the interest of the family they have created are personal rights. The so-called personal goods (interests) such as health, freedom, dignity, freedom of conscience, surname or pseudonym, image, secrecy of correspondence are also of a personal character. The above are therefore not a part of the estate. As a general rule, real and obligational (contractual, tortious, unjustified enrichment) rights and duties are of a proprietary character.

C. Rights and Duties Strictly Connected with the Deceased

546. Some rights and duties are so closely connected with a particular physical person that it would be undesirable or even incorrect for them to exist after the death of that person. Damages for an unjust conviction and imprisonment can only be claimed by the aggrieved person and do not devolve to his or her heirs. The right to receive or the duty to pay alimony is also strictly connected with identified persons and does not form a part of the estate. However, alimony payments that became due before the death of the obliged person are duties of the estate and the person entitled to alimony may claim these payments from the heirs of the deceased.

547. Contractual rights and duties can also be strictly connected with the parties to the contract. If this is the case, they will not devolve to heirs. A contract for the performance of specified work will be terminated upon the death of the party, whose personal performance was essential for the proper fulfilment of the contract (e.g., a contract to paint a portrait will be terminated upon the death of the artist). Sometimes particular provisions clearly stipulate that a given right is terminated upon the death of a person (e.g., personal easements – Article 299 PCC; usufruct, if the holder of the right is a physical person – Article 266 PCC).

D. Rights and Duties Which Do Not Devolve to Indicated Persons

548. Some rights and duties devolve to particular persons, regardless of whether they are the heirs of the deceased or not. The acquisition of such rights by particular

263. E. Kremis, 'Szczególne składniki spadku', in E. Gniewek, P. Machnikowski (eds) *Kodeks Cywilny. Komentarz*, ed. (C.H. Beck: Warsaw, 2014), 1663; A. Kawałko, 'Article 922 Commentary', in M. Habdas, M. Fras (eds), *Kodeks cywilny. Komentarz. Tom VI. Spadki (art. 922-1087),* (Warszawa: Wolters Kluwer, 2019), 69–70.

persons occurs on the basis of *legi speciali*. First and foremost this concerns the institution of the *legatum per vindicationem*, regulated in Articles 981^1–981^6 PCC. This institution causes the legatee to acquire the bequeathed object or right at the moment of the opening of the succession, regardless of whether that person is an heir or not. Therefore a person indicated by the deceased acquires objects or rights regardless of succession mechanisms that regulate to whom the state devolves.

549. Important provisions also concern residential leases. According to Article 691 §1 PCC upon the death of a lessee of residential premises, the spouse who was not a co-lessee, children of the lessee and of the lessee's spouse, other persons the lessee was obliged to maintain or pay alimony to, and the person the lessee actually cohabited with, become the new lessees. The above only applies to those persons, who actually lived in the premises together with the deceased until his or her death.

550. Another significant regulation is to be found in the Banking Law Act 1997 (Articles 56 and 57),[264] where it is stipulated, that the holder of an individual savings bank account may indicate a person, to whom the bank will pay out money from the account upon the account holder's death. The indicated person must be either the account holder's spouse, his or her ascendant, descendant or sibling. The amount to be paid out may not exceed twenty times the average monthly income in the businesses sector published by the Main Office of Statistics for the month preceding the death of the person in question. If any money remains in the account, it is included in the estate.[265]

551. It is also worth mentioning that according to Article 831 §1 PCC, the holder of a life or an accident insurance policy may indicate one or more persons entitled to receive the sum specified in the policy in the case of an insured person's death. In §3 of the mentioned provision, it is stipulated that the sum specified in the policy that is to be paid to a designated beneficiary is not be included in the estate of the insured person.

552. Article 922 §3 PCC, quoted above, provides that the estate also includes duties that were not obligations of the deceased. These duties arise upon his or her death and are specified in the mentioned provision (i.e., bearing the costs of the deceased person's funeral to the extent in which that funeral complies with the customs prevailing in a given society, the costs of the inheritance proceedings, the duty to satisfy the claims for legitim, the duty to carry out the bequests (legacies) and testamentary burdens) as well as in other provisions of Book IV PCC. These other provisions include Articles 923 §1, 938, 939 and 966 PCC. Only the first of the mentioned provisions applies to all instances of succession, whereas the middle two provisions concern only intestate succession, and the last provision relates to testamentary succession. They will be discussed in the relevant chapters.

264. Act of 29 Sep. 1997, consolidated version: Journal of Statutes 2018, item 2187 with subsequent amendments.
265. T. Czech, 'Przynależność środków pieniężnych na indywidualnym rachunku bankowym do majątku wspólnego małżonków', *Prawo Bankowe*, no. 7–8 (2008): 37 et seq.

553. Article 923 §1 PCC provides, that the spouse and other persons, who were close to the deceased and lived with him or her until the day of his or her death, are entitled, during three months after the opening of the succession, to use his or her home (dwelling) together with the household equipment in the same manner as they have done before his or her death. The disposition of the deceased precluding or limiting that right is null and void. The intention of this provision is to give the spouse and persons, who were close to the deceased, time to organize their accommodation arrangements. Both the spouse and persons, who were close to the deceased must have lived with him or her until his or her death.

554. A spouse is a person who had remained married to the deceased until his or her death and therefore had a formal, legal relationship with the deceased. This condition is met even if divorce proceedings had ended before the opening of the succession, but the judgment did not become binding before or at that moment. If the spouse had been legally (not merely factually) separated from the deceased at the moment of his or her death, it seems that he or she should be treated as if he or she had been divorced since according to Article 61^4§1 FGC a judicial separation brings about most of the effects that a divorce does.

555. Persons, who were close to the deceased are ones who had an emotional, but not necessarily a formal, relationship with the deceased. They may include lifetime partners (de facto spouses) of different or the same sex as the deceased, children that he or she was bringing up, friends or distant relatives to whom he or she was attached, an ex-spouse or a judicially separated spouse, that the deceased remained close to.

556. Living with the deceased until his or her death denotes using his or her dwelling for the purposes of satisfying one's own residential needs. Long or short visits or moving in temporarily for the purpose of being able to care for the deceased while he or she requires assistance or care will not be regarded as living with the deceased in the understanding of Article 923 §1 PCC.

557. The right to use the dwelling and household equipment may be exercised regardless of whether the spouse or other persons, who were close to the deceased had been: appointed to inherit, held unworthy to inherit, disinherited or whether they had: waived the estate, or renounced succession. The right may not be effectively extinguished by the deceased in a testament or any other legal act. One should add that the entitlement lasts only three months and it is debatable, whether this period is long enough for the mentioned people to have the chance to organize their new accommodation if such a need arises. Opinions that this period should be lengthened to at least six months have already been voiced in academic writings and in the PCCCL working group.[266]

---

266. M. Habdas, 'Pozycja prawna małżonka spadkodawcy na tle prawnoporównawczym', *Rejent*, no. 2 (2006): 58–82.

§2. PREMISES OF SUCCESSION

558. In order to be an heir, three conditions must be met. The potential heir must: (1) have the capacity to inherit; (2) be appointed to inherit; and (3) cannot be unworthy to inherit.

I. The Capacity to Inherit

559. The capacity to inherit is an element of legal capacity. According to Polish law, every physical person from the moment of birth has the legal capacity (Article 8 PCC). Legal capacity denotes the capacity to hold rights and incur debts but must be distinguished from the legal capacity to perform acts in law. The latter allows one to personally perform acts in law and depends on the age a given person has attained (*see* Articles 11–22 PCC).

560. Although the PCC does not currently contain express provisions on the legal capacity of the *nasciturus* (i.e., a child that has been conceived but not yet born), it is accepted by academics and the courts that a *nasciturus* has conditional legal capacity.[267] The condition is a condition precedent that the *nasciturus* will be born alive. According to Article 9 PCC, there is a rebuttable presumption that a child is born alive. Consequently, a born child attains legal capacity, even if it dies soon after birth.

561. Legal capacity of juristic persons is not distinguished from their capacity to perform acts in law. Juristic persons attain legal capacity once they come into legal existence according to provisions which regulate their creation.

562. A physical person has the capacity to inherit if he or she is already alive and still alive at the time of the opening of the succession. In other words, a potential heir must outlive the deceased person (Article 927 §1 PCC). An exception is made with respect to the nasciturus. A child that had been conceived before the death of the deceased person has the capacity to inherit on the condition that it is born alive (Article 927 §2 PCC). The mentioned presumption of Article 9 PCC applies.

563. It is also important to remember that according to Article 32 PCC if several persons lose their lives as a result of facing a common danger *(commorientes)*, they are presumed to have died simultaneously. This presumption can be rebutted (usually by medical evidence) if it is proven that one person outlived another. If there is no such evidence, the victims will not have the capacity to inherit from one another.

564. A juristic person has the capacity to inherit if that person already exists and still exists at the time of the opening of the succession. An exception concerns a

267. A. Dyoniak, 'Pozycja nasciturusa na obszarze majątkowego prawa prywatnego', *RPEiS*, no. 3 (1994): 49 et seq.

foundation which has been established by the testator in a testament.[268] Such a foundation has the capacity to inherit on the condition that is entered in the appropriate register within two years of the opening of the succession. If such an entry occurs after these two years have elapsed, the foundation will not have attained the capacity to inherit.

II. The Appointment to Inherit

565. Once the capacity to inherit from a given person has been ascertained, one must show that he or she has been appointed to inherit. According to Article 926 §1 PCC, the appointment to inherit may arise from statute (intestate succession) or a testament (testamentary succession); however, in light of Articles 926 §2 and 959 PCC, it is apparent, that the appointment to inherit may be mixed and be derived partly from testament and partly from the statute.[269]

566. Priority is given to testamentary succession as this reflects the accepted principle of the freedom of testamentary disposition and the belief that the holder of the estate should be able to arrange for its devolution according to his or her personal wishes. If the testator has appointed heirs to the whole estate and all of them can inherit (i.e., have the capacity to inherit and are not unworthy of inheriting) and want to inherit (i.e., do not waive the estate), then succession is based on the testament exclusively.

567. Intestate succession of the whole estate occurs when there is no valid testament or none of the appointed heirs can inherit or want to inherit. Intestate succession may apply only to a part of the deceased person's estate. This occurs when the testator appointed heirs only to a part of his or her estate or when he or she appointed heirs to the whole estate but some heirs cannot inherit or do not want to inherit. In such a situation testamentary and intestate successions occur simultaneously.[270]

III. Unworthiness to Inherit

568. The institution of unworthiness to inherit eliminates from the circle of heirs those persons, who have behaved in such a way that allowing them to inherit would be wrong from a moral point of view. Currently, Polish law does not allow for unworthiness to take effect *ipso inure* and the probate court does not take it into account ex officio. Unworthiness is acknowledged and takes effect only when a

268. E. Niezbecka, 'Status majątku fundacji a zdolność do dziedziczenia fundacji ustanawianej w testamencie', *Rejent*, no. 12 (1992): 22 et seq.
269. *See* Supreme Court decision issued on 9 Oct. 1996, II CKU 25/96, LEX no. 560913.
270. H. Witczak, 'Article 926 Commentary', in M. Habdas, M. Fras (eds), *Kodeks*, 117.

court issues an appropriate ruling. The ruling may only be issued in separate proceedings concerning unworthiness. Such proceedings may be instigated by any person who has an interest in doing so. The interest does not have to be connected with a legal reason or a proprietary right; it may be a personal or an emotional reason. The mentioned proceedings must be instigated within one year from the day on which the person concerned learned about the cause of unworthiness, but no later than three years from the opening of the succession (Article 929 PCC).[271] The one-year time limit does not start to run until the opening of the succession.

569. The law precisely defines the reasons for finding an heir unworthy to inherit, and therefore it is impossible to apply the regulation to other similar situations. According to Article 928 §1 PCC, the court may hold an heir to be unworthy to inherit if:

(1) he or she intentionally committed a grave criminal offence against the deceased;[272]
(2) he or she induced the deceased by deceit or threat to draw up or to revoke a testament or in the same manner prevented him or her from performing one of these acts;
(3) he or she intentionally concealed or destroyed the deceased's testament, forged or altered that person's testament or knowingly benefited from a testament forged or altered by another person.[273]

570. Unworthiness may apply to all heirs, regardless of whether intestate or testamentary succession takes place. It is also applicable to a legatee through Article 972 PCC according to which, the provisions on the appointment of the heir, the capacity to inherit and unworthiness apply *mutatis mutandis* to legacies.

571. An heir held to be unworthy to inherit is excluded from succession as if he or she had not outlived the deceased person (Article 928 §2 PCC). The court ruling creates a new legal situation and is effective *ex tunc*, that is, from the moment of the opening of the succession. The unworthy heir must return the objects he or she received from the estate to the remaining heirs and possibly pay costs connected with using, damaging and taking fruits from the object while it was in his or her possession (*see* Articles 225 and 226 PCC). He or she is to be treated as a possessor in bad faith.

572. An heir cannot be held to be unworthy if the deceased forgave him or her. The act of forgiveness is not a juridical act (act in law); therefore, it is not required that the one who forgives has the capacity to perform such acts. The law requires that the one who forgives acts with sufficient awareness. However, the fact that one has full capacity to perform acts in law does not automatically denote that he or she

271. J. Zrałek, 'Niegodność dziedziczenia - uwagi de lege ferenda', *Rejent*, no. 2 (2006): 203 et seq.
272. J. Wierciński, 'O przestępstwie jako przyczynie niegodności dziedziczenia', *Kwartalnik Prawa Prywatnego*, no. 2 (2010): 555 et seq.
273. *See* Supreme Court decision issued on 10 May 1977, I CR 207/77, OSNC 1978/2/34.

is acting with sufficient awareness. If he or she is senile or suffers from dementia but has not been incapacitated, he or she will not be acting with the required awareness even though, technically speaking, he or she will still possess full legal capacity to perform acts in law. The one who forgives has to be aware of the fact that he or she is forgiving. Consequently, he or she needs to know who they are forgiving and what they are forgiving. Forgiveness is an act that may be expressed in an explicit or an implicit way, but it has to be executed personally by the one who forgives.[274]

§3. Renouncement of Succession

573. Polish succession law in Article 1047 PCC contains a general ban on creating contracts concerning the estate of a person who is still alive. This ban includes, but is not limited to, the contract of succession (i.e., a *mortis causa* contract in which parties appoint heirs of the estate held by a person, who is still alive), a contract concerning an expected estate (inheritance), which is concluded between potential heirs of an identified physical person, and a contract concerning an expected estate (inheritance), which is concluded between the potential heir of an identified physical person and a third party.

574. The ban introduced in Article 1047 PCC reflects the principle of freedom of testamentary dispositions. It seems impossible to reconcile this freedom (particularly the freedom to revoke a testament) not only with the contract of succession but also with the other contracts mentioned above. It should be noted that the contract of succession does not, as a rule, allow for its termination by a unilateral act of the estate holder, as this would violate the *pacta sunt servanta* principle. Consequently, the contract of succession violates the fundamental principle, that a person must stand free to a succession that had not yet been opened. Therefore, the Polish legislator has rejected contracts of succession as an admissible title to succeed, that could exist alongside intestate and testamentary succession.[275]

575. As an exception to the above, Polish succession law allows concluding contracts that renounce succession, although such contracts definitely concern the estate of a person who is still alive.[276] According to Article 1048 PCC, a statutory heir may, by a contract with a person from whom he or she would inherit in the future, renounce succession from the latter. A contract to renounce succession may be described as a negative contract of succession since its purpose is to exclude from succession a future heir. The contract applies to intestate successions only; therefore, a person who renounces succession does not lose his or her capacity to inherit

274. M. Krajewski, 'Przebaczenie i inne okoliczności wyłączajace możliwość uznania spadkobiercy za niegodnego', *Państwo i Prawo*, no. 5 (1997): 65 et seq.
275. G. Wolak, 'Article 1047 Commentary', in M. Habdas, M. Fras (eds), *Kodeks*, 834–835.
276. M. Pazdan, 'Umowa o zrzeczenie się dziedziczenia w polskim prawie spadkowym', *Rejent*, no. 4 (1997): 184 et seq.

and may inherit in testamentary succession. Furthermore, it is irrelevant, whether the testament was made prior to the contract to renounce succession or not.

576. In order to be valid, the contract must be concluded in the form of a notarial deed. Its content should specify whether the descendants of the one who renounces succession are to be excluded from the effects of renunciation. Contentious issues concerning the content of the contract to renounce include the admissibility: to reserve a condition, to renounce the succession in favour of an identified third party, to renounce the succession only in part and to renounce only the right to legitim.[277] In practice, the contract to renounce succession is usually concluded as a result of another contract, that the potential heir has concluded or is going to conclude with the person from whom he or she would inherit through intestate succession. Often the parties in question conclude a contract to renounce succession in connection with a contract of donation.

577. Renouncing succession has the effect of excluding from succession the person who renounced it, as well as his or her descendants. They are treated as if they had not lived until the opening of the succession (Article 1049 §2 PCC). The contract of renouncing succession may stipulate, that the renouncement does not include the descendants of the person who renounces (Article 1049 §1 PCC).

578. Renouncing succession also causes the loss of the right to legitim, *as the* latter is available only to those persons, who would have inherited in intestate succession if testamentary succession had not taken place. Similarly, the right provided for in Article 939 PCC (*see* below Chapter 2) will also be lost. The PCC does not, however, expressly regulate the possibility to renounce the right to legitim. Although, as explained above, renouncing succession automatically causes the renouncement of legitim, it is not clear whether pursuant to Article 1048 PCC it is possible to only renounce legitim, without renouncing the whole succession. This matter has been resolved in a resolution of the Supreme Court,[278] where it was explained that since it is possible to renounce the whole succession, a statutory heir should not be precluded from renouncing the legitim. Since the statutory heir is entitled to do "more" s/he must have the competence to do "less". According to the court, this reasoning does not violate the principle established in Article 1047 PCC (a ban on creating contracts concerning the estate of a person who is still alive) and brings about necessary flexibility of succession law, which should allow persons to more precisely plan the devolution of their estate. This view has not been uniformly accepted in academic writings, where attention is drawn to the fact that legitim is not a part of succession, but merely an additional entitlement, which is lost upon the renouncement of succession. This happens as a side effect of the renouncement which causes the renouncing party to lose the status of a person 'who would have inherited in intestate succession if testamentary succession had not taken place'. That status is necessary to be entitled to legitim. Consequently, since the legislator,

277. A. Malinowski, 'Umowa o zrzeczenie się dziedziczenia w ujęciu Kodeksu cywilnego', *Nowy Przegląd Notarialny*, no. 4 (2004): 34 et seq.
278. Resolution of 17 March 2017, III CZP 110/16, LEX no. 2248747.

as an exception to Article 1047 PCC, allows in Article 1048 PCC only the renouncement of succession, but not the legitim, and the latter is not an element of the former, but a separate institution, the application of Article 1048 is questioned.[279]

579. The renunciation of succession may be overruled by a contract (concluded in the form of a notarial deed) between the person who renounced succession and the person whose succession was renounced (Article 1050 PCC). In such an event, the person who renounced succession regains his or her position as a potential heir in intestate succession.

279. T. Justyński, Uchwała Sądu Najwyższego – Izba Cywilna z dnia 17 marca 2017 r., III CZP 110/161. Glosa, OSP no. 11 (2018): 3 et seq.

Chapter 2. Intestate Succession

580. According to the remarks made above, the appointment to inherit may arise from statute (intestate succession) or a testament (testamentary succession), with priority given to testamentary succession. Despite this, intestate succession is a common phenomenon not only because a testament does not always exist or is valid, but also because testamentary succession is sometimes supplemented by intestate succession (*see* above: The Appointment to Inherit). The rules of intestate succession are a substitute for the actual will of the deceased that had either not been expressed or had not been validly expressed in a testament. Their aim is to reflect the most probable will of a deceased person.[280]

§1. Relatives' Right of Succession

581. Intestate succession is based on blood ties; therefore, the relatives of the deceased are entitled to inherit from him or her in the absence of a valid testament. Although the surviving spouse is not, strictly speaking, a relative of the deceased, his or her right to inherit in intestate succession is not contested. The relatives appointed to inherit in intestate succession are as follows: the spouse of the deceased, his or her descendants (children, grandchildren, and so on), his or her parents, his or her siblings and their descendants, his or her grandparents and their descendants, and the children of the deceased person's spouse (stepchildren), if both of their parents have died.

582. It is important to note that a *spouse* is a person, who had been married to the descendant at the moment of the opening of the succession. In Polish law, there are no marriages between same-sex couples and no regulations on heterosexual couples who are not formally married. Such partners may not be treated as spouses; however, they may be treated as persons who were close to the deceased.

583. If before the opening of the succession a divorce judgment became binding, the person in question is not a spouse. If, however, a divorce judgment had been issued but was not yet binding at the moment of the opening of the succession, the person in question is still a spouse. Divorce proceedings instigated by either of the spouses are discontinued if one of them dies (Article 446 PCPC); therefore, it is impossible for a divorce to take place after one of the spouses has died.

584. As a rule, it is also impossible to nullify a marriage after the death of one spouse, however, it is important to distinguish between two situations. The first one occurs if proceedings to nullify a marriage have been instigated before the death of either of the spouses. In such cases, the court may nullify the marriage even after one of them had died (Article 450 PCPC). The second situation concerns instigating proceedings to nullify a marriage after the death of either of the spouses

---

280. J. Wierciński, 'Uwagi o teoretycznych założeniach dziedziczenia ustawowego', *Studia Prawa Prywatnego*, no. 2 (2009): 82 et seq.

(Articles 447–449 PCPC). This is admissible only in two instances regulated in Article 18 FGC, namely: the annulment of a bigamous marriage and the annulment of a marriage between people who are lineal descendants, no matter how remote, or between siblings. An annulment of marriage takes effect *ex tunc*, which means that the marriage is assumed to have never existed. Consequently, if a marriage is nullified after the opening of the succession, the spouse who inherited from the deceased loses the inheritance, as that person can no longer be considered to have ever been the spouse of the deceased.

585. The *children* of the deceased are appointed to intestate succession regardless of whether they were born in or out of wedlock. The only important factor is that filiation of a given child to his or her parent has been ascertained according to provisions of the FGC.

586. In cases of *adoptio plena* and *plenissima*, adopted children have the same succession rights as natural children of the deceased. According to Article 936 §1 PCC, an adopted child inherits from his or her adoptive parent and the relatives of the latter as if he or she were a child of the adoptive parent, and the adoptive parent and his or her relatives inherit from the adopted child as if the adoptive parent were a parent of the adopted child. In §2, it is clarified that an adopted child does not inherit from his or her natural ascendants and their relatives, and they do not inherit from him or her. For obvious reasons, in §3 it is stipulated, that in the event where one of the spouses has adopted a child of his or her spouse, the provision of §2 shall not apply to such spouse and to his or her relatives.

587. Different rules apply to the so-called partial adoption *(adoptio minus-plena)* which does not extinguish all legal relations of the adopted child with his or her natural relatives (*see* Article 124 FGC). Therefore, according to Article 937 PCC if the effects of the adoption consist of establishing a relationship between the adoptive parent and the adopted child exclusively, the following rules apply:

(1) the adopted child shall inherit from the adoptive parent as if the former were a natural child of the latter, and the descendants of the adopted child shall inherit from the adoptive parent according to the rules that apply to the succession of more remote descendants of the deceased;
(2) the adopted child and his or her descendants shall not inherit from the relatives of the adoptive parent, and the relatives of the adoptive parent shall not inherit from the adopted child and his or her descendants;
(3) the natural parents of the adopted child shall not inherit from him or her; their place is taken by the adoptive parent; the adoption shall not otherwise overrule the appointment to succession based on blood ties.

§2. The Classes of Heirs

588. Relatives that may potentially inherit from the deceased in intestate succession are divided into five classes. Each consecutive class may inherit only if there are no heirs from the preceding class who can or want to inherit.[281]

The classes of heirs are as follows:

(1) the surviving spouse and the deceased person's descendants (primary heirs);
(2) the surviving spouse and the deceased person's parents, siblings and their descendants (secondary heirs);
(3) the deceased person's grandparents and their descendants (tertiary heirs);
(4) the children of the deceased person's spouse (stepchildren), if their both parents have died;
(5) the local authority or the State.

I. Primary Heirs

589. According to Article 931 §1 PCC, the children of the deceased and his or her spouse shall, by virtue of statutory law, be appointed to inherit first and they shall inherit in equal parts. However, the part inherited by the spouse cannot be lesser than one-fourth of the entire estate.

590. Consequently, if the deceased left a spouse and two children, each inherits one-third of the estate. If he or she left a spouse and three children, each inherits one-fourth of the estate. If, however, apart from the spouse, there are four children, the spouse inherits one-fourth of the estate, and the remaining three-fourths of the estate are to be equally divided among the four children (i.e., each will inherit three-sixteenth of the estate). If a child did not outlive the deceased, the share of the estate, which would have been inherited by that child, passes to his or her children in equal parts. This provision applies respectively to more remote descendants (Article 931 §2 PCC). If there is no surviving spouse, the whole estate is inherited in equal parts by the children of the deceased and their descendants.

591. In this context, it is important to point out, that according to Article 935^1 PCC, provisions on intestate succession of the surviving spouse do not apply to a spouse who had been in judicial separation (*see* Article 61^{1-6} FGC) with the deceased at the date of the opening of the succession. Although judicial separation does not end the marriage, the legislator has expressly provided, that the surviving spouse, who had been in judicial separation with the deceased at the time of the opening of succession is excluded from intestate succession.

281. M. Pazdan, 'Neuregelung der gesetzlichen Erbfolge im polnischen Recht', in M. Habdas, A. Wudarski (eds), *Festschrift fur Prof. Stanislawa Kalus. Ius est ars Boni et aequi*, (Frankfurt am Main: Peter Lang Verlag, 2010), 375–384.

592. It is also important to note, that special provisions regulate situations in which divorce or separation proceedings have been instigated, but have not ended before the death of a spouse. In such circumstances, the surviving spouse is still technically married to (or not judicially separated from) the deceased at the moment of the latter's death, so as a rule he or she is appointed to inherit in intestate succession. The legislator allows excluding such a surviving spouse from succession under the condition that the deceased had, before his or her death, brought before the court an action for divorce or separation and had claimed that the break-up of marriage was entirely or at least partly the fault of the surviving spouse.[282] Furthermore, the demand for a divorce or separation due to the surviving spouse's fault for marriage break-up must have been justified (Article 940 §1 PCC).[283] For the above provision to apply, it is irrelevant whether the deceased had been the plaintiff or the defendant in the divorce or separation proceedings. If at any stage of the proceedings the deceased agreed to abandon his or her claim concerning the fault for the break-up of the marriage, the exclusion of the surviving spouse from succession will not be possible.

593. If conditions set out in Article 940 §1 PCC are met, each of the heirs that is appointed to inherit concurrently with the surviving spouse may demand that the court issue a judgment, which excludes the surviving spouse from succession. The mentioned demand cannot be brought before the court after the lapse of six months from the day on which an heir learned of the opening of the succession. This period may not end later than one year from the opening of the succession (Article 940 §2 PCC).[284] The court judgment is effective *ex tunc* and excludes the surviving spouse from intestate succession, as well as extinguishes his or her rights of legitim and ones mentioned in Article 939 PCC (*see* below).

594. Finally, it is necessary to indicate, that upon the death of a spouse, property that he or she held jointly with the surviving spouse (joint marital property) is converted into co-ownership. The surviving spouse retains a share of half of that property. The other share of half, together with the deceased person's property that was not included in the joint marital property, is subject to succession.[285]

II. Secondary Heirs

595. The second class of heirs inherits in intestate succession only when the deceased left no children or their descendants. According to Article 932 §1 PCC, in the absence of the descendants of the deceased, his or her spouse and parents are

---

282. *See* Supreme Court resolution issued on 2 Jul. 1985, II CZP 39/85, OSNC 1986/5/68 and on 19 Aug. 1983, III CZP 38/83, OSNC 1984/2-3/27.
283. L. Stecki, 'Wyłączenie małżonka od dziedziczenia ustawowego (Art. 940 k.c.)', *RPEiS*, no. 1 (1990): 79 et seq.
284. *See* Supreme Court judgment issued on 12 Apr. 2002, I CKN 1345/99, LEX no. 55556.
285. B. Kucia, 'Article 931 Commentary', in M. Habdas, M. Fras (eds), *Kodeks*, 198–200.

appointed to inherit by virtue of statutory law. The share in the estate of the spouse who inherits concurrently with the deceased's parents equals half of the estate (Article 933 §1 PCC).

596. The share in the estate of each parent who inherits concurrently with the deceased person's spouse amounts to one-fourth of the entire estate. If a man's paternity had not been established (in other words, the father is unknown in the understanding of the law), the share in the estate of the deceased person's mother who inherits concurrently with the surviving spouse is equal to half of the entire estate (Article 932 §2 PCC). The parents of the deceased inherit the entire estate in equal parts in the absence of descendants and the surviving spouse (Article 932 §3 PCC).

597. The siblings of the deceased are appointed to inherit if at least one of the deceased person's parents had died before the opening of the succession. The share the deceased parent would have had in the estate passes to the siblings of the deceased in equal parts (Article 932 §4 PCC). If any of the deceased person's siblings died before the opening of the succession but had left descendants, the latter inherit in equal parts the share in the estate that would have gone to the deceased sibling. It is important to remember, that the share in the estate of the surviving spouse who inherits concurrently with the deceased person's parents and/or siblings and their descendants is always equal to half (Article 933 §1 PCC).

598. The surviving spouse will inherit the entire estate only in the absence of the deceased person's descendants, parents, siblings or their descendants (Article 933 §2 PCC). This solution is controversial because when the parents of the descendant have not outlived him or her, the spouse inherits together with the sideline of the deceased husband's or wife's family. This not only complicates probate proceedings but also leads to questionable results of the spouse having to share the inheritance with rather distant members of the family, who usually have in no way contributed to the wealth creation of their sibling. In the case of the spouse inheriting together with the parents of the deceased, some justification is provided by arguing that it is the parents who usually have some input into their child's assets, however, that justification does not apply if the spouse is to inherit with the deceased person's siblings or their children. Thus the legislator should consider amending the groups of heirs and introduce siblings and their children as statutory heirs only in the absence of the spouse.

599. With respect to the surviving spouse, one should also mention his or her additional entitlements provided for in Article 939 §1 PCC.[286] The surviving spouse who inherits under statutory succession concurrently with other heirs may demand that they transfer to him or her the ownership of household equipment which during the deceased person's life, the surviving spouse used together with the deceased or

286. Habdas, 'Pozycja', 67–74.

alone.[287] This demand is additional to the surviving spouse's statutory share in the estate. The provision does not apply if the surviving spouse inherits concurrently with the descendants who lived with the deceased at the moment of his or her death. Finally, the surviving spouse is not entitled to the mentioned household equipment if the cohabitation of the spouses ceased during the life of the deceased (Article 939 §2 PCC).

600. The demand is time-barred and provisions on bequest apply *mutatis mutandis*. Consequently, the claim for transferring the household equipment must be made no later than five years from the moment it became due, the latter being no earlier than the moment in which it was ascertained who the heirs are (*see* Article 981 PCC).

601. The term 'household equipment' denotes all kinds of objects which serve as furnishings and equipment of the house. It includes objects such as furniture, carpets, paintings, cutlery, crockery, kitchen and bathroom appliances (refrigerator, microwave oven, washing machine) as well as other electronic appliances (television set, radio). It does not include objects which are more of an investment, than a household appliance (e.g., a collection of valuable paintings). In practice, the classification of a given object as a piece of household equipment may be a contentious issue, particularly if such equipment is valuable and makes up a large part of the estate.

602. The surviving spouse will not be able to benefit from Article 939 PCC if the succession is in its entirety a testamentary one, the surviving spouse: has renounced succession, has been held to be unworthy to inherit, has been disinherited, has waived the estate, or Article 940 PCC is applicable. Similarly, Article 939 PCC will not apply if the deceased excluded the surviving spouse from inheriting through a negative testament, excluded his or her Article 939 PCC entitlements in a testament or bequeathed the household equipment mentioned in Article 939 PCC to others. Finally, the surviving spouse may accept the estate but reject Article 939 PCC entitlement; however, he or she cannot accept the latter and reject the estate.

III. Tertiary Heirs

603. The third class of heirs inherits in intestate succession only if there are no primary or secondary heirs, that is, the deceased left no descendants, spouse, parents, or siblings and their descendants. It is then that the grandparents of the deceased inherit the estate in equal parts (Article 934 §1 PCC). This denotes that the estate is divided into four equal parts (grandparents from the mother's side and grandparents from the father's side). If any of the deceased person's grandparents

287. S. Wójcik, 'Ochrona interesów jednostki w polskim prawie spadkowym w zakresie powołania do dziedziczenia', *Zeszyty Naukowe Uniwersytetu Jagiellońskiego – Prace Prawnicze*, no. 98 (1981):189; J. Gwiazdomorski, 'Prawo spadkowe w kodeksie cywilnym PRL', *Państwo i Prawo*, no. 5–6 (1965): 710.

died before the opening the estate, the share the deceased grandparent would have had in the estate passes to his or her descendants and is to be distributed among them in accordance with the principles which govern the division of the estate among the descendants of the deceased (Article 934 §2 PCC). In essence, this means that the estate will be passed down not through lineal descendants but through collateral relatives. If the grandparent who predeceased left no descendants, his or her share passes in equal parts to the surviving grandparents.

604. It is also necessary to note, that although grandparents may inherit as tertiary heirs, they have a special entitlement provided for in Article 938 PCC if, in a given situation, they have not been appointed to inherit. According to that provision, the grandparents of the deceased, who live in poverty and cannot obtain their due means of subsistence from persons obliged by statute to provide them with such means, may demand that an heir, who is not obliged by statute to provide the mentioned means, does supply the grandparents with the necessary means of subsistence in proportion to the value of his or her share in the estate. The heir may also satisfy the grandparents' claim by paying them a sum of money equal to the value of one-fourth of his or her share in the estate.

IV. Further Heirs

605. If the deceased left no primary, secondary or tertiary heirs, his or her stepchildren (i.e., the children of his or her spouse) inherit the estate in equal parts under the condition, that none of their parents remains alive (Article 934^1 PCC). It is irrelevant, whether the stepchildren come from a marriage which existed at the time of the opening of the estate or from a previous marriage or marriages of the deceased. In other words, children of all spouses that the deceased had during his or her life are appointed to inherit, if both of their natural parents are no longer alive at the time of the opening of the succession. If one of the stepchildren had predeceased, the other stepchildren inherit the whole estate in equal parts, as the legislator does not provide for succession of a stepchild's descendants.

606. Finally, in the absence of the spouse of the deceased, his or her relatives and children of the deceased person's spouse, the estate is inherited by the local authority (commune) or the State. The former inherits after a person, whose last place of residence was located within the territory of that local authority. If the last place of residence of the deceased in the Republic of Poland cannot be established, or if his or her last place of residence was outside Poland, the estate is inherited by the State (Article 935 PCC).[288]

607. If the local authority or the state is appointed to inherit in intestate succession they may not waive the estate. They accept the estate with the benefit of inventory by virtue of law.

288. M. Pazdan, 'Dziedziczenie gminy i Skarbu Państwa – po nowelizacji kodeksu cywilnego w 2003 r.', *Rejent*, no. 2 (2003): 13 et seq.

Chapter 3. Testamentary Succession

608. As has already been mentioned, testamentary succession has priority over intestate succession, but in order for the former to take place, there must be a valid testament/will. The term 'testament' has two meanings. The first meaning denotes a document, which comprises the last will of the testator. The second meaning denotes an act in law.

609. The testament as an act in law is a disposition *mortis causa* so its effects are postponed until the testator dies. This disposition also has other, special characteristics. It is a unilateral act in law that may be revoked by the testator at any time before the opening of the succession. The testator may choose to revoke the whole testament or just some of its dispositions (Article 943 PCC) in an express or implied way. The disposition is formal in the sense that a testament must be made in one of the forms prescribed by legal provisions. It is also a disposition that must be made personally by the testator (Article 944 §2) and not by his or her proxy or any other persons.

610. Additionally, according to Article 942 PCC, the will may include dispositions of only one testator. Consequently, joint wills are prohibited in the Polish law of succession. The main reason for the above is that a joint will may potentially violate the principle of the freedom of testamentary dispositions. Moreover, joint wills limit the freedom to revoke a will, and this is viewed as contrary to the essence of a testament as an act in law. Polish courts have not allowed for any exceptions to this principle.[289]

611. Finally, due to the fact that contracts of succession are impermissible in Polish law, a testament is the only act in law which allows making *mortis causa* dispositions.

§1. The Validity of a Will

I. Premises of Validity

612. In order for a will to be valid, the following conditions must be met:

(1) the testator must have the capacity to make a will;
(2) the testator must act *cum animi testandi*;
(3) the will must be made in the prescribed form;
(4) there may not be any deficiencies in the declaration of intent;
(5) the will must have a specified content.

289. *See* Supreme Court decision issued on 24 Mar. 1998, I CKU 6/98, Prokuratura i Prawo -wkł. 1998/9/27 and on 17 Mar. 2004, II CK 67/03, LEX no. 602409.

613. The capacity to make a will exists only if the testator has full capacity to perform acts in law (Article 944 §1 PCC). The existence of this capacity is to be evaluated with respect to the moment the will had been made. A later loss of full legal capacity to perform acts in law does not influence the validity of a will. A will made by a testator who had no capacity to make a will is void and cannot be validated by any later actions. As has already been mentioned, the will must be made by the testator personally (944 §2).

614. The testator must act with the intent to make *mortis causa* dispositions of his or her estate. He or she must be aware of the fact, that his or her dispositions will become effective upon his or her death and that they will be the basis for distributing that estate among heirs and other persons.

615. The will must take one of the forms prescribed by law. Polish law divides wills into ordinary and extraordinary ones. The first category includes holograph, notarial and allograph wills. The second category includes a verbal will, a will made while travelling on a sea vessel or in an aircraft, and a military will.

616. Certain deficiencies in the declaration of intent cause the will to be void. According to Article 945 §1 PCC, a will is null and void if it was made:

(1) in a state precluding a conscious or free decision and declaration of intent;
(2) as a result of a mistake which justifies the supposition that had the testator not been mistaken he or she would not have drawn up such a will;[290]
(3) under threat (undue influence).[291]

617. If any of the circumstances enumerated above existed when the testament was being made, any person who has a legal interest in doing so may claim that the will is void.[292] Despite the fact that the will is void by operation of law, the legislator introduces a time limit for relying on such a claim. According to Article 945 §2 PCC, the invalidity of a testament for the above reasons cannot be claimed after the lapse of three years from the day on which one found out about the cause of invalidity. This period may not end later than ten years after the opening of the succession. It seems that these limitation periods were introduced in order to avoid complications that would arise if the invalidity of the will was claimed a long time after the opening of succession when there would be significant difficulties in providing proof as well as in indicating new heirs and invalidating the testamentary succession.[293]

618. Finally, the will may only contain dispositions which do not violate general rules on acts in law as well as rules of succession law. According to Article 58 PCC,

290. *See* Supreme Court decision issued on 29 Oct. 2003, III CK 325/02, LEX no. 602262.
291. *See* Supreme Court decision issued on 21 Apr. 2004, III CK 523/02, LEX no. 585812.
292. A. Mączyński, 'Wpływ wad oświadczenia woli na ważność testamentu', *Rejent*, no. 7–8 (1991): 24 et seq.
293. *See* Supreme Court decision issued on 8 Aug. 2008, I CSK 140/07, OSNC 2008/10/118.

an act in law which is inconsistent with statutory law, the principles of community life, or is designed to circumvent the law is null and void unless appropriate provisions provide otherwise, in particular, that those provisions of the act in law which are null and void are replaced by the appropriate provisions of statutory law. If only a part of an act in law is affected by nullity, the act shall remain valid as to its remaining parts unless it follows from the circumstances, that without the provisions affected by nullity the act would not have been performed.

619. The testator must also conform with specific rules regarding succession law which allow for the will to contain, among others, the following dispositions:

(1) the appointment of an heir;
(2) a legacy (bequest);
(3) a testamentary burden;
(4) the appointment of a testamentary executor;
(5) the exclusion of an heir appointed to inherit in intestate succession (if it is the only disposition of the will, the latter is referred to as a negative testament);
(6) disinheritance;
(7) the establishment of a foundation.

II. Revocation of a Will

620. As has already been mentioned, a will is an act in law which may be revoked by the testator at any time before his or her death. The revocation of a will has *mortis causa* effects and may be done in an explicit or implicit way.[294] The legislator provides in Article 946 PCC that the testament may be revoked if:

(1) the testator makes a new testament;
(2) in order to revoke a testament, the testator destroys it or deprives it of features which account for its validity (e.g., erases his or her signature on a holograph testament);
(3) the testator alters the testament in a manner which indicates his or her intention to revoke the disposition contained in the will (e.g., the testator crosses out or scribbles out written dispositions).

621. If the testator drew up a new testament without stipulating therein that he or she is revoking a previous testament, only those provisions of the latter which are inconsistent with the contents of the new testament are revoked (Article 947 PCC).

294. T. Juszyński, 'Glosa do postanowienia SN z dnia 8 stycznia 2002 r., I CKN 482/00', *Państwo i Prawo*, no. 11 (2005): 114 et seq.

§2. THE INTERPRETATION OF A WILL

622. Most testaments are made without the involvement of persons with legal knowledge. Therefore, dispositions contained in wills are often imprecise and expressed in words which do not correspond to legal terminology. Consequently, a proper interpretation of the deceased person's testament is of paramount importance if freedom of testamentary disposition is to have a practical and not only theoretical meaning.

623. *Favour testamenti*, referred to as benevolent interpretation, is the main principle relating to the interpretation of a will. According to Article 948 §1 PCC, a testament must be interpreted in a way which ensures the fullest possible compliance with the testator's will. If a testament can be interpreted in various ways, the interpretation which allows to carry out the testator's dispositions and gives them reasonable meaning is to be applied (Article 948 §2 PCC). This rule of interpretation employs both individual and objective elements. The former are taken into account when the interpretation is applied in order to discover the actual intent and will of the testator. The latter are reflected when the interpretation is aimed at finding a reasonable meaning of the testator's dispositions that will allow to give them practical effect, as it is natural to assume, that the testator would not include unreasonable dispositions in his or her will.[295]

624. The interpretation concerns only the content of the testament and cannot be expanded to include the question of observing the required form of a will or possessing full legal capacity. The interpretation of the testament's content excludes the possibility of supplementing or modifying the existent dispositions through interpretation, even if they are incomplete.

625. In cases of doubt, the sense of the testator's dispositions is to be discovered with the use of common rules of interpreting statements expressed in a given language. Words are to be understood in their general, everyday meaning, unless the testator has used words or phrases which are connected with jargon, dialect, etc. In the latter case, one should apply the rules of interpreting that special language, before employing the general interpretation rules. This also applies if the testator himself or herself consistently used a given language in a non-standard way.

626. It is also possible to take into account circumstances external to the will if they can be helpful in its interpretation since according to Article 948 §1 PCC it is necessary to strive for 'the fullest possible compliance with the testator's will'. Therefore, the first rule of interpreting a testament is shaped by individual, and not objective, elements. The mentioned circumstances can be proven by any means admitted in court proceedings.[296]

---

295. Z. Radwański, 'Wykładnia testamentów', *Kwartalnik Prawa Prywatnego*, no. 1 (1993): 5 et seq.
296. *See* Supreme Court decision issued on 13 Feb. 2001, II CKN 378/00, LEX no. 550937.

627. The second paragraph of Article 948 PCC allows reinterpreting the legal position of a person indicated in the testament in a way which is not consistent with the actual terminology that the testator has employed. This may only be done in order to give the dispositions a reasonable meaning and consequently to give them practical effect.

628. In addition to the above, the legislator formulates rules of interpretation in the following matters:

(a) *Appointment of an heir*: A testator often employs the verb 'to bequeath' in order to indicate, that he or she would like to appoint certain persons to be his or her heirs. This occurs frequently since the Polish language does not have a verb which would allow expressing in one word the desire to make someone an heir. Therefore, according to Article 961 PCC, if the testator bequeathed in his or her testament to a given person particular material objects which exhaust almost the entire estate, that person shall be, in case of doubt, considered to be an heir appointed to inherit the entire estate and not a mere legatee. If such a testamentary disposition was made in favour of several persons, they shall be, in case of doubt, considered as appointed to inherit the entire estate in fractions, which correspond to the proportions that the value of the bequeathed objects has with respect to the value of the whole estate.
(b) *Interpretation of conditions*: The appointment of an heir cannot be subject to a condition or a time limit and if the latter have been introduced, they are treated as non-existent. However, if the contents of the testament or circumstances indicate that the heir would not have been appointed without the condition or time limit, the appointment of the heir shall be null and void. This does not apply to cases, in which the condition was satisfied or remained definitively unsatisfied or the time limit has elapsed before the opening of the succession (Article 962 PCC).
(c) *Lack of clarity about the size of inheritance*: If the testator appointed several heirs to inherit the estate or a certain part thereof without determining their respective shares in the estate, they inherit in equal parts (Article 960 PCC).

§3. Different Types of Wills

629. The Polish legislator divides wills into ordinary and extraordinary ones. The former ones are available to everyone, as no special conditions must exist in order to make them. However, the latter ones may only be made under circumstances described in the relevant provisions. If a will lacks certain formal requirements mandatory for a given type of will but fulfils the requirements of another type of will, it is a valid disposition.

I. Ordinary Wills

630. There are three types of ordinary wills. The testator may choose to observe any of these forms according to his or her preferences. No special conditions must exist in order to make an ordinary testament.

A. Holograph Testament

631. This type of testament must be entirely handwritten by the testator, signed by him or her and must have a date. The above requirements are clearly expressed in Article 949 §1 PCC. The lack of a date does not result in the invalidity of a handwritten testament if there are no doubts as to the testator's capacity to draw up a testament, the contents of the testament and the relationship among several testaments (Article 949 §2 PCC).

632. The holograph testament may only be made by persons who can read and write. The entire will must be handwritten, so any completely, as well as partially typed or printed wills will be invalid. The testament may be written on any material (paper, leather, wood, etc.) with the use of any utensils, as long as they are permanent enough for the testament to last at least until the opening of the succession. The testament may contain dispositions of one person only, as joint wills are forbidden. A will written on a piece of paper, where one side contains a will of one person, and the other side contains a will of another person is not a joint will. Similarly, two wills may be written on the same side of a sheet of paper if they are separate wills, and each has a date and a signature.

633. The signature of the testator reflects not only *animus testandi* but also provides information as to who the testator is. A signature should consist of the testator's full first and last name. If the testator used a pseudonym it can serve as the signature. The courts have been rather lenient in interpreting the requirement of a signature in the sense, that they have accepted incomplete signatures (e.g., providing an initial instead of the full first name, using a term of endearment that the testator was called or used, using a term which indicates the family relation of the testator – father, mother, sister, etc.). The signature should be placed immediately under the written dispositions, so a signature placed on the envelope in which the will is placed will not fulfil the legal requirements. It is, however, accepted that a valid will may form a part of a letter, even if the dispositions are not separated from the text of the letter and the signature is placed under the letter and not the actual dispositions.[297]

634. The date should consist of an indication of the day, month and year when the testament was made, however, if there is only one testament made in a given year, it would be enough to indicate the month or just the time of year. The date may also be provided in a descriptive manner, for example, on my 60th birthday. The

297. *See* Supreme Court resolution issued on 28 Apr. 1973, III CZP 78/72, OSNC 1973/12/207.

lack of date will not result in the testament's invalidity if there are no doubts as to the testator's legal capacity (e.g., he was never incapacitated and did not suffer from any mental disorders), the content of the testament (e.g., the testator only had one wife and stayed married to her until his death) and the relation among testaments that the testator had made (the testator destroyed his previous testaments).

635. If a holograph testament had been destroyed (but not revoked) or lost and there is evidence the will existed and what its content was, it is possible to prove the existence of the will and rely on its dispositions in probate court proceedings concerning the certificate of estate acquisition.[298]

B. Notarial Testament

636. According to Article 950 PCC, a testament may be drawn up in the form of a notarial deed. PCC does not include any other provisions regarding this type of will, therefore further regulations are to be found in the Law of Notaries Act 1991 (LNA),[299] Articles 79–95. The mentioned provisions concern all acts in law that take the form of a notarial deed.

637. This type of a will may be made by any person, including persons who cannot read or write, persons who are blind, deaf or both.[300] A notary is a person of public trust who will refuse to perform an act which is contrary to law. He or she is also obliged to inform his or her clients about the performed act and to protect the rightful interests of the parties involved (*see* Article 80 LNA).

638. This type of will is preferable for a number of reasons. First, the notary has legal knowledge necessary to write down the dispositions of the testator in compliance with the rules and terminology of succession law. Second, the chances of someone exerting undue influence on the testator are negligible. Third, later attempts of the heirs to have the testament invalidated are unlikely to take place or be successful.[301]

C. Allograph (Official) Testament

639. This type of a will cannot be utilized by persons who are mute or deaf, as it requires them to verbally express their last will and then listen to a reading of a written record that contains the testator's will. According to Article 951 §1 PCC, the testator may make his or her testament by verbally declaring, in the presence of two

298. *See* Supreme Court decision issued on 20 Jul. 2005, I CK 2/05, LEX no. 152531 and on 16 Apr. 1999, II CKN 255/98, OSNC 1999/11/194.
299. Act of 14 Feb. 1991, consolidated version: Journal of Statutes 2020, item 1192 with subsequent amendments.
300. B. Kucia, 'Article 931 Commentary', in M. Habdas, M. Fras (eds), *Kodeks*, 301.
301. R. Sztyk, 'Testament notarialny. Wybrane zagadnienia', *Rejent*, no. 9 (2005): 128 et seq.

witnesses, his or her last will to the head of a borough (mayor, president of a city), a staroste, a marshal of a voivodeship, a secretary of a poviat or commune or the Registrar General. The testator's declaration is recorded in a written document with the indication of the date on which it was drawn up. The document is read out loud to the testator in the presence of the witnesses. It must then be signed by the testator, the person to whom the will was declared, and the witnesses. If the testator cannot sign the document, that fact must be mentioned therein and the reason for the lack of the signature must be given (951 §2 PCC). The public official and the witnesses must always sign the written record.

640. The allograph testament is also called the official testament, as it is made in the presence of public officials, namely the executive officers of local authorities or the Registrar General. In this context, its advantage is that the testator is unlikely to be under undue influence and it would be difficult to hold that the testament is invalid due to deficiencies of the testator's declaration of intent. This type of testament does, however, involve a number of formal requirements and it is not made in the presence of persons who possess legal knowledge about succession law. Therefore, these testaments are often invalid due to the lack of observing all the formal requirements mentioned in Article 951 §1 PCC.[302]

II. Extraordinary Wills

641. Extraordinary testaments may only be made if there are special circumstances which justify abandoning the ordinary form of testament. Moreover, the validity of such testaments is always limited in time.

A. *Verbal Testament*

642. According to Article 952 §1 PCC if there is a fear of the testator's imminent death or if due to extraordinary circumstances it is impossible or very difficult to observe the ordinary form of the testament, the testator may verbally declare his or her last will in the presence of at least three witnesses.

643. It is a contentious issue whether the fear of the testator's imminent death should be justified by objective factors (e.g., a terminal illness, a life-threatening injury) or by the testator's individual assessment of the situation (e.g., he or she is convinced that he or she will soon die, although in medical terms his or her condition is not life-threatening). It seems that purely individual but irrational feelings of the testator do not warrant making a verbal testament. His or her individual feelings are to be taken into account when it was justified for him or her to assume that

302. *See* Supreme Court decision issued on 27 Apr. 2001, III CKN 396/00, LEX no. 550964 and on 12 Jan. 1993, I CRN 208/92, LEX no. 146210.

his or her death is imminent, even though objectively he or she was not in such danger (e.g., the medical diagnosis was incorrect).[303] Consequently, although the fear of imminent death must be related to objective circumstances, the individual conviction of the testator should also be taken into account.[304] The fear of imminent death must exist at the moment the testament is being made and is in itself enough to warrant making a verbal will. The mentioned fear does not have to bring about the difficulty or impossibility of observing an ordinary form of a will.

644. The verbal will may also be made when, due to extraordinary circumstances, it is impossible or very difficult to observe the ordinary form of the testament. This means that it is impossible or very difficult not only to make a notarial or an official will but also to make a holograph will and the impossibility or difficulty is caused by extraordinary circumstances.

645. If the above-mentioned circumstances exist, the testator can verbally communicate his or her last will in the presence of at least three witnesses.

646. Although the verbal testament is made at the moment the testator declares his or her will,[305] in order for it to be legally effective, its contents must be confirmed in a written document. This may be done in two ways. The first one requires that one of the witnesses or a third party writes down the contents of the will, indicating the place and the date the declaration was made and the place and the date the contents of the will were written down. The document must then be signed by the testator and two witnesses or by all the witnesses. This written confirmation of the verbal will may be done while the testator is still alive or after his or her death (only the witnesses sign the document) but in any case no later than one year from the moment the verbal will was made (Article 952 §2 PCC). It should be pointed out that some scholars and courts do not allow for this type of confirmation after the testator's death claiming, that in such cases only the procedure mentioned below is admissible.

647. The second way to confirm the verbal will is for the witnesses to testify in front of a court as to the contents of the testament. If it is impossible for one of the witnesses to testify in front of the court or hearing his or her testimony is hindered by obstacles that are difficult to overcome, the court may rely on the consistent testimonies of two witnesses. This type of confirmation of the verbal will may only take place if the will had not been confirmed in a document signed by the witnesses and/or the testator and if the time that has elapsed from the opening of the succession does not exceed six months (Article 952 §3 PCC).

---

303. A. Łazarska, 'Prawno-medyczna wykładnia 'obawy rychłej śmierci' jako przesłanka ważności testamentu ustnego', *Prawo i Medycyna*, no. 2 (2007): 86 et seq.
304. *See* Supreme Court decision issued on 8 Feb. 2006, II CSK 128/05, LEX no. 192038 and on 17 Feb. 2004, III CK 328/02 LEX no. 602713.
305. L. Żyżylewski, 'Glosa do uchwały SN z dnia 22 marca 1989 r., III CZP 22/89', *Nowe Prawo*, no. 1–3 (1991): 167 et seq.

B. *Wills Made While Travelling on a Sea Vessel or an Aircraft*

648. According to Article 953, it is possible to make a will while travelling on a Polish sea vessel or an aircraft. The testament is made by a verbal declaration of the will to the commander of the sea vessel/aircraft or his or her deputy in the presence of two witnesses. The commander or his or her deputy records the will of the testator in a document and indicates the date of making the document. He or she then reads the document to the testator in the presence of the witnesses, whereupon the text is signed by the testator, the witnesses, and the commander or deputy commander of the sea vessel/aircraft. If the testator cannot sign the document, the cause of the lack of the testator's signature is indicated in the text. If observing this form of a will is impossible, an oral testament may be made.

649. The described type of a will may be made while one is travelling on a sea vessel or aircraft, and it is not required that any extraordinary circumstances exist or that making an ordinary will is impossible or difficult.

C. *Military Will*

650. This type of a will may only be made during a war, a state of military mobilization or while being held as a prisoner of war. Special provisions are contained in an Ordinance of the Minister of Defence 1965.[306] Persons who may make a military will include soldiers, military personnel and civilians involved in the Red Cross, religious and other activities connected with providing services during the time of war. Other civilians may make such a will if they are located in an area under the exclusive supervision of military forces.

651. The testator may declare his or her will:

(1) to a military judge;
(2) in the presence of two witnesses;
(3) in the presence of three witnesses if the testator cannot sign the written record containing his or her will;
(4) in cases of imminent death, the testator may declare his or her will to two witnesses who do not have to be simultaneously present.

D. *Loss of Validity*

652. Extraordinary testaments are always prepared when special circumstances indicated in succession law exist. Therefore, these testaments are not valid indefinitely. According to Article 955 PCC, an extraordinary testament loses its validity

---

306. Ordinance of 30 Jan. 1965, Journal of Statutes 1965, no. 7, item 38.

after six months from the moment that circumstances which justified the non-observance of the ordinary form of a testament ceased to exist. This does not apply if the testator had died before the lapse of those six months. The six-month period is suspended for a time during which the testator does not have the possibility of making an ordinary testament.[307]

653. It should also be mentioned, that during its term the PCCCL working group had questioned the necessity of maintaining six different forms of testaments, finding that it is not constructive or practical to do so. The group was proposing to keep not only the holograph, notarial and military testament but possibly also the oral testament. The latter would have to be subject to more restrictions in order to be permitted only in absolutely exceptional circumstances. The group had also been considering the possibility of introducing joint wills for spouses.[308] No final drafts had been prepared, before the dissolution of PCCCL in 2015.

III. Witnesses of a Will

654. Whenever the legislator requires witnesses to be present in the process of making a will (allograph, verbal and travel testaments), they must meet criteria set out in the relevant provisions. According to Article 956 PCC, the following persons cannot be witnesses in the process of drawing up a will:

(1) those who do not have full capacity to perform acts in law;
(2) those who are blind, deaf, or mute;
(3) those who are illiterate;
(4) those who do not know the language in which the testament is made;
(5) those who have been validly convicted by the court for giving false evidence.

655. Additionally, according to Article 957 §1 PCC, a person for whom any benefit has been provided in the testament cannot be a witness. The following persons are also excluded from serving as witnesses: the testator's: spouse, persons related to him or her by blood or affinity of the first and second degree, as well as persons whom he or she adopted or by whom he or she was adopted.

656. If one of the persons mentioned above was a witness, the testamentary disposition which provides benefits for that person, his or her spouse, persons related to him or her by blood or affinity of the first and second degree, and persons whom he or she adopted or by whom he or she was adopted is invalid. However, if the contents of the testament or other circumstances show, that without that invalid provision the testator would not have made the testament, it shall be null and void in its entirety (Article 957 §1 PCC).

307. *See* Supreme Court decision issued on 2 Jun. 2000, II CKN 523/00, LEX no. 532088.
308. W. Klyta, 'Testamenty wspólne', *Rejent*, no. 2 (2006): 98 et seq.

IV. The Publication of the Testament

657. If it is probable or certain that the testator had made a testament, it is of utmost importance to find the testament and ascertain whether it is valid and what its contents are. Consequently, in Article 646 §1 PCPC, the legislator obliges anyone who holds the testament to present it in court as soon as that person learns of the testator's death unless the testament has already been deposited with a notary. Anyone who, without justification, neglects to do so is liable for the loss suffered by others as a result of such behaviour and he or she may be fined by the court (Article 646 §2 PCPC). The court may also demand explanations as to whether there is a testament and where it may be found (Article 647 PCPC). If the court finds out that the testament is held by a specified person, that person may be ordered to present the testament in court within a specified amount of time (Article 648 PCPC).

658. The testament is opened and made public (announced), once the court or the notary has proof that the testator has died (Article 649 PCPC). If there is more than one testament, all of them are opened and made public. The opening and the publication of the testament is confirmed in a written record of these events.

659. The opening and the publication of the testament have a mostly formal and informational function. The purpose of these events is to make the contents of the testament known to persons included in testamentary dispositions and to the executor of the testament if he or she has been appointed. The testament's validity is not dependent on the opening and the publication of the testament, and the testament's validity is not examined at that time. These events are important, for example, when determining the prescription of legitim claims (*see* below §5: Legitim) or identifying the moment after which the execution of a legacy may be demanded (*see* below §4, II, A.: Legacy).

§4. Provisions in a Will

660. Polish succession law does not specify the necessary content of a will, although one of the most important dispositions made by the testator is the appointment of an heir or heirs. Nevertheless, it is possible to draw up a negative testament, that is, one that only contains:

- a disposition of excluding from succession one of the statutory heirs; or
- dispositions of a non-proprietary kind (e.g., a description of the manner in which the funeral should be performed).

661. In such cases, the testament is treated as a reflection of the fact that the testator accepts the order of succession regulated in intestate succession provisions.

I. The Appointment of an Heir

662. In practice, the appointment of an heir is one of the most important dispositions made in a will. The testator may appoint one or several persons to inherit the entire estate or a part thereof (Article 959). The heirs do not have to possess any special features or traits apart from having the capacity to inherit (*see* Article 927 PCC and Chapter 1, §2: Premises of Succession). The heir may be identified in any way that allows ascertaining who he or she is. He or she may be appointed by his or her full name, part of the name, nickname or a description through family ties (e.g., my eldest son).[309] As has already been mentioned (*see* Chapter 3, §2: The Interpretation of a Will) the appointment of an heir may not be made subject to a condition or a time limit (Article 962 PCC).[310] It is, however, possible to appoint a substitute heir if either a statutory or testamentary heir does not want to or cannot inherit. If a provision of substituting one heir with another is made, then the share of the heir who does not want to or cannot inherit is inherited by the indicated substitute.

663. If no substitute heir has been indicated, then the fate of his or her share is determined by Article 965 PCC. According to this provision, the 'vacant' share is used to proportionally increase the shares of those testamentary heirs, who do inherit the estate. If, however, the testator has explicitly excluded the mechanism of proportionally increasing the shares of other heirs and no substitute heir has been indicated, then the share is inherited in accordance with intestate succession rules.

664. It is not possible to appoint an heir who will be obliged to hold the inherited estate on trust for another person (no fiduciary substitution – *fidei commissum).*[311] If such a disposition had been made, its sole effect is that the potential 'beneficiary of the trust' is treated as being appointed a substitute heir. However, if the testator would not have appointed the heir, had he or she known about the inadmissibility of a fiduciary substitution, the appointment of that heir is null and void (Article 964 PCC).

665. It is interesting to note, that in socialist times, the prohibition of fiduciary substitution was justified by the view, that it was a remnant of feudal times and was used to preserve big fortunes by wealthy families. In socialist Poland, such a mechanism could not be permitted. Currently, fiduciary substitution is seen as a means of including a condition or a time limit in the appointment of a testamentary heir and therefore is viewed as being incompatible with rules on testamentary succession. There are, however, discussions about introducing changes to succession law that would allow for this type of substitution as it may be argued that it is consistent with

---

309. P. Dzienis, 'Glosa do postanowienia SN z dnia 13 czerwca 2001 r., II CKN 543/00', *Palestra*, no. 11–12 (2002): 231 et seq.
310. E. Skowrońska, 'Z problematyki powołania spadkobiercy w testamencie', *Palestra*, no. 1–2 (1993): 5 et seq.
311. M. Zachariasiewicz, 'Ustanowienie trustu w testamencie lub za pomocą innej czynności prawnej mortis causa pod rządami polskiego prawa spadkowego', *Rejent*, no. 2 (2009): 163 et seq.

the freedom of testamentary dispositions and that allowing for an undivided estate to remain in a family is useful for the society.

II. Legacy (Bequest) and Testamentary Burdens

A. Legacy

666. A *legacy* is a type of a testamentary disposition by means of which a statutory or testamentary heir is to perform a proprietary obligation for a specified person (Article 968 §1 PCC). The legatee himself or herself may also be charged with a legacy (sub-legacy – Article 968 §2 PCC). If the estate is inherited by several heirs, they are responsible for the execution of the legacy in proportion to the amount of their respective shares in the estate unless the testator decided otherwise. This applies accordingly to a sub-legacy (Article 971 PCC).

667. A legacy may only be made in a testament and its effect is the creation of an obligational relationship. Unlike the appointment of an heir, a legacy may be created subject to a condition or a time limit (Article 975 PCC).[312]

668. The legatee has a claim against the heir charged with the legacy. The claim denotes the legatee's demand that the legacy be performed. The claim can be enforced in court proceedings. If the testator did not decide otherwise, the legatee may demand the execution of the legacy immediately after the publication of the testament. However, a legatee obliged to provide a sub-legacy may withhold its execution until the legacy has been executed by the heir (Article 970 PCC).

669. The legatee obliged to provide a sub-legacy may release himself or herself from this duty in two ways. He or she can either transfer gratuitously to the sub-legatee the rights acquired from the legacy or he or she can assign to the sub-legatee the claim against the heir to execute the legacy (Article 974 PCC). The claim is subject to a prescription period of five years (Article 981 PCC) from the day on which the legacy became enforceable (i.e., the day specified in Article 970 PCC).

670. The legacy requires a performance of a proprietary obligation, which includes, but is not limited to the following:

(1) transferring ownership of a thing to the legatee;
(2) creating a limited real right for the benefit of the legatee;
(3) paying a specified sum of money to the legatee;
(4) supplying a specified service to the legatee;
(5) assigning a claim to the legatee;
(6) releasing the legatee from a debt.

312. E. Niezbecka, 'Ustanowienie spadkobiercy i zapisobiorcy w testamencie', *Rejent*, no. 6 (1992): 36 et seq.

671. The legacy of a thing specified as to its identity is ineffective if the thing is not a part of the estate at the moment of the opening the succession or if the testator was, at the moment of his or her death, obliged to transfer that thing to another person (Article 976 PCC). The testator may, however, decide that the legacy is to be effective in such circumstances. This means that the heir should acquire the identified thing and transfer its ownership to the legatee. If this is impossible, the obligation will be extinguished according to general rules on the performance of obligations (Article 475 §1 PCC), unless the testator further provided that in such a situation, the heir is to pay a specified sum to the legatee.

672. It is important to note that if the heir charged with the legacy does not want to or cannot inherit, this duty passes to the statutory, substitute, or testamentary heir that has acquired the 'vacated' share (or its portion) in the estate. The testator may exclude the application of this rule (Article 967 PCC). Finally, it is necessary to point out, that according to Article 972 PCC provisions on the appointment of an heir, the capacity to inherit and the unworthiness to inherit are to be applied to the legatee *mutatis mutandis* (Article 972).

B. Legatum Per Vindicationem

673. An ordinary legacy described in the preceding paragraphs only creates an obligation and the legatee does not acquire the bequeathed object or right but has a claim against the heir. A new type of a legacy has, however, been introduced by an amendment of the PCC, which came into force on 23 October 2011.[313] This amendment introduced the *legatum per vindicationem* in Articles 981^1–981^6 PCC. This new institution functions alongside the ordinary legacy but unlike the latter, it does not create only obligational effects. Instead, the legatee acquires the bequeathed object or right at the moment of the opening of the succession (Article 981^1§1 PCC). This mechanism is a close reflection of the society's perception of what a legacy is; however, it is also a rather noticeable exception to the rule of universal succession which is a leading principle of succession law.[314]

Legatum per vindicationem may only be provided in a notarial testament and its objects have been exhaustively listed by the legislator in Article 981^1§2 PCC. The testator may therefore decide that a thing specified as to its identity, a transferrable property right, an enterprise or an agricultural farm is to be acquired by the legatee at the moment of the opening of the succession. The testator may also employ this mechanism to create the right of usufructus or an easement for the benefit of the legatee. *Legatum per vindicationem* is not to be effective if at the moment of the opening of the succession the object of this legacy does not belong to the testator, or the testator was obliged to transfer it to another person. Similarly, if a thing which was to be encumbered by usufructus or an easement does not belong to the testator

313. Act of 18 Mar. 2011, Journal of Statutes 2011, no. 85, item 458, published on 23 Apr. 2011.
314. A. Dyszlewska-Tarnawska, 'Article 981^1 Commentary', in M. Habdas, M. Fras (eds), *Kodeks*, 407–408.

at the moment of the opening of the succession, or the testator was obliged to transfer it to another person, the legacy is ineffective (Article 981^2 PCC).

Legatum per vindicationem cannot be subject to a condition or a time limit, and if the latter have been introduced, they are treated as non-existent. However, if the contents of the testament or circumstances indicate that the heir would not have provided for a *legatum per vindicationem* without the condition or time limit, the mentioned legacy shall be null and void. This does not apply to cases, in which the condition was satisfied or remained definitively unsatisfied or the time limit has elapsed before the opening of the succession (Article 981^3§1 PCC). If the *legatum per vindicationem* is null and void due to the stipulation of a condition or a time limit, it is to be treated as an ordinary legacy, which has been made subject to a condition or a time limit, unless the contents of the testament or circumstances indicate otherwise (Article 981^3§2 PCC). The testator may charge a legatee of the *legatum per vindicationem* with an ordinary legacy (Article 981^4§2 PCC).

Provisions on the appointment of an heir, the acceptance and waiver of the estate, the capacity to inherit and the unworthiness to inherit are to be applied to *legatum per vindicationem mutatis mutandis*. Issues not regulated by the above-mentioned provisions on *legatum per vindicationem* are to be resolved by a *mutatis mutandis* application of provisions on the ordinary legacy (Articles 981^5–981^6 PCC).

674. Ideas to include *mortis causa* donations[315] in succession law have also been voiced in academic writings. This requires further deliberations as it is necessary to decide whether *legatum per vindicationem* and *mortis causa* donations should both function or whether the legislator should retain only one of these institutions, which is currently the *legatum per vindicationem*. Discussions concentrate on perceptions of the society and the need to reflect them in succession law, as well as on issues connected with the extent to which the freedom of testamentary dispositions and the principle of universal succession may be limited.

C. Testamentary Burden

675. A testamentary burden is an obligation placed on the heir or the legatee to behave in an indicated manner. Although the burden indicates the parties charged with its performance, there is no corresponding beneficiary or entitled person (Article 983 PCC). Consequently, a testamentary burden does not create an obligational relationship, because there is no creditor. The burden is a debt that forms a part of the estate. Often the burden requires the charged person to spend the inherited money in a given way, to care for the testator's grave, to conduct the funeral in a specified manner, to volunteer for charity work, etc.

676. If the person charged with the burden is a legatee, he or she may withhold the performance until the legacy is executed by the heir. This rule is to be applied

315. E. Drozd, 'Darowizna na wypadek śmierci', *Rejent*, no. 1 (1992): 74 et seq.; J. Górecki, 'Umowa darowizny na wypadek śmierci', *Rejent*, no. 2 (2006): 29 et seq.

accordingly to situations in which the person charged with the burden is a sub-legatee (Article 983 PCC). If an heir was charged with a legacy and the legatee, who was charged with a burden, does not want to or cannot be a legatee, the heir who has been released from the duty to execute the legacy should perform the burden, unless the testator decided otherwise. The above applies accordingly to a burden placed on a sub-legatee (Article 984 PCC).

677. Although creating a testamentary burden does not make anyone a creditor, the legislator allows for particular persons to demand the performance of a burden.[316] According to Article 985 PCC, any heir, as well as the executor of the testament, may demand the performance of a testamentary burden unless its sole aim is to benefit the person charged with the burden (e.g., the person charged is to undergo medical treatment, continue his or her education, complete a training). If the burden is connected with a public interest, its performance may also be demanded by the competent public authority (Article 985 PCC).

III. The Executor of the Testament

678. The appointment of the executor of the testament is a testamentary disposition. If no executor has been appointed, his or her duties are performed by the heirs themselves. This may be a task which they find difficult to perform, particularly if there are many testamentary dispositions.[317] Also, although the heirs cannot change the will of the testator, they do to a large extent shape the fate of the estate and how it will be utilized and divided. If the testator wants to ensure that his or her will is carried out according to his or her wishes, he or she should appoint an executor (or executors) of the testament. The role of the latter is to administer the inherited estate, pay the inherited debts, in particular, execute the legacies and testamentary burdens, and then release the inherited estate to the heirs in accordance with the will of the testator and with statutory law (Article 988 §1 PCC). The testator may also appoint the executor to manage the estate, its part or a specified object within that estate (Article 986^1 PCC). The executor is not, however, entitled to divide the estate or file a motion to the probate court for such a division to be made. The testator may modify these duties and add other ones. After the entry into force of the PCC amendment which introduced the *legatum per vindicationem*, he may, in particular, appoint an executor to manage the object of the *legatum per vindicationem* until it is retrieved by the legatee (Article 990^1 PCC). It should also be mentioned that the executor is also responsible for handing over the object of the *legatum per vindicationem* to the entitled legatee (Article 988 §3 PCC).

679. The appointment of the executor must be done by the testator himself or herself. The testator cannot provide that the choice will be made by one of the heirs or by the court. The testator may indicate a substitute executor if the one originally appointed would not or could not assume his or her duties. The executor must have

316. *See* Supreme Court decision issued on 19 Apr. 2004, III CZP 19/02, LEX no. 74583.
317. K. Skubisz-Kępka, 'Article 986 Commentary', in M. Habdas, M. Fras (eds), *Kodeks*, 455.

full legal capacity to perform acts in law. He or she may be one of the heirs, a legatee or a third person. Since the legislator does not stipulate that it must be a physical person, it seems acceptable to allow for the executor to be a juristic person. This would be particularly beneficial if that juristic person happens to specialize in the management of assets, particularly real estate.

680. The appointment of the executor becomes effective at the moment of the opening of the succession but is not yet definite. If the person appointed as the executor does not wish to assume that duty, he or she must make a declaration to the court or in front of a notary (Article 987 PCC). It seems, that if the person appointed to be the executor actually began performing his or her duties, he or she cannot later decline being an executor on the basis of Article 987 PCC; however, the court has discretion to discharge the executor if important reasons to do so exist (Article 990 PCC).

681. The executor of the testament has a unique legal position. It cannot be denied that he or she does not act in his or her own interest, but he or she does act in his or her own name. In this respect, he or she is not a proxy of the heirs. His or her legal position does not resemble a proxy (who acts in the name and interest of the represented person) but an indirect substitute and should be viewed as a separate institution of succession law.

682. The executor may ask that a notary or a court of probate issue a certificate which confirms that he or she has been appointed the executor of the estate and stipulates the testator's: name, last place of residence, the date and place of the death (Article 665 PCPC). The executor may sue and be sued in matters resulting from the administration of the estate. He or she may also sue in matters concerning the rights belonging to the estate and be sued in matters concerning the inherited debts. He or she is entitled to remuneration, which constitutes a debt of the inherited estate. Other costs of administration of the estate are also included in the debts of the estate (Article 989 §2 PCC). The executor may, in particular, demand that an inventory of the estate be made (Article 637 §1 PCPC), demand that the objects belonging to the estate are disclosed (Article 655 §1 PCPC) and apply for a certificate of the acquisition of the estate by the heirs (Article 1025 §1 PCPC).

683. Once the executor begins performing his or her duties, an obligational relationship is created between him or her and the heirs. This relationship is to be governed by provisions on the remunerated mandate which are to be applied *mutatis mutandis* (Article 989 §1 PCC, also *see* Articles 734–751 PCC). If the executor's actions cause the heirs to suffer loss, his or her civil liability will be based on provisions concerning contractual liability (Articles 471 PCC and the following ones).

IV. The Succession Manager

684. The succession of businesses ran by sole traders, also known as self-employed entrepreneurs, poses unique challenges when the business owner dies.

Succession law mechanisms are not sufficient to ensure a smooth continuation of business activities and their transition to heirs. Without special legislation, upon the death of the sole trader: employment contracts automatically expire, the name of the enterprise that contains the name of the deceased can no longer be used, administrative decisions/licenses required to conduct certain types of business activities expire, access to bank accounts connected with the business is limited, etc.[318] In recognition of these difficulties, the legislator has introduced a new institution, namely the succession manager, whose legal position is regulated in the act of 5 July 2018 on the succession management of an enterprise of a physical person (ASM),[319] which entered into force on the 25 November 2018. The object of these provisions is to ensure a temporary management and continuation of the business by the succession manager, until the time that it can be taken over by the new owners. The act applies to sole traders who are physical persons and whose business activity is registered in a Central Register of Economic Activity (CREA).

685. The succession manager may be appointed in one of two ways. First, the sole trader may appoint the succession manager, by indicating the appropriate person or by stipulating that the commercial proxy will become the succession manager. This must be done in writing and the indicated person must express his/her consent, also observing the written form. The appointment must then be entered in the CREA (Articles 6 and 9 ASM). The appointment of the succession manager is a *mortis causa* juridical act of the sole trader that brings about legal effects upon his/her death.[320] The succession manager must be a physical person who has full legal capacity and who has not been banned (through a conviction or pursuant to bankruptcy law) from performing business activities (Article 9 ASM). There can only be one succession manager, however, the sole trader may appoint a succession manager, who will perform the function in the case the first succession manager has resigned or for other reasons cannot be the succession manager (i.e., has died or lost full legal capacity) (Article 11 ASM).

686. If the succession manager has not been appointed by the sole trader in the manner indicated above, that manager may be appointed by: the deceased sole trader's spouse, who has a share in the enterprise, by an intestate heir who has accepted the estate, by a testamentary heir, who has accepted the estate, or by the legatee per vindicationem, who has accepted the legacy, if the latter two have a share in the enterprise pursuant to the contents of the announced testament (Article 12 section 1 ASM). However, after the certificate of estate acquisition or the certificate of inheritance or the European certificate of inheritance has been issued and have become binding, the succession manager may only be appointed by the new owner of the enterprise (Article 12 section 2 ASM). The above persons may appoint the succession manager only if there has not been a previous appointment made by the sole

318. K. Wojarska-Aleksiejuk, P. Aleksjejuk, 'Ustawa o zarządzie sukcesyjnym w kontekście sukcesji firm rodzinnych w Polsce', *Nowy Przegląd Notarialny*, no. 1 (2019): 46.

319. Journal of Statutes 2018, item 1629.

320. K. Kopaczyńska-Pieczniak, 'Status prawny zarządcy sukcesyjnego', *Przegląd Prawa Handlowego* (no. 12): 4.

trader and no later than within two months from the date of the sole trader's death (Article 12 section 10 ASM). The appointment must, in this case, take the form of a notarial deed and the notary is obliged to file a motion for the entry of the succession manager in the CREA (Article 12 section 9 ASM).

687. The succession management of the business encompasses the whole or a part of the enterprise that belonged to the sole trader at the time of his/her death (Article 2 ASM). The succession manager acts in his/her own name, but for the account of the owners of the enterprise or its part that is the object of succession (Article 21 section 1 ASM). The business is conducted under its previous name with an added phrase 'in succession' (Article 17 section 1 ASM). The succession manager is entitled and obliged to undertake all factual and legal activities connected with running the business, including activities in front of courts and other public bodies (Article 21 ASM). However, all activities which classify as exceeding ordinary management require the consent of the enterprise owners and, in lack thereof, of the court (Article 22 ASM).[321] The succession manager is not entitled to sell the enterprise or a share then, as this exceeds his/her competencies of 'running the business' and is the sole prerogative of the owners of the enterprise.

688. An important aspect of succession management is the fact that the succession manager performs all rights and duties of the sole trader that relate to the business. This includes performing ongoing contracts, deciding on their termination, continuing the employment of business employees (Articles 29–31 ASM). Finally, the legislator delimits the competencies of a succession manager and those of the executor of the testament. Should both these positions exist (e.g., the executor of the testament was appointed in the testament and the succession manager was appointed by persons indicated in Article 12 sections 1–2 ASM), the executor of the testament acts within competencies specified in Articles 986–990^1 PCC, however with the exclusion of the enterprise, which remains within the sphere of the succession manager's competencies (Article 24 PCC).

689. Since the succession manager acts for the account of the enterprise owners, the latter are liable to creditors for the performance of contracts or other obligations, while the succession manager is free from such liability. The latter is liable to enterprise owners for loss resulting from inadequate performance of the duties specified by the legislator in ASM (Articles 32–35). The legislator also included detailed provisions on the possibility to continue the validity of administrative decisions/licenses that the sole trader had obtained in order to conduct a particular type of business activity. Succession management allows time (few months) to apply for such decisions to be confirmed as valid towards new enterprise owners. This may not always be possible if a business must be run by an individual with specified qualifications that new enterprise owners do not have (e.g., a pharmacy). In many cases, however, the validity of decisions will be confirmed or the business

321. *Also see* R. Kapkowski, M. Kaufmann, 'Charakter prawny zarządcy sukcesyjnego na tle pokrewnych instytucji zarządu masą spadkową', *Rejent,* no. 7 (2019): 54–88.

owners will have time to employ an individual with required qualifications, before the expiry of the license (*see* Articles 36–45 ASM).

690. Succession management is a temporary solution aimed at allowing the continuance of business activities before succession matters and new ownership issues are resolved. As a consequence, succession management is limited in time and expires or terminates upon the occurrence of specified events. First, the succession manager may be removed by the new business owner or by the court. The succession manager may also resign or lose his/her function as a result of losing full legal capacity or being convicted for particular crimes (*see* Articles 51–58 ASM). Second, succession management will expire:

(1) after two months from the death of the sole trader if during that period none of the heirs has accepted the estate or a legatee per vindicationem has not accepted the legacy containing the enterprise or a share therein unless the succession manager is acting on behalf of the sole trader's spouse who has a share in the enterprise;
(2) on the day the certificate of estate acquisition or the certificate of inheritance or the European certificate of inheritance has become binding if only one heir or legatee per vindicationem has acquired the whole enterprise;
(3) on the day the whole enterprise has been acquired by one of the persons listed in Article 3 section 3 ASM;
(4) after one month from deleting the succession manager from the CREA, unless during that time a new succession manager has been appointed;
(5) on the day the entrepreneur is declared insolvent;
(6) on the day a division of the estate, including the business, is effected;
(7) after two years from the death of the sole trader.

691. To summarize the institution of succession management, one should point out that it is a temporary arrangement with the purpose of managing a particular object, namely the enterprise (or its part) that is a part of the inherited estate. A succession manager is always a physical person whose role is to manage a specified part of the inherited estate, i.e., the enterprise. This allows the business activity of the deceased sole trader to be continued, particularly in the context of commercial contracts and employment contracts, as well as to secure further validity of administrative licences/consents required for particular types of business activities. The competencies of the succession manager are prescribed in legislation and they cannot be restricted.

§5. Legitim

692. The freedom of testamentary disposition is one of the most important rules in Polish succession law; however, if the testator's dispositions completely exclude his or her relatives from the estate, there is a danger that the interests of his or her closest family will be infringed. Meanwhile, succession law is based on the assumption that the estate of the deceased should first and foremost devolve to his or her family since in most cases they are the ones who contributed to its creation. Therefore, it would be unjust for third parties to acquire the estate with the complete exclusion of at least some members of the testator's closest family.[322]

693. The Polish institution of legitim is not based on the French system of forced heirship, in which the forced heir is in fact an heir of the estate and has a share in that estate. The Polish legitim does not cause the protected persons to become heirs of the estate but instead grants them a claim to receive a sum of money equivalent to the value of a part of the share they would have inherited in intestate succession. This system may be described as forced heirship by calculation (as opposed to the French system of forced heirship by fraction).

694. The legitim does not compromise the principle of the freedom of testamentary dispositions in the sense that the testator may effectively provide for all of his or her estates to devolve to third persons and completely exclude members of the family from inheriting. It does, however, oblige the heirs to pay a sum of money to the persons entitled to legitim and in this way allows them to benefit from the succession after their close relative. Only disinheriting the persons entitled to legitim will prevent them from acquiring any benefits from the succession, but the reasons for disinheritance are specified in succession law and cannot be extended to include situations not enumerated by the legislator.[323]

I. Persons Entitled to Legitim

695. The persons entitled to legitim are specified in Article 991 PCC. According to §1 of that provision, the above include the descendants, the spouse and the parents of the deceased. The latter are entitled only if they would have been appointed to inherit in statutory succession. This means that parents are entitled to legitim only when there are no descendants of the deceased. Parents are secondary heirs and may inherit jointly with the surviving spouse, but not with the deceased person's descendants.

696. Persons specified in Article 991 PCC are entitled to legitim regardless of whether the testator completely omitted them in his or her testament or whether they have been appointed as heirs or legatees in that testament. If they have not received the equivalent of the legitim either through testamentary succession, legacy or a donation the testator had made during his or her lifetime, they may demand the payment of a sum which will cover the legitim or supplement it.

697. Similarly, persons who have received certain benefits from the deceased during his or her lifetime will not be entitled to legitim at all or partially. According

322. W. Borysiak, 'O prawie spadkobierców ustawowych do zachowku – polemicznie', *Państwo i Prawo*, no. 5 (2008): 111 et seq.; T. Juszyński, 'Glosa do wyroku SN z dnia 7 kwietnia 2004 r., IV CK 215/03', *Państwo i Prawo*, no. 6 (2005): 111 et seq.

323. M. Załucki, 'Article 991 Commentary', in M. Habdas, M. Fras (eds), *Kodeks*, 480–481.

to Article 996 PCC, a donation or a *legatum per vindicationem* made by the deceased to a person entitled to a legitim is to be set off against that legitim. If the person entitled to a *legatum per vindicationem* is a more remote descendant of the deceased, the donation or a *legatum per vindicationem* made by the deceased to the ascendant of the entitled person is also to be set off against legitim. Additionally, if the person entitled to a legitim is a descendant of the deceased, the costs borne by the testator to bring him or her up and to allow him or her to receive a general or vocational education are to be set off against his or her legitim if such costs exceeded the average level accepted in a given society (Article 997 PCC). Obviously, if the benefits mentioned above amount to the value of the legitim, the person in question is not entitled to legitim at all.

698. The entitlement to legitim does not apply to persons who have been held unworthy to inherit, the surviving spouse who has been excluded from succession on the basis of Article 940 PCC (*see* above Chapter 2, §2, I: Primary Heirs), and heirs who have renounced succession or who have waived the estate in intestate succession.

II. The Calculation of Legitim

699. The sum that persons entitled to legitim may claim depends on two factors. The first one is connected with personal features of the entitled person. If that person is permanently unable to work or is a descendant who is still a minor (the moment of the opening of the succession is decisive in determining these circumstances), he or she is entitled to receive two-thirds of the value of the share he or she would have inherited in intestate succession. In all other cases, that fraction is equal to half of the mentioned share.

700. The second factor is the share the entitled person would have inherited, had intestate succession taken place. The calculation of this share is subject to special rules. According to Article 992 PCC, the share is calculated as if persons who have been held unworthy to inherit or have waived the estate did in fact inherit, however, statutory heirs who have renounced succession or have been disinherited are not taken into account.

701. Once the shares of potential statutory heirs of a given succession have been calculated according to the rules mentioned above, the share of the person entitled to legitim should be multiplied by either two-thirds or half.

702. The next step is to calculate the value of the estate, as the mentioned fraction is to be applied to that amount.[324] The value of the estate is determined by subtracting the value of the debts of the estate from the value of the assets of the

324. A. Szpunar, 'Uwagi o obliczaniu wysokości zachowku', *Rejent*, no. 4 (2002): 13 et seq.

estate.[325] The value of the debts does not include the value of legacies and testamentary burdens although they are debts of the estate (Article 993 PCC). The value of the assets of the estate is increased by the value of donations and the *legatum per vindicationem* the testator had made. Some donations are not added to the value of the estate. This is regulated in Article 994 PCC where it is stipulated that:

(1) minor donations which are customarily made in a given society, as well as ones made more than ten years before the opening of the succession to persons who are neither heirs nor are entitled to legitim, are not added to the value of the estate;
(2) when calculating the legitim due to a descendant, the donations made by the deceased at a time when he or she had no descendants are not added to the value of the estate, unless they had been made less than three hundred days before the birth of the descendant;
(3) when calculating the legitim due to the surviving spouse, the donations made by the deceased before he or she got married are not added to the value of the estate.

703. The value of the donations is to be determined with reference to the factual state at the time the donation had been made, but according to prices existent at the moment of calculating legitim (Article 995 §1 PCC). The value of the *legatum per vindicationem* is to be determined with reference to the factual state at the moment of the opening of the succession, but according to prices existent at the moment of calculating legitim (Article 995 §2 PCC). The value of the estate is to be determined with reference to the factual state at the moment of the opening of the succession, but according to prices existent at the moment of calculating legitim. Once the value of the estate has been calculated according to the mentioned rules, it is to be multiplied by a fraction derived in the manner described above.

III. Debtors of Legitim

704. The debtors of legitim are first and foremost testamentary heirs, as according to Article 992 §2 PCC the person entitled to legitim may claim the payment of a sum of money required to cover the legitim or to supplement it from the heir. The rules on being liable for legitim are further elaborated on in other provisions. Unfortunately, their application is not always clear and often reveals many contentious issues. The rules concerning the donees as debtors of legitim are particularly difficult to apply in practice. The above issues are regulated as follows.

705. If the person entitled to legitim is appointed to succession, he or she is liable for the legacies and testamentary burdens only to the amount which exceeds

325. *See* Supreme Court judgment issued on 14 Mar. 2008, IV CSK 509/07, LEX no. 445279.

the value of his or her own share in the estate. The share is to be calculated according to the rules of calculating a share for the purpose of legitim. This applies respectively when the legacy benefits a person entitled to legitim and the legacy was charged with a sub-legacy, testamentary burdens or was made subject to a condition or a time limit (Article 998 PCC). If an heir, who is obliged to pay legitim, is himself or herself entitled to legitim, his or her liability is limited to the amount which exceeds the value of his or her own legitim (Article 999 PCC).

706. After the entry into force of the PCC amendment which introduced the *legatum per vindicationem*, if the person entitled to legitim cannot obtain it from the heir, he may claim it from a person, who benefitted from the *legatum per vindicationem*, which has been added to the value of the estate. However, such a legatee is obliged to pay the mentioned sum only within the limits of the enrichment resulting from the legacy. If the mentioned legatee is himself entitled to legitim, his liability for legitim of other entitled persons is limited by the amount which exceeds the value of his own legitim. The legatee may discharge himself from the duty to pay legitim by handing over the object of the *legatum per vindicationem*. If there are several persons, who benefitted from the *legatum per vindicationem*, their liability is joint and several (Article 999^1 PCC). If the person entitled to legitim cannot obtain it from the heir or the person who benefited from the *legatum per vindicationem*, he or she may claim it from a person, to whom the testator had made a donation, which has been added to the value of the estate. However, the donee is obliged to pay the mentioned sum only within the limits of the enrichment resulting from the donation. If the donee is himself or herself entitled to legitim, his or her liability for legitim of other entitled persons is limited by the amount which exceeds the value of his or her own legitim. The donee may discharge himself or herself from the duty to pay legitim by handing over the object of the donation (Article 1000 PCC). If there are several donees, the entitled person should make his or her claim against the one who received his or her donation most recently. Access to less recent donees is admissible only when more recent ones cannot satisfy the claim of the person entitled to legitim (Article 1001 PCC).

707. Special rules apply to decreasing legacies and testamentary burdens if the heirs obliged to pay legitim are also obliged to perform legacies and testamentary burdens. These regulations reflect the view that legatees and persons entitled from testamentary burdens should also participate in satisfying legitim claims. Consequently, the heirs liable for the satisfaction of a legitim claim may themselves claim a proportional reduction of legacies and testamentary burdens (Article 1003 PCC). Again, there are practical difficulties in the proper interpretation and application of the following provisions.

708. The reduction of legacies and testamentary burdens is made proportionally to their respective values unless the testator decided otherwise in the testament. In the case of a reduction of a legacy burdened with a sub-legacy or a testamentary burden, that sub-legacy or burden is subject to a proportional reduction (Article 1004 PCC).

709. If an heir liable for the satisfaction of a legitim claim is himself or herself entitled to legitim, he or she may claim the reduction of the legacies and testamentary burdens to an extent necessary to retain his or her own legitim. If a legatee is himself or herself entitled to legitim, the legacy made to him or her is subject to a reduction only to the amount exceeding the value of his or her own legitim (Article 1005 PCC). If the reduction applies to a legacy of an indivisible object, the legatee may claim that the legacy be fully executed in return for an adequate payment made by the legatee to the person who was charged with the legacy (1006 PCC).

710. The claims for legitim as well as for the reduction of legacies and testamentary burdens are subject to a prescription period of five years from the moment of the publication of the testament. However, a claim to supplement the legitim directed against the donee or a person who benefited from the *legatum per vindicationem* is subject to that same prescription period from the moment of the opening of succession (Article 1007 PCC).[326]

IV. Disinheritance

711. Being disinherited by the testator denotes a disposition, which has the effect of depriving the entitled persons of their right to legitim. This technical meaning of being disinherited is not usually recognized by members of the Polish society, who most often identify being disinherited with either not being appointed to inherit in a testament or with being excluded from intestate succession through a negative testament.[327]

712. The testator may disinherit persons entitled to legitim only in a valid testament, and a testament may only consist of the disposition on disinheriting the persons entitled to legitim. The testator does not have to apply the verb 'to disinherit', but it must be clear from what has been written, that the testator wanted to deprive the entitled parties of their right to legitim.[328]

713. In Polish succession law, the reasons for disinheriting persons entitled to legitim are stipulated exhaustively (and cannot be subject to an extensive interpretation) in Article 1008 PCC, according to which the testator may in his or her testament deprive his or her descendants, spouse and parents of their respective legitim, if the entitled person:

(1) contrary to the will of the testator persistently behaved in contravention of the principles of community life;

326. A. Szpunar, 'Przedawnienie uprawnień z tytułu zachowku', *Rejent*, no. 9 (2001): 61 et seq.
327. E. Niezbecka, 'Skutki prawne testamentu negatywnego i wydziedziczenia', *Rejent*, no. 7–8 (1992): 16 et seq.
328. M. Pogonowski, 'Wydziedziczenie. Zarys problematyki', *Rejent*, no. 4 (2005): 121 et seq.

(2) committed with respect to the testator or one of the persons closest to him or her an intentional offence against life, health or freedom, or a glaring insult to their dignity;
(3) persistently neglects family duties with respect to the testator.

714. An heir may be both unworthy to inherit on the basis of Article 928 §1 PCC and be disinherited.

715. In the first of the mentioned grounds for disinheriting, it is important to note that the behaviour must not only be contrary to the will of the testator but must also be persistent and violate the principles of community life. Therefore, if the testator's daughter had, against his or her will, persistently pursued her career, postponing marriage and having children, she cannot be disinherited, because such a choice is not contrary to the principles of community life. The grounds mentioned in the second point should be understood in the context of penal law; however, persons who are considered to be the testator's closest companions should not be identified with the penal law definition of a 'close person'. The testator's closest companions are persons who were so close to him or her, that an offence against one of them would be treated by the testator as an offence against him or her. Such persons can include more or less distant relatives, de facto spouses, same-sex partners of the testator, his or her long-time friends, etc. Finally, grounds for disinheriting mentioned in the third point include a wide range of duties resulting from family ties, like not only supplying the testator with means necessary for a decent existence, helping him or her in everyday life but also just keeping in touch with him or her, informing him or her of important matters so that he or she does not worry unnecessarily, etc.[329] Neglecting such duties must be persistent. This ground for disinheriting an heir is perhaps one of the more frequently encountered one. It should be noted, however, that parents who have deserted their children have been held not to have grounds for disinheriting a child by showing that s/he had neglected family duties. In cases where children deserted by a parent are not, later in their life, interested in developing a relationship with a person who has effectively become a stranger to them and does not participate in care for that parent when s/he is elderly, they cannot be disinherited. According to the Roman principle of *nemo turpitudinem suam allegans auditur*, one must conclude that a person who is responsible for breaking family ties cannot reap benefits from that fact and cannot transfer negative consequences to the innocent party.[330]

716. The legislator requires that the reason for disinheriting a person entitled to legitim be evident from the contents of the testament (Article 1009 PCC). Disinheriting an heir will not be effective if: the reason for disinheriting is not evident; although the reason is evident, it does not reflect the factual state of affairs; and the

329. *See* Supreme Court judgment issued on 7 Nov. 2002, II CKN 1397/00, LEX no. 75286.
330. *See* Supreme Court judgment issued on 23 Mar. 2018, I CSK 424/17, LEX no. 2510953; similar judgments of: Court of Appeals in Poznań judgment issued on 5 Apr. 2018, I Aca 1095/17, LEX no. 2546257; Court of Appeals in Białystok judgment issued on 11 Sep. 2018, I Aca 612/17, LEX no. 2574885.

reason is evident but is not included in the grounds for disinheritance stipulated in Article 1008 PCC. In such cases, it would be constructive to carefully interpret the testator's will to see if his or her dispositions could be understood as a negative testament, that is, the testator also wanted to exclude an heir from intestate succession.

717. The testator cannot disinherit a person entitled to legitim if he or she had forgiven him or her. The act of forgiveness is not an act in law but is a demonstration of feelings. Therefore, it is not required that at the time of forgiving, the testator had full legal capacity to perform acts in law. It is enough if the testator had acted with sufficient understanding of his or her actions (Article 1010 PCC). Forgiveness should take place before disinheriting in a testament persons entitled to legitim, but after learning about circumstances which justify disinheriting a statutory heir. A contentious issue concerns the effects of the act of forgiveness that occurred after the testator had already disinherited persons entitled to legitim. There are opinions that if forgiveness occurs after the disinheritance, it does not remove its effects and the testator should make a new testament or amend the one in which he or she disinherited persons entitled to legitim if he or she does not want them to remain disinherited. Others argue that such forgiveness will effectively override the disinheritance and it does not require the observation of any form.[331]

718. Finally, it is necessary to note, that the descendants of the disinherited descendant shall be entitled to their respective legitim even if the disinherited descendant survived the testator (Article 1011 PCC).

331. J. St. Piątowski, *Prawo spadkowe. Zarys wykładu* (Warszawa: PWN, 1973), 278; E. Skowrońska -Bocian, *Prawo spadkowe* (Warszaw: C.H. Beck, 2018), 115; Supreme Court resolution issued on 14 Jun. 1971, III CZP 24/71, OSNC 1972/2/23.

Chapter 4. The Legal Position of the Heir

719. As has already been mentioned, the devolution of the estate occurs 'automatically' at the moment of the opening of the succession. The heirs inherit the estate of the deceased but the acquisition is temporary because the heirs have rights which allow them to shape their legal position. The decisions that they make will affect their liability for the debts of the estate but will also allow them to express their desire to remain heirs of the estate or not.

§1. Waiver and Acceptance of the Estate

720. Each heir can decide whether to accept the estate or not. An acceptance may be one in which there is no limitation of liability for debts of the estate (simple acceptance) or one, which limits the liability for debts up to the value of the estate's assets (acceptance with the benefit of inventory). An heir may also decide to waive the estate, in which case he or she is treated as if he or she had predeceased (Article 1020 PCC). All interested parties who, according to available information, are appointed to inherit as more remote heirs must be informed about the acceptance or waiver of the estate (Article 643 PCPC). Although the legislator does not specify whether this is a task of the probate court or of the notary who obtained the heir's declaration, it seems that the former is charged with this duty.

I. Types of Acceptance and Waiver

721. As a rule, an heir cannot partly accept the estate and partly waive it (Article 1014 §3 PCC). There are, however, some exceptions. First, the acceptance or waiver of a share in the estate that the heir receives as a result of substitution may occur regardless of an acceptance or waiver of a share in the estate which the heir receives as a result of other succession law mechanisms (Article 1014 §1 PCC). Second, an heir may waive his or her proportion of a 'vacant' share (i.e., one which is divided to proportionally increase the shares of testamentary heirs who do inherit) but may accept the share that he or she receives through his or her appointment as an heir (Article 1014 §2 PCC). It is not possible to do the opposite, since, in order to be entitled to a portion of the vacant share, one must be a testamentary heir. Consequently, a waiver of the share received as a result of being appointed as an heir precludes the possibility of accepting a portion of the vacant share. Third, an heir who has been appointed to inherit as both a testamentary and a statutory heir, may waive his or her testamentary share but accept his or her statutory one (Article 1022 PCC). Although the legislator does not expressly permit to do the opposite, there are no reasons for not allowing the heir to accept his or her statutory share and waive the testamentary one.

722. The situation of the local authority or the State who are heirs of the estate is slightly different. These juridical persons cannot waive an estate that they have inherited as statutory heirs, because Polish succession law does not allow for the creation of estates with no owners. If the local authority or the State are statutory heirs, they do not make a declaration as to the acceptance of the estate. That acceptance is always one with the limitation of debts up to the value of the estate's assets (Article 1023 PCC). The local authority or the State may waive a testamentary share. It also seems that it would be impossible for a foundation created in a testament in order to inherit the estate of the deceased to waive that estate. This would be incompatible with the purpose of creating such a foundation, particularly since its existence is derived from a *mortis causa* disposition.

723. If the heir waived the estate to the disadvantage of his or her creditors, each of the creditors whose receivable debt existed at the time of the waiver may demand for it to be considered ineffective with respect to him or her in accordance with the provisions on the protection of the creditors in the case of the debtor's insolvency (Article 1024 §1 PCC). The demand may be made within six months from the time the creditor had learnt about the waiver, but no later than three years after the waiver had been made (Article 1024 §2 PCC).

II. Time and Form of the Acceptance and Waiver

724. The legislator introduces a six-month time period within which the heirs may make their declarations about the acceptance or waiver of the estate. The time starts running separately for each heir and is connected with the day on which an heir has learnt about his or her title to inherit (Article 1015 §1 PCC; this may happen simultaneously for all heirs but does not have to).[332] Learning about the title to inherit must first and foremost be connected with a positive knowledge of the deceased person's death. Moreover, if succession is based on a testament, the heir must know that such a testament exists and that he or she has been appointed as an heir. If succession is based on statute, the heir must know that he or she is a relative of the deceased, for example, that he or she is his or her child. Sometimes it will be important to know that a testament has been held to be invalid and intestate succession is taking place or that others have waived the estate and more remote heirs become appointed to succession.[333]

725. The declaration must be made in front of a notary or the probate court. It cannot be subject to a condition or a time limit, otherwise, it is null and void. Once the declaration has been made it cannot be revoked (Article 1018 PCC). The declaration may be made by persons who have full legal capacity to perform acts in law or by representatives of persons who do not have such capacity. The declaration may be made by a proxy, who has been appointed in a written document with the represented person's signature endorsed by a public official. If parents wish to successfully waive the estate on behalf of their child (e.g., because it contains

332. J. Pisuliński, 'Niektóre problemy związane z terminem do złożenia oświadczenia o przyjęciu lub odrzuceniu spadku', *Rejent*, no. 6 (1992): 54 et seq.
333. Supreme Court judgment issued on 15 Jan. 1991, III CZP 75/90, OSNC 1991/5-6/68.

numerous debts), they must have prior consent from the court. Such an act is considered to exceed matters of ordinary management and thus requires the parents to approach the court for consent (Article 101§3 FGC). Although there have been conflicting judgments, the most recent opinion of the Supreme Court is that when parents apply for the court's consent to waive the estate, the six-month time limit stops running until the court delivers its decision.[334]

726. If the six months' period is not observed and no declaration about the waiver or acceptance of the estate has been made by the heir, this results in a definite acceptance of the estate. Due to the October 2015 PCC amendment, the effects of the acceptance are different for estates opened before 18 October 2015 and for ones opened on or after that date (*see* Chapter 1, §1, I). In the former situation, no declaration within the six-month period brings about a simple acceptance of the estate, that is, one with no limitation of liability for debts of the estate. However, if the heir is a person who does not possess full capacity to perform acts in law, there are grounds to fully incapacitate him or her, or he or she is a juristic person, the lack of a declaration denotes an acceptance of the estate with the benefit of the inventory (Article 1015 §2 PCC prior to the October 2015 amendment). Moreover, if at least one of the heirs has accepted the estate with the benefit of inventory (either expressly or by virtue of the application of Article 1015 PCC prior to the October 2015 amendment), it is recognized that all heirs who have not made their declaration in the specified time limit have accepted the estate in the same way.

In cases of estates opened on or after 18 October 2015, the lack of a declaration within the six-month period results in accepting the estate with the benefit of the inventory. Consequently, the heir is liable only up to the estate's assets' value (Article 1015 §2 current version).

727. If the heir died before the lapse of six months within which he or she could have accepted or waived the estate but had made no such declaration, it can be made by his or her heirs. This mechanism is called transmission because the right to make the declaration is transmitted to the heirs of the original heir.[335] The time limit they have to make the declaration cannot end before the time limit these heirs have to accept or waive the estate of the deceased (Article 1017 PCC).

III. Mistake and Threat

728. Although the acceptance or waiver of the estate cannot be revoked, the declaration may have deficiencies caused by the existence of a mistake or threat (undue influence). In such circumstances, the heir who made the defective declaration may avoid its legal effects by a stipulation made before the probate court. Simultaneously, the heir must also declare whether and how he or she accepts the estate. This also applies to an heir who as a result of an error or threat made no declaration within the specified time limit about the acceptance or waiver of the inheritance.

334. Supreme Court decision issued on 20 Nov. 2014, OSNC 2014/9/93, LEX.

335. K. Matuszyk, 'Kilka uwag o transmisji spadku', *Palestra*, no. 11–12 (2006): 97 et seq.

The stipulation made before the court must be approved by that court (Article 1019 PCC). Provisions on mistakes and threats contained in Book I of PCC apply *mutatis mutandis* (*see* Articles 84–88 PCC). This denotes that the mistake should be relevant in the sense that had the heir possessed proper information about the estate, he or she would not have accepted it. Also, the heir should make his or her stipulation before the court of probate within one year of finding out about his or her mistake or from the moment when the threat ceased to exist.

729. In practice, there are a lot of cases where heirs would like to avoid the legal effects of accepting the estate (usually due to the lapse of the six-month period mentioned above) when they realize that it contains debts that amount to or even exceed the value of the estate's assets. Even though currently heirs inherit the estate with the benefit of the inventory, if it is encumbered with substantial debts, they may not be interested in being part of legal proceedings brought by the creditors who may try to show that there is some money in the estate to cover the debt. Even if the heirs successfully show that debts exceed the value of the estate or that they have already satisfied creditors up to the amount of the balance of the assets and debts, they will have spent considerable time and money on legal proceedings. This will not be worth the gain if the debts are almost as high as the value of the assets of the estate. In such situations, it will be safer for the heirs to waive the estate.

730. The question that arises is whether a mistake as to the contents of the estate, in particular the debts that it includes, is indeed a legally relevant mistake that enables one to rely on Article 1019. The mistake may in fact concern two issues. The first one is an issue connected with the assessment of facts, i.e., a mistake as to what actually constitutes a given estate. The second one is an issue of legal assessments, i.e., the mistake was caused by the fact that the heir did not know he or she would be liable for the debts of the deceased or thought that no activity to accept the estate results in its waiver.

The first issue has been considered in various court judgments. Judges accept that a mistake as to the contents of the estate, in particular the debts it comprises, is relevant and may warrant the application of Article 1019 PCC. The courts emphasize that the heir's lack of knowledge about the debts of the estate despite reasonable and possible efforts to learn about the deceased person's obligations does qualify as a mistake under Article 1019 PCC.[336] The mistake as to the debts of the estate cannot, however, be caused by neglecting to find out whether the estate does contain debts. By being negligent, the heir bears the risk and consequences of being mistaken. The lack of knowledge about the debts must therefore be justified by the circumstances of the case.[337] It is thus necessary to examine whether there were acts that the heir could have reasonably taken to find out about the debts of the estate. These acts must have been factually and legally possible to undertake as well as reasonably expected from an heir in given circumstances.[338]

336. Supreme Court decision issued on 5 Jul. 2012, IV CSK 612/11, LEX no. 1224805.
337. Supreme Court decision issued on 1 Dec. 2011, I CSK 85/11, LEX no. 1147725.
338. Supreme Court decision issued on 29 Nov. 2012, II CSK 172/12, LEX no. LEX no. 1299156.

A more difficult situation concerns the mistake about the legal provisions regulating the heirs' liability for the debts of the deceased. The question that arises is whether one should apply the Roman principle of *ignorantia iuris nocet* (being unaware of the law hurts) or not. It seems that the courts have allowed for a mistake as to the law to be taken into account under Article 1019 PCC as long as it is relevant and justified by circumstances of a given case. In particular, the court held that a daughter's mistake as to not inheriting her father's debts was relevant and justified by the circumstances. The daughter acquired the age of majority a couple of months before her father's death and was informed by her mother that due to the separation of property regime between her and the deceased husband, the daughter could not inherit debts from her father. The court held that the daughter who had just acquired the age of majority could not have been reasonably expected to understand marital property regimes and question her mother's information about the effects of succession.[339]

IV. The Inventory

731. Making an inventory of the estate is very important when the estate has been accepted with the benefit of inventory, that is, with the limitation of liability up to the estate assets' value. For estates opened after 18 October 2015 acceptance with the benefit of the inventory takes place automatically, if the heir did not declare otherwise within a period of six months from learning about his title to inherit. For estates opened before that date, the benefit of the inventory as a rule requires an explicit declaration from the heir (*see* II above).

The limitation of liability for the debts of the estate will have no practical effect if an inventory is not prepared. There is no obligation or penalty for not preparing an inventory; however, its lack prevents the heir from successfully relying on his or her limited liability for the debts of the estate. For inventory proceedings initiated but not concluded before 18 October 2015, the currently repealed Article 644 PCPC will still apply. According to that provision, the probate court will ex officio request that an inventory be made if the estate has been accepted with the benefit of inventory and the latter has not yet been made (Article 644 PCPC) or a curator of the estate has been appointed (Article 666 PCPC). This does not apply to situations in which the acceptance with the benefit of inventory occurred *ex lege* on the basis of Articles 1015 §2 and 1023 §2 PCC.

732. If there is no court ruling requesting the inventory to be made, the court will give such a ruling upon the request of a person who shows that he or she is a potential heir, legatee or one entitled to legitim. This request may also be made by the executor of the testament, a creditor whose claim against the deceased is evidenced in writing or a tax revenue office (Article 637 PCPC). The party entitled to

339. Supreme Court decision issued on 29 Nov. 2012, II CSK 171/12, LEX no. LEX no. 1294475.

request the making of an inventory can approach the bailiff directly, who will immediately start his or her activities and inform the probate court so that a ruling on the making of an inventory may be given. Without it, the inventory made by the bailiff will have no legal effects.

733. A new version of provisions PCC and PCPC applies to inventory proceedings which have not been initiated before 18 October 2015. Due to the fact that from 18 October 2015 the acceptance of the estate with the benefit of the inventory is the default, automatic option, the legislator decided to amend and develop provisions concerning the inventory. Currently, the inventory may take two different forms, namely: the list of inventory or the register of inventory. The value of inventory items indicated in either the list or the register is the upper limit of the heir's liability for the estate's debts. This limitation does not apply if the heir fraudulently did not indicate objects that are a part of the estate or have been designated as objects of the *legatum per vindicationem* or fraudulently indicated debts that do not exist (Article 1031 §2 PCC).

734. The list of inventory may be prepared and presented to a notary or the probate court by each heir, the executor of the testament or the person entitled to the *legatum per vindicationem* (Article 1031^1 §1 PCC). This means that more than one list may be prepared. The above persons may jointly prepare such a list (Article 1031^1 §2 PCC). The list of inventory is to be prepared with due diligence and indicate all assets of the estate together with their value according to their state and prices at the date the succession was opened. In addition, the list should contain all debts of the estate together with an indication of their value according to the state at the date the succession was opened (Article 1031^1 §3 PCC). If additional items of the estate are discovered after the inventory had been presented to a notary or the probate court, those who prepared it are obliged to update the list (Article 1031^1 §4 PCC).

Persons who prepared a list of inventory are to pay the debts of the estate in accordance with that list, but they cannot rely on the lack of knowledge about other lists of inventory prepared by other heirs, the executor of the testament or persons entitled to *legatum per vindicationem* (Article 1031^3 PCC). More detailed provisions concerning the preparation of the list of inventory are contained in an ordinance of 22 September 2015 r. concerning the template for inventory lists.[340]

735. Unlike the list of inventory, the preparation of the register of inventory is ordered by the probate court at the request of anyone who shows the probability of being an heir, a person entitled to legitim, a person entitled to a legacy, or the executor of the testament as well as at the request of a creditor who has written proof of his or her claim against the deceased person (Article 637 PCPC). The request to prepare the register of the inventory may also be made directly to the bailiff (Article 637^1 PCPC). In both cases, it is the bailiff who prepares the register, indicating all assets (including objects of the *legatum per vindicationem*) and debts of the estate

340. Journal of Statutes 2015, item 1537.

along with their values (Article 638^8 PCPC). If the register needs to be supplemented due to new information on assets or debts not previously included, the court orders such a supplement (Article 638^{11} PCPC).

736. The preparation of inventory lists and registers is announced by the court on its website and on bulletin boards in the courthouse (638^1 PCPC). Anyone who justifies the need to examine the inventory list will be allowed to do so. The announcement of the preparation of the register contains information that anyone who shows the probability of being an heir, a person entitled to legitim, a person entitled to a legacy, or the executor of the testament, as well as a creditor who has written proof of his or her claim against the deceased person, may take part in the bailiff's activities in the process of preparing the register of inventory.

§2. The Certificate of Estate Acquisition and the Certificate of Inheritance

737. The acquisition of the estate by the heirs occurs *ex lege* and therefore may potentially cause doubts as to who is an heir and in what proportion. Moreover, the heirs will not be able to prove their rights to third parties if the only document they can present is a physical person's act of death since it does not in any way show who the heir is and what type of succession (intestate or testamentary) has taken place. Consequently, it is necessary for the heirs to obtain a certificate of estate acquisition (issued by the court of probate) or a certificate of inheritance (issued by a notary).[341]

738. The importance of the above is also connected with a rule according to which, with respect to a third party, who does not claim any rights to the estate by virtue of inheritance, the heir may prove his or her rights resulting from succession only by presenting a certificate of estate acquisition or a registered certificate of inheritance (Article 1027 PCC). This is particularly important when real estate has been inherited and the heirs would like to have their names entered in the land register as the new owners.

739. The certificates are connected with the presumption, that the person who has obtained them is in fact an heir of the deceased (Article 1025 §2 PCC). If both documents have been issued, the presumption derived from the probate court certificate of estate acquisition overrides the presumption derived from the notarial certificate of inheritance (Article 1025 §3 PCC).

740. The presumption is rebuttable only in special court proceedings. Anyone wishing to prove that the person who obtained a certificate of estate acquisition or a certificate of inheritance is not an heir or has a different share in the estate must instigate proceedings to revoke or amend these certificates. If the applicant took part

341. M. Blok, 'Notarialny akt poświadczenia dziedziczenia a sądowe stwierdzenie praw do spadku', *Rejent*, no. 7–8 (2010): 9 et seq.

in the process of issuing the certificates he or she may not demand their revocation or amendment unless his or her claim is based on grounds that could not have been presented in that process. His or her request must be brought no later than one year after the applicant has gained the possibility to rely on such grounds (Article 679 PCPC). Applicants other than the above do not have a time limit within which to instigate the mentioned proceedings. They include anyone who has an interest in revoking or amending the issued certificate.

741. The probate court will revoke a registered certificate of inheritance if a certificate of estate acquisition has been issued with respect to the same estate. If more than one certificate of inheritance has been registered, the court will revoke all of them and issue a certificate of estate acquisition at the request of an interested party (Article 669^1 PCPC).

742. It is necessary to point out, that certificates cannot be issued before the lapse of six months from the opening of the succession unless all known heirs have already made their declarations concerning the acceptance or waiver of the estate (Article 1026 PCC). The certificates do not bring about a change of legal rights and duties but merely acknowledge and evidence the effects of the opening of the succession.

I. Procedure

A. Probate Court

743. The court instigates proceedings at the request of anyone who has an interest in obtaining a certificate of estate acquisition.[342] This definitely includes, but is not limited to, the heirs, a person who has acquired the estate from the heirs, the creditors of the deceased or of the heir. The right to request a certificate of acquisition is not a claim; therefore, it is not subject to prescription. General rules of making an application in non-litigation proceedings apply, with the exception that the request must indicate all parties interested in the case (Article 511 PCPC).

744. This is further expanded on in Article 669 PCPC where it is stipulated that the court conducts a hearing to which all potential testamentary and statutory heirs are subpoenaed. The court examines ex officio who the heirs are and in particular examines whether the deceased had left a testament. If so, the court requires the person who most probably has the testament to submit it in court. Once the testament is submitted, the court opens and publishes it (Article 670 PCPC). If there is a dispute concerning the validity of the testament, the court resolves it during these proceedings. The court may not, however, make decisions as to the unworthiness of an heir to inherit (this requires separate litigious proceedings) or determine the components of the estate.

342. *See* Supreme Court decision issued on 6 Feb. 2008, II CSK 433/07, LEX no. 497677.

745. The court may accept as evidence an assurance made by an heir that there are no other heirs. This assurance should also include all other circumstances relating to the existence of other heirs that would inherit concurrently or as more remote relatives and to the testaments made by the deceased. The court informs the heir that his or her assurance is subject to penal liability and is equivalent to testifying under oath (Article 671 PCPC).

746. If the mentioned assurance has not been made or it is not accepted by the court as sufficient, the certificate may be issued only after a subpoena of other heirs through an announcement (Article 672 PCPC). The latter is to be published in a paper which is read in the whole country, and additionally, it should be made available to the public in the deceased person's last place of residence (Article 674 PCPC). If no persons had responded to the announcement within six months of its publication, the court will issue the certificate of estate acquisition. The certificate must determine the legal situation of the estate in a comprehensive manner, that is, all the heirs and their respective shares in the estate must be indicated (Article 677 PCPC).

B. The Notary

747. A certificate of inheritance issued by a notary is regulated in Article 95a–p LNA. It is a fairly new institution in Polish succession law since the respective legal provisions came into force on 2 October 2008.[343] Its introduction has been positively assessed by the courts, notaries, but above all the citizens, because access to a notary is much simpler, faster and less stressful than instigating court proceedings, not to mention that it is also very inexpensive. The notary costs for issuing the certificate of inheritance cannot exceed PLN 50 (approximately EUR 12.50), and the mandatory preparation of the written record of inheritance costs up to PLN 100 (approximately EUR 25).

748. The notary may issue the certificate for both intestate and testamentary successions, excluding successions based on extraordinary testaments. Before issuing the certificate of inheritance, the notary prepares a written record of inheritance in the presence of all persons who are potential testamentary or statutory heirs. The certificate may only be issued upon the unanimous request of all the persons present (*see* Article 95c §2 LNA).[344]

749. The notary is not entitled to ex officio examine who the heirs are but must rely on statements made by the potential heirs. The latter are obliged to reveal the existence or non-existence of all persons who may potentially inherit as well as

343. Act of 24 Aug. 2007, Journal of Statutes 2007, no. 181, item 1287.
344. M. Manowska, 'Wybrane zagadnienia dotyczące poświadczenia dziedziczenia', *Nowy Przegląd Notarialny*, no. 3 (2008): 16 et seq.

information about the existence or non-existence of testaments. Persons making statements before the notary must tell the truth and face penal liability for perjury (Article 95c §1 LNA).

750. The certificate of inheritance identifies the heirs and their shares in the estate. A list of all the components of such a certificate is contained in Article 95f LNA. Immediately after the preparation of the certificate, the notary registers it in an electronic register of certificates of inheritance. The registration number and date is shown on the certificate of inheritance (Article 95h §4). If the certificate issued by the notary relates to an estate which has already been the object of a different certificate of inheritance, the system will not register a new certificate (Article 95h §5). The certificate becomes binding once it has been successfully registered.

After the entry into force of the PCC amendment which introduces the *legatum per vindicationem*, the certificate of estate acquisition and the certificate of inheritance will also include information of the person who acquired a given object or a right by virtue of *legatum per vindicationem*.

II. Legal Effects

751. An heir may prove his or her rights resulting from succession only by presenting a certificate of estate acquisition or a registered certificate of inheritance. Therefore, in relation to third parties, including public offices, the certificate is the only proof of having inherited an estate. The heir does not need to have the certificate in disputes where other heirs or persons who claim that they are heirs are involved. The certificates are not necessary for an heir to take possession of the estate and manage it. The creditors of the deceased, legatees, persons entitled to legitim can sue the heirs regardless of whether a certificate has been issued or not. This also applies to persons who acquired objects by *legatum per vindicationem*.

752. The certificate also performs an important role in the protection of persons who are in good faith and conclude an act in law relating to a component of the estate with the person who, according to the certificate, is an heir. According to Article 1028 PCC, a person who is in good faith and has relied on the certificate will acquire a right or be discharged from a duty, even if the contracting party is not an heir. The provision only applies to the protection of third parties, that is, to persons who are not themselves heirs.

§3. The Protection of Succession

753. A special claim is available to an heir who is not in custody of the estate or of some of its elements. He or she may demand the return of the estate or its elements from a person who is not an heir but controls the estate or its elements as if he or she were the heir (Article 1029 §1 PCC). The claim may be brought by an heir as well as his or her heirs, a person who acquired the estate, the executor of the testament or the curator of the estate. The claim is directed against a person who controls at least one element of the estate as if he or she were the heir. The entitled party demands that the estate or its elements be returned to him or her and therefore his or her claim should include a detailed account of the objects he or she wishes to recover.

754. The claimant does not have to possess a certificate of estate acquisition or of inheritance because in the proceedings he or she can prove his or her succession by providing the relevant evidence. He or she does not have to prove that the deceased was in fact the owner of the objects in question but must simply show that the latter had them in his or her control at the time of his or her death. The claim will not be successful if the defendant proves, that he or she is the owner of the object or that the plaintiff is not an heir.

755. Provisions on the claims between the owner and the autonomous possessor of a thing apply respectively to the claims of the heir for remuneration for the use of objects belonging to the estate, for the return of the fruits or for the payment of their value, and also for the redress of the damage caused by wear and tear, deterioration or loss of those objects, and to claims against the heir for the return of outlays (Article 1029 §2 PCC).

756. The claim derived from Article 1029 §1 PCC is subject to a prescription period of six years from the time the heir was deprived of control over the estate or its objects. If the heir never had such control, that time limit begins to run from the day of the opening of the succession.

§4. The Heir's Liability

757. The estate comprises not only rights but also duties or obligations of the deceased as well as some duties which arise upon the death of the testator. Therefore, the heirs upon the acquisition of the estate (at the moment of the opening of the succession) immediately become liable for the debts of the testator. The extent of their liability is shaped by the acceptance or waiver of the estate as well as the later division of the estate. It is also necessary to remember that the initial acquisition of the estate is not definite, because the heir may waive the entire estate. Consequently, an analysis of the heirs' liability will differ depending on whether one considers the period before or after declarations of acceptance and waiver can be made and whether a division of the estate has taken place.

I. Liability Before the Acceptance or Waiver of the Estate

758. The initial acquisition of the estate is provisional in the sense that an heir may, within a specified time limit, waive the estate. The liability of heirs who still have time to declare whether they want to accept or waive the estate is strictly connected with the estate itself and does not extend to the heir's other property. This rule is expressed in Article 1030 PCC and it denotes that the liability of the heir is limited to the deceased person's estate. This is a *cum viribus hereditatis* limitation.

759. Creditors of the deceased who wish to satisfy their claims may only demand execution from the components of the inherited estate. At the same time, creditors of the heir may not satisfy their claims from those components (Article 836 PCPC). In practice, this type of liability occurs when the debtor dies during execution proceedings and the heirs cannot be identified. The creditors of the deceased may request that the court appoint a curator of the estate, which will allow them to continue execution from the components of the estate.

II. Liability after the Acceptance of the Estate

A. *Simple Acceptance*

760. Once an heir has declared a simple acceptance of the estate or the time to accept or waive the estate has elapsed without any declaration on the part of the heir (for successions opened before 18 October 2015), his or her liability for the inherited debts is no longer limited to the estate. The heir now answers to the creditors with his or her entire estate, which includes the assets that he or she had before succession occurred and the inherited share in the estate. This rule applies regardless of whether the acceptance of the estate was a simple one or one with the benefit of inventory. The type of acceptance is however important in determining a monetary limit of the heir's liability. Obviously, if the *acceptance was a simple one*, the heir's liability is not in any way limited (Article 1031 §1 PCC) and the creditors have access to all of his or her property in accordance with provisions on execution proceedings. Notwithstanding the above, the liability for legitim and legacies is always limited to the value of estate assets (Article 1033 PCC). If their value exceeds the value of estate assets, they are to be proportionally decreased.

B. *Acceptance with the Benefit of Inventory*

761. If the acceptance was made with the benefit of inventory (either expressly or, for successions opened on or after 18 October 2015, automatically, if the heir made no declaration), the heir's liability is limited by the value of the estate's assets identified in the inventory. The creditors do have access to all of the heir's property, but they cannot execute claims in excess of the estate assets' value *(pro viribus hereditatis* limitation). For successions opened before the October 2015 amendment of the PCC, this limitation of the heir's liability does not apply if the heir fraudulently did not indicate objects that are a part of the estate or have been designated as objects of the *legatum per vindicationem* or fraudulently indicated debts that do not exist (Article 1031 §2 PCC).

762. The practical application of the *pro viribus hereditatis* limitation of liability may be difficult for an heir, particularly if the estate debts exceed the estate assets. Polish succession law does not have institutions such as setting the estate apart (like the German *Nachlassabsonderung*), the public citation of creditors (a public summons to creditors to file their claims), the liquidation of the estate or summoning a creditors' meeting. There are also no indications relating to the order in which the creditors should be satisfied. Moreover, the heir has no legal means of finding out what the debts of the estate are and at the same time is not obliged to take any actions in order to ascertain the actual debts.[345] The legislator does, however, distinguish two situations.

763. In the first situation, an heir whose liability is limited to the estate assets' value has paid some of the estate debts not being aware of the existence of other estate debts. His or her liability will be limited to the difference between the value of the estate assets (as stated in the inventory) and the value of all the debts he or she has paid, regardless of whether that difference is enough to actually satisfy the remaining creditors. The legislator protects the heir's limitation of liability to the value of estate assets (Article 1032 §1 PCC).

764. In the second situation, an heir whose liability is limited to the estate assets' value has paid some of the estate debts while being aware of (or having the possibility to find out about) the existence of other estate debts. His or her liability may exceed the estate assets' value, but it may not exceed the sum that he or she would have paid, had he or she properly satisfied the claims of the creditors. This does not apply to an heir who does not have full capacity to perform acts in law or there are bases for incapacitating him or her (Article 1032 §2 PCC). For successions opened on or after 18 October 2015, the legislator stipulates that the heir satisfies creditors in accordance with the prepared list of inventory, also taking into account lists of inventories that may have been prepared by other heirs, the executor of the testament or persons entitled to a *legatum per vindicationem* (Article 1031^3 §1 PCC). However, from the moment a register of inventory has been prepared, the heir is obliged to satisfy the debts in accordance with that register (Article 1031^3 §2 PCC). The register is therefore binding and excludes the application of previously prepared inventory lists. Unfortunately, the legislator did not elaborate on what it means to satisfy creditors in accordance with the inventory list or register. In particular, it is not certain, whether the heir should pay creditors in the order they are listed or if there are any other priority rules. In academic writings, it has been accepted that a proper payment of debts in situations when the assets are not enough to satisfy the creditors, would denote that the prudent heir should pay these debts proportionally. If the value of the estate assets (which defines the limit of the heir's liability) is 1,000 and there are two debts, each worth 1,000, the heir should pay each creditor 500. If knowing about the existence of both debts, the heir paid the first creditor the full 1,000, he or she will still be liable to the second creditor for 500, as this is how much the latter would have received, had the heir satisfied the claims prudently.[346]

345. G. Gorczyński, 'Article 1012 Commentary', in M. Habdas, M. Fras (eds), *Kodeks*, 536–539.
346. Skowrońska – Bocian, *Prawo*, 168–169.

765. As can be seen, these provisions cannot be viewed as satisfactory and the need to introduce a new and more comprehensive regulation of these matters is perceptible. It is interesting to note that more complex provisions were in force before World War II, but they were considered obsolete and unnecessary in a communist country. It would seem that the existent market economy and a democratic legal system would require revisiting these issues.

766. The limitation of liability has no application with respect to a pledge and a mortgage, which are real securities that may be realized regardless of who the owner of the encumbered thing is.

C. Liability of More Than One Heir

767. The general rule is that heirs are *jointly liable for debts if the estate has not been divided*. This means that any creditor may satisfy his or her claim from any of the heirs, the latter having redress claims to the remaining heirs for amounts that he or she has paid that exceed his or her share in the estate. (Article 1034 §1). This rule is easiest to apply when simple acceptance of the estate relates to all the heirs.

768. If all the heirs accepted the estate with the benefit of the inventory and the debts do not exceed the value of estate assets, the heir who is approached by a creditor should pay the entire debt and then utilize his or her redress claims. However, if the debts exceed the value of estate assets, the heir approached by the creditor should pay the debt up to the mentioned value and again claim redress from the remaining heirs for amounts exceeding his or her share in the estate.

769. The problem that needs to be highlighted is that accepting the estate with the benefit of the inventory may not be enough to protect the interests of an heir when the estate is overburdened with debts or the debts are nearly as high as the value of the assets. First, the heir needs to bear in mind that any creditor may bring an action against him or her for the payment of a debt, regardless of how high that debt is and whether the assets of the estate are valuable enough to cover that debt. Moreover, the creditor with a valid claim, will be awarded the claim by the court and win the proceedings, meaning that the defendant heir will have to pay the entire costs of the proceedings and these may be substantial.

The limitation of liability will only come into play during execution proceedings when the heir will show that the creditor may successfully execute only a part of the claim that does not exceed the value of the estate's assets. Unfortunately, at this point, the heir may be surprised by the fact that due to the joint and several liability of all heirs before the division of the estate, he or she will have to undergo the execution based on the entire value of the estate's assets and not just the share that he or she has actually inherited in the estate. The heir may, of course, utilize redress claims towards other heirs, but if they do not voluntarily repay the debt according to their shares in the estate, the defendant heir will have to instigate new court proceedings to reclaim the money paid to the creditor. This means more costs, time and effort, and possible problems with recovering money if the other heirs have financial difficulties.

Due to the current default rule of accepting the estate with the benefit of the inventory, it is of the utmost importance for legal professionals to correctly advise their clients. If there is a risk of the estate containing too many debts (as has been mentioned above, there are no legal institutions in place that allow one to find out exactly how many creditors the deceased person had and what their claims are), in most cases it may be more beneficial to waive the entire estate than to be subjected to proceedings (and their costs) instigated by creditors even when the value of the estate is very low. Another important matter that needs to be clarified to the client is that only the division of the inherited estate ends the joint and several liability of the heirs and allows each heir to answer for debts proportionally to the value of the share in the estate. Before the division, the heir who has the best financial situation or assets easy to seize and sell in execution proceedings is likely to be exclusively targeted by the creditors.

These issues are not intuitively understood by citizens who are usually convinced that inheriting with the benefit of the inventory will prevent them from losing their money for the deceased person's debts. Unfortunately, in cases of estates that contain substantial debts, this institution does not provide enough protection and may subject the heir to high costs of court proceedings and of legal representation, as well as problems of regaining money from other heirs and the inconvenience of execution proceedings that may be directed to the heir's whole property and not just the inherited items.

770. It is also possible for some of the heirs to have accepted the estate with the benefit of inventory, while others have expressly accepted the estate without such limitation. If the creditor approaches an heir who benefits from liability limitation, he or she will only obtain a payment which does not exceed this limit. If an heir with no limitation of liability is approached, the creditor may demand payment of the entire debt. The heirs still have redress claims which must be proportional to the shares in the estate, but heirs with limited liability will not return more, than the value of estate assets.

After the entry into force of the PCC amendment which introduces the *legatum per vindicationem*, the persons who benefitted from the mentioned legacy will be liable jointly with the heirs for the debts of the estate until the division of the estate takes place. This liability is proportional to the value of the objects or rights acquired through the legacy (Article 1034^1 PCC).

771. Once the estate has been divided, the heirs are no longer liable jointly, but each is liable proportionally to the share he or she has in the estate (Article 1032 §2). The creditor now has to collect (usually only after instigating court proceedings against each and every heir) money due from each heir proportionally to the held shares. The same rule applies to persons who benefitted from *legatum per vindicationem*. Additionally, their liability is limited to the value of the objects or rights acquired through the legacy calculated according to their factual state and prices at the moment of the opening of the succession (Articles 1034^2–1034^3 PCC).

Chapter 5. Ownership of the Estate

§1. Community of the Estate

772. It is most often the case, that there is more than one heir to the estate. The question that needs to be addressed concerns the type of proprietary relationship that exists among the heirs with respect to the estate. In Polish succession law, the heirs are co-owners of the estate.[347] Each heir has a share in the estate and consequently in each of the elements which comprise that estate. The share is expressed as a fraction. The legislator stipulates, that provisions on co-ownership of things (Articles 195–221 PCC and 617–625 PCPC) are to be applied *mutatis mutandis* to the co-ownership of the estate unless succession law stipulates otherwise.

773. In co-ownership of the estate, there is no presumption of equal shares and the heirs are not allowed to make dispositions of their shares without the consent of other heirs, so Articles 197 and 198 PCC concerning the ownership of things will not apply to co-ownership of the estate at all. There are, however, no reasons not to apply Article 200 PCC according to which each co-owner is entitled to and obliged to manage the common things. Acts of management which do not exceed ordinary management are taken when the majority of heirs consent (majority is calculated according to shares). Acts which exceed extraordinary management are taken when all the heirs' consent (Articles 199 and 201 PCC). Each heir is entitled to individually take any actions indented to protect the common right (Article 209 PCC). This includes bringing *rei vindicatio or actio negatoria* claims. As a rule, all heirs are entitled to the possession and use of things comprised in the estate (Article 206 PCC). The above competencies and entitlements of heirs are limited if an executor of the testament (Article 988 PCC) or a curator of the estate (Articles 667 §2 and 935 §1 PCPC) has been appointed because his or her role is to manage the estate.

774. An important modification of co-ownership in succession law relates to making dispositions of a share that an heir has in an object belonging to the estate. Although a co-owner of an object can do this individually, without the consent of other co-owners, a co-owner of the estate is obliged to obtain consent from all other heirs (Article 1036 PCC). It is important to note that this rule does not apply to making dispositions of a share in the estate, which is subject to a different provision (Article 1051 PCC, *see* below §3: Contracts Concerning the Estate). Other heirs may give their consent before, during or after the disposition of a share in an object belonging to the estate occurs, however in the latter situation, the disposition will not be legally effective until such consent has been granted. If one or more of the remaining heirs do not consent, the disposition of a share in an object belonging to

347. W. Kurowski, 'Stosunki między współspadkobiercami przed działem spadku – uwagi *de lege ferenda*', *Rejent*, no. 2 (2006): 133 et seq.

the estate is valid. The legislator does, however, provide, that the disposition is ineffective with respect to the heir who did not consent, insofar as it would infringe his or her rights resulting from the provisions on the division of the estate (Article 1036 PCC).[348]

§2. Division of the Estate

775. Co-ownership of the estate, like co-ownership of things (material objects), is indented by the legislator to be a temporary state which will ultimately be terminated. This termination is achieved through the dissolution of the co-ownership of things (Articles 210–221 PCC) and in the case of the estate, through its division.[349] A request to divide the estate is not subject to prescription.

776. According to Article 1037 §1 PCC, the estate may be divided either by way of a contract concluded by all heirs or by a court decision issued upon the demand of any heir. If the estate comprises an immovable (real estate), the contract of division must be concluded in the form of a notarial deed (Article 1037 §2 PCC). Consequently, it is up to the heirs to decide which option to choose. They should bear in mind, that the division of the estate by the court as rule concerns the entire estate. It may be limited to its part only if important reasons justify such a division. A division by the court usually occurs when the heirs are in disagreement. A contractual division of the estate may, depending on the heirs' preferences and needs, either cover the entire estate or be limited to a part thereof. The contract will only be valid if all the heirs took part in its conclusion.

777. In order to divide the estate, it is necessary to know the value of the estate assets. That value is multiplied by the share (expressed as a fraction) of an heir and consequently, the value of that share is identified. As a result of dividing the estate, the heir should receive objects which are equal in value to the value of his or her share. However, upon the demand of two or more heirs, the court may define their respective shares inherited in their entirety or in parts in such manner that it awards them a certain object or objects of the estate in co-ownership, with shares expressed as fractions (Article 1044 PCC).

778. The court divides the estate only at the request of an heir. If there is no agreement among all the heirs, the court is not, technically speaking, bound by the proposed manner of dividing the estate. Succession law does not explicitly oblige the court to follow the testator's instructions of dividing the estate, but it seems that the general rule on ensuring the fullest possible compliance with the testator's will does bind the court in its decision of dividing the estate (Article 948 §1 PCC).[350]

---

348. *See* Supreme Court decision issued on 16 Feb. 2001, IV CKN 1212/00, OSNC 2001/9/140 and on 1 Dec. 2000, V CKN 1298/00, OSNC 2001/6/94.
349. M. Fras, 'Dzial spadku. Uwagi *de lege lata* i *de lege ferenda*', *Rejent*, no. 2 (2006): 19 et seq.
350. T. Felski, 'Wpływ woli testatora na sposób podziału majątku spadkowego', *Palestra*, no. 12 (1994): 5 et seq.

Consequently, if the heirs agree on the division of the estate or the testator has indicated his or her wishes as to the division of the estate, the court's decision should reflect these solutions unless they violate the law, principles of socio-economic justice or would be unfair to one or more heirs.[351]

779. The division of the estate may be connected with the obligation to take into account donations and *legatum per vindicationem* made by the deceased. This applies only when there is intestate succession of primary heirs, namely the surviving spouse and the descendants or just the descendants. Such heirs are mutually obliged to include in their inherited shares the donations and the mentioned legacies received from the deceased unless it follows from the declaration of the deceased or from the circumstances that the donation was released from the duty of being included in the estate. The deceased may impose the duty of including the donation and the mentioned legacy in the inherited share also upon a statutory heir who is not a primary heir. Minor donations customarily accepted in a given society are not subject to inclusion in the estate (Article 1039 PCC).[352]

780. If the value of the donation or the *legatum per vindicationem* subject to the inclusion in the estate exceeds the value of the inherited share, the heir is not obliged to return the surplus. In such case, neither the donation, the mentioned legacy, nor the heir obliged to include it in the inherited share shall be taken into consideration in the division of the estate (Article 1040 PCC). A more remote descendant of the deceased is obliged to include in the inherited share a donation and the mentioned legacy made by the deceased to his or her ascendant (Article 1041 PCC).

781. The provisions on the inclusion of donations and the mentioned legacies in the inherited share apply respectively to the costs incurred by the deceased in connection with the upbringing and the general or vocational education of his or her descendant if such costs exceed the average level accepted in a given society.

782. An heir may rely on mistakes to avoid the legal effects of concluding a contract on the division of the estate only if the mistake concerned a factual state that the parties considered to be beyond any doubts (Article 1044 PCC). After the division of the estate, the heirs are mutually liable under warranty for physical and legal defects in compliance with the provisions on the warranty on sale. The warranty concerning the inherited, receivable debts shall also cover the solvency of the debtor (Article 1045 PCC).

§3. Contracts Concerning the Estate

783. Contracts concerning the estate may be divided into two categories, namely: contracts concerning the estate of a person who is still alive and contracts

351. *See* Supreme Court decision issued on 19 Sep. 2009, II CSK 243/09, LEX no. 564969.
352. *See* P. Zdanikowski, 'Article 1039 Commentary', in M. Habdas, M. Fras (eds), *Kodeks*, 816–821.

concerning the estate of a person who has already died. As has been mentioned above in Chapter 1, §3: Renouncement of Succession, Polish succession law forbids concluding contracts concerning the estate of a person who is still alive, with the exception of the contract of renouncing succession.

784. A different approach is taken with respect to contracts concerning the estate of a person who has already died. Such contracts include the transfer of the estate or a part thereof (this also applies to the transfer of a share in the estate), the transfer of a share in the ownership of an object belonging to the estate and the contract of the estate division. The latter have already been discussed in §1 and §2 above.

I. The Object of the Transfer

785. The transfer of the estate (or a share therein) may consist of transferring the entire estate or just a part of the estate to the purchaser (Article 1051 PCC). The transfer of a part of the estate is a transfer of a share in the estate and not a transfer of specified objects belonging to the estate. Similarly, if there is more than one heir, the transfer may concern an heir's entire share in the estate or a part of that share. If an heir inherits both in testamentary and intestate succession, he or she may transfer his or her testamentary share in the estate without transferring the statutory share and vice versa, or he or she may transfer both shares. It is important to distinguish the transfer of a share in the estate (or a part of that share) from the transfer of a share in an object belonging to the estate. The former does not require the consent of other heirs, while the latter does. In practice, it is sometimes difficult to ascertain which of the two contracts was actually concluded.

II. The Time of Transfer

786. The transfer may only take place after the estate has been accepted by the heir in question, either through an express declaration of acceptance or after the time to waive the estate has elapsed. If the contract is concluded before the acceptance, it is null and void. The parties should also bear in mind that other heirs may waive the estate, be found unworthy to inherit, etc., so the shares of the remaining heirs may change. Therefore, it is wise to transfer a share in the estate after a certificate of estate acquisition or of inheritance has been issued, because the risk of any changes within the circle of heirs is greatly reduced.

III. The Effects of the Transfer

787. The transfer is a contract which has both obligational and proprietary effects, unless the parties decided otherwise (Article 1052 §1 PCC). This means that the purchaser acquires the estate at the moment the contract is concluded and no other acts need to follow. The contract requires the existence of a valid *causa* (Article 1052 §2 PCC), however, in Polish civil law, this is a rule which applies to all acts in law. The contract must take the form of a notarial deed (Article 1052 §3 PCC) regardless of whether the parties conclude just one contract with both obligational and proprietary effects or two separate contracts – one purely obligational and the other one – purely proprietary (i.e., one which brings about the actual change of the estate holder).

788. The acquirer of the estate succeeds to the rights and duties of the heir (Article 1053 PCC), so the acquisition is not singular, but a universal succession. Consequently, the acquirer steps into the shoes of the heir, from whom he or she acquired the estate. Therefore, according to Article 1055 PCC, the acquirer of the estate is liable for the inherited debts to the same extent as the transferor. Their liability with respect to the creditors is joint and several. Notwithstanding the above, the acquirer is liable to the transferor for preventing the creditors from demanding from the latter any performances intended to satisfy the inherited debts.

789. The legislator also imposes a number of duties on the heir who transfers his or her estate. According to Article 1054 PCC, the transferor of an estate is obliged to release anything which, as a result of a transfer, loss or damage of objects belonging to the estate, was obtained in exchange for those objects (including damages). If consideration for the transfer of the estate was given, the transferor is also obliged to make up for the decrease in value resulting from wear and tear or the gratuitous disposal of the objects belonging to the estate. However, the transferor may demand that the acquirer reimburse expenses and outlays the transferor had made with respect to the estate.

790. The transferor is not liable under warranty for physical and legal defects of particular objects belonging to the estate (Article 1056 PCC), because the contract concerns the estate and not particular objects. The transferor is liable for legal defects of the transferred estate according to provisions regulating the type of contract utilized to transfer the estate (e.g., sale, donation, exchange). The benefits and encumbrances connected with the objects belonging to the estate as well as the risk of their accidental loss or damage pass to the acquirer at the time of the conclusion of the contract of transfer of the inheritance unless the parties agreed otherwise (Article 1057 PCC).

Chapter 6. Inheriting Agricultural Farms

791. In the communist era, inheriting an agricultural farm was subject to restrictive provisions. The legislator wanted to avoid the division of farms and to make it easier for the State to become their owner. Farms were treated as a separate part of the estate that should have a distinct regulation. Restrictions applied to both intestate and testamentary successions. Not everyone could be an heir of an agricultural farm because it was required that the heir was either involved in agricultural production or was educated in agricultural production.

792. A noticeable liberalization of provisions on the inheritance of agricultural farms took place in 1990, after Poland's shift to a democratic system and a market economy. Restrictions concerning the appointment of heirs were abandoned; however, some restrictions in intestate succession remained in force.[353] More radical changes occurred after a Constitutional Tribunal judgment of 31 January 2001[354] in which the Tribunal decided that Articles 1059, 1060, 1062, 1064 and 1087 PCC violate the Constitution with respect to successions opened after 14 February 2001 (i.e., the publication date of the judgment).[355]

793. Currently, the remaining legislation on the succession of agricultural farms seems obsolete and incomplete, since some provisions were repealed, while others are no longer binding due to the Constitutional Tribunal judgment mentioned above.[356] Nevertheless, according to Article 1058 PCC statutory succession of agricultural farms including farmland of an area exceeding one hectare is regulated by succession law, with modifications resulting from the provisions following Article 1058 PCC.[357] These are as follows:

- in the case of the division of an agricultural farm which belongs to the estate, the provisions on the division of agricultural farms during the dissolution of co-ownership apply *mutatis mutandis* (Article 1070 PCC);
- in case of transferring a share in the estate which comprises an agricultural farm, Article 166, as well as Articles 3 and 4 of the Act of 11 April 2003 on shaping the agricultural system (Journal of Statutes 2003, no. 64, item 592) apply;
- if, in addition to the agricultural farm, the estate includes other objects, the heirs' shares in the agricultural farm are included in their respective shares in the whole estate;
- after the division of the estate, the heir who received the farm as a result of the division, as well as the heirs he or she was to pay off, are liable for the inherited

353. *See* D. Łobos-Kotowska, M. Stańko, 'Article 1058 Commentary', in M. Habdas, M. Fras (eds), *Kodeks*, 953 et seq.
354. P 4/99, OTK 2001, no. 1, item 5.
355. A. Lichorowicz, 'Szczególny porządek dziedziczenia gospodarstw rolnych w Polsce po orzeczeniu Trybunału Konstytucyjnego z dnia 31.I.2001 r.', *Rejent*, no. 9 (2001): 88 et seq.
356. B. Wierzbowski, 'Glosa do wyroku TK z dnia 31 stycznia 2001 r., P 4/99', *Przegląd.Sejmowy*, no. 5 (2001): 103 et seq.
357. W. Grabarek, 'Określenie nieruchomości podlegającej dziedziczeniu na zasadach dziedziczenia gospodarstw rolnych', *Nowy Przegląd Notarialny*, no. 2 (2005): 39 et seq.

debts connected with running the farm. Each of those heirs is liable in proportion to the value of the share received. For all other debts of the estate, the heirs are liable according to the general succession law principles (Article 1081 PCC);

- if the estate includes an agricultural farm, the calculation of the legitim is carried out according to succession law provisions and to Article 216 PCC (Article 1082 PCC);
- the provisions on inheriting an agricultural farm also apply to estates which include a contribution of land to an agricultural production cooperative (Article 1086 PCC).

Selected Bibliography

§1. Family Law

I. Textbooks

Andrzejewski, M. *Prawo rodzinne i opiekuńcze* [*Family and Guardianship Law*]. Warszawa: C.H. Beck, 2014.

Grzybowski, S. *Prawo rodzinne. Zarys wykładu* [*Family Law. Coursebook*]. Warszawa: PWN, 1980.

Ignaczewski, J. *Małżeńskie prawo majątkowe* [*Matrimonial Property Law*]. Warszawa: C.H. Beck, 2017.

Ignatowicz, J., M. Nazar. *Prawo rodzinne* [*Family Law*]. Warszawa: Lexis Nexis, 2016.

Smyczyński, T. *Prawo rodzinne i opiekuńcze* [*Family and Guardianship Law*]. Warszawa: C.H. Beck, 2018.

Sokołowski, T. *Prawo rodzinne. Zarys wykładu* [*Family LAW. Coursebook*]. Poznań: Ars boni et aequi, 2008.

Strzebinczyk, J. *Prawo rodzinne* [*Family Law*]. Warszawa: Wolters Kluwer, 2016.

Szer, S. *Prawo rodzinne* [*Family Law*]. Warszawa: PWN, 1969.

Walaszek, B. *Zarys prawa rodzinnego i opiekuńczego* [*An Outline of Family and Guardianship Law*]. Warszawa: PWN, 1971.

Winiarz, J. & J. Gajda. *Prawo rodzinne* [*Family Law*]. Warszawa: PWN, 1999.

Zieliński, A. *Prawo rodzinne i opiekuńcze w zarysie* [*An Outline of Family and Guardianship Law*]. Warszawa: Muza, 2000.

II. Commentaries

Breyer, S. *Kodeks rodzinny i opiekuńczy* [*The Family and Guardianship Code*]. Warszawa: Wydawnictwo Prawnicze, 1966.

Dolecki, H., Sokołowski, T. *Kodeks rodzinny i opiekuńczy* [*The Family and Guardianship Code*]. Warszawa: Wolters Kluwer, 2013.

Gajda, J. *Kodeks rodzinny i opiekuńczy. Akty stanu cywilnego. Komentarz* [*The Family and Guardianship Code. Births, Marriages and Deaths Register. A Commentary.*]. Warszawa: C.H. Beck, 2002.

Gromek, K. *Władza rodzicielska. Komentarz.* Warszawa: C.H. Beck, 2008.

Gromek, K. *Kodeks rodzinny i opiekuńczy. Komentarz* [*The Family and Guardianship Code. A Commentary*]. Warszawa: C.H. Beck, 2018.

Gudowski, J. *Kodeks rodzinny i opiekuńczy* [*The Family and Guardianship Code*]. Kraków: Zakamycze, 1998.

Haak, H. *Kodeks rodzinny i opiekuńczy. Władza rodzicielska. Komentarz* [*The Family and Guardianship Code. Parental Authority. Commentary*]. Toruń: TNOiK, 1995.

Haak, H. *Pochodzenie dziecka, Komentarz* [*The Child's Affiliation, A Commentary*]. Toruń: TNOiK, 1997.

Habdas, M., Fras, M. (eds). Kodeks cywilny. Komentarz. Tom I. Część ogólna (art. 1-125) [*The Civil Code. A Commentary. Vol. I. The general part]*. Warszawa: Wolters Kluwer, 2018.

Ignatowicz, J. *Pietrzykowski J. Kodeks rodzinny i opiekuńczy z komentarzem* [*The Family and Guardianship Code with a commentary*]. *Warszawa*: *Wydawnictwo Prawnicze*, 1993.

Ignaczewski, J. *Pochodzenie dziecka i władza rodzicielska po nowelizacji* [*The Child's Affiliation and Parental Authority after Amendments*]. Warszawa: C.H. Beck, 2009.

Krzemiński, Z. *Alimenty i ojcostwo. Komentarz* [*Alimony and Paternity. A Commentary*]. Warszawa: Wolters Kluwer, 2008.

Krzemiński, Z. Rozwód. *Praktyczny komentarz* [*Divorce. A Practical Commentary*]. Warszawa: Wolters Kluwer, 2007.

Piasecki, K. (ed.). *Kodeks rodzinny i opiekuńczy z komentarzem* [*The Family and Guardianship Code with Commentary*]. Warszawa: Lexis Nexis, 2011.

Piątowski, J.St. (ed.). *System Prawa Rodzinnego i Opiekuńczego* [*The System of Family and Guardianship Law*]. Wrocław (et al.): Ossolineum 1985.

Pietrzykowski, J. (ed.) *Kodeks rodzinny i opiekuńczy z komentarzem* [*The Family and Guardianship Code with a Commentary*]. Warszawa: C.H. Beck, 2018.

Smyczyński, T. (ed.). *System prawa prywatnego. Tom 11. Prawo rodzinne i opiekuńcze* [*The System of Private Law. Vol. 11*, *Family and Guardianship Law*]. Warszawa: C.H. Beck, 2014.

Smyczyński, T. (ed.). *System prawa prywatnego. Tom 12. Prawo rodzinne i opiekuńcze* [*The System of Private Law. Vol. 12*, *Family and Guardianship Law*]. Warszawa: C.H. Beck, 2011.

III. Monographs

Bladowski, B. *Obowiązek alimentacyjny* [*The Alimony Obligation*]. Warszawa: Wydawnictwo Prawnicze, 1983.

Holewińska-Łapińska, E. *Uznanie dziecka według kodeksu rodzinnego i opiekuńczego* [*The Acknowledgment of a Child According to the Family and Guardianship Code*]. Warszawa, Wydawnictwo Prawnicze, 1979.

Ignaczewski, J. *Małżeńskie ustroje majątkowe* [*Marital Property Regimes*]. Warszawa: C.H. Beck, 2005.

Kalus, S. *Opieka nad osobą całkowicie ubezwłasnowolniona* [*Guardianship over a Completely Incapacitated Person*]. Katowice: Wydawnictwo Uniwersytetu Śla̧skiego, 1989.

Piątowski, J.St. *Stosunki majątkowe między małżonkami* [*Property Relations Between the Spouses*]. Warszawa: ZPP 1955.

Stojanowska, W. *Rozwód a dobro dziecka* [*Divorce and the Well-Being of a Child*]. Warszawa: Wydawnictwo Prawnicze, 1979.
Winiarz, J. *Małżeńskie stosunki majątkowe* [*Marital Property Regimes*]. Warszawa: Wydawnictwo Prawnicze 1967.
Zielonacki, A. *Zawarcie małżeństwa* [*The Conslusion of a Marriage*]. Wrocław (et al.): Ossolineum, 1982.

§2. Succession Law

I. Textbooks

Biernat, J. & P. Cybula. *Prawo spadkowe: pytania, kazusy, tablice* [*Succession Law: Questions, Cases, Tables*]. Warszawa: C.H. Beck, 2015.
Doliwa, A. *Prawo spadkowe* [*Succession Law*]. Warszawa: C.H. Beck, 2012.
Gwiazdomorski, J. *Prawo spadkowe w zarysie* [*An Outline of Succession Law*]. Warszawa: PWN, 1990.
Kaltenbek, L. & W. Iurek. *Prawo spadkowe* [*Succession Law*]. Warszawa: Wolters Kluwer, 2016.
Księżak, p. *Prawo spadkowe* [*Succession Law*]. Warszawa: Wolters Kluwer, 2017.
Piątowski, J. & B. Kordasiewicz. *Prawo spadkowe. Zarys wykładu* [*An Outline of Succession Law*]. Warszawa: Lexis Nexis, 2011.
Skowrońska-Bocian, E. *Prawo spadkowe* [*Succession Law*]. Warszawa: C.H. Beck, 2018.
Witczak, H. & A. Kawałko. *Prawo spadkowe* [*Succession Law*]. Warszawa: C.H. Beck, 2014.
Zając, A. *Prawo cywilne. Spadki. Kazusy* [*Succession Law. Cases*]. Warszawa: Lexis Nexis 2012.

II. Commentaries

Gniewek, E. (ed.). *Kodeks cywilny. Komentarz* [*The Civil Code. A Commentary*]. Warszawa: C.H. Beck, 2014.
Habdas, M., Fras, M. (eds). Kodeks cywilny. Komentarz. Tom VI. Spadki (art. 922–1088) [*The Civil Code. A Commentary. Vol. VI. Succession]*. Warszawa: Wolters Kluwer, 2019.
Ignaczewski, J. *Prawo spadkowe. Art. 922 – 1088 KC. Komentarz* [*Succession Law. Art. 922-1088. A Commentary*]. Warszawa: C.H. Beck, 2004.
Kordasiewicz, B. (ed.). *System Prawa Prywatnego. Tom 10. Prawo spadkowe* [*The System of Private Law. Vol. 10, Succession Law*]. Warszawa: C.H. Beck, 2015.
Kidyba, A. & E. Niezbecka. *Kodeks cywilny. Komentarz. Spadki. Tom IV* [*The Civil Code. A Commentary. Successions. Vol. IV*]. Warszawa: Wolters Kluwer Polska, 2015.
Piątowski, J.St. *System prawa cywilnego: prawo spadkowe* [*The System of Private Law: Succession Law*]. Wrocław (et al.): PAN Ossolineum, 1986.
Pietrzykowski, K. (ed.) *Kodeks cywilny. Tom II. Komentarz* [*The Civil Code. Vol. I. A Commentary*]. Warszawa: C.H. Beck, 2018.
Skowrońska-Bocian, E. *Nowelizacja prawa spadkowego. Komentarz* [*The Amendment of Succession law. A Commentary*]. Warszawa: Lexis Nexis, 2010.

Skowrońska-Bocian, E. *Komentarz do kodeksu cywilnego. Księga czwarta. Spadki* [*A Commentary to the Civil Code. Book Four. Successions*]. Warszawa: Lexis Nexis, 2011.
Skowrońska-Bocian, E. Odpowiedzialność za długi spadkowe. *Komentarz* [Liability for debts of the estate. *A Commentary*]. Warszawa: Wolters Kluwer, 2018.

III. Monographs and Handbooks

Babiarz, S. *Spadek i darowizna w prawie cywilnym i podatkowym* [*The Estate and the Donation in Civil and Tax Law*]. Warszawa: Lexis Nexis, 2019.
Biernat, J. *Ochrona osób bliskich spadkodawcy w prawie spadkowym* [*The Protection of Persons Close to the Deceased Person in Succession Law*]. Toruń: Wydawnictwo Adam Marszałek, 2002.
Biernat, J. *Umowa o dział spadku* [*The Contract of the Estate Division*]. Warszawa, Kraków: Wolters Kluwer, 2008.
Borysiak, W. *Dziedziczenie. Konstrukcja prawna i ochrona* [Succession. Legal shape and protection]. (Warszawa: Lexis Nexis, 2013).
Dyoniak, A. *Ochrona rodziny w razie śmierci jednego z małżonków* [*The Protection of Family in Case of One Spouse's Death*]. Warszawa, Poznań: PWN 1990.
Kłos, M. *Wspólność majątku spadkowego* [*The Community of the Inherited Estate*]. Warszawa: Lexis Nexis, 2004.
Księżak, P. *Zachowek w polskim prawie spadkowym* [*The Legitim in Polish Succession Law*]. Warszawa: Lexis Nexis, 2012.
Margoński, M. *Kurator spadku* [*The Curator of the Estate*]. Warszawa: Lexis Nexis, 2009.
Niezbecka, E. *Zapis* [*The Bequest*]. Lublin: Wydawnictwo Uniwersytetu Marii Curie-Skłodowskiej, 1990.
Niedośpiał, M. *Swoboda testowania* [*The Freedom of Testation*]. Bielsko-Biała: Wydawnictwo Sto, 2004.
Osajda, K. *Testamenty wspólne* [*Joint Testaments*]. Warszawa: C.H. Beck, 2005.
Skowrońska, E. *Forma testamentu w prawie polskim* [*The Form of the Testament in Polish Law*]. Warszawa: Wydawnictwa UW, 1991.
Skowrońska, E. *Testament w prawie polskim* [*The Testament in Polish Law*]. Warszawa: LexisNexis, 2004.
Stempniak, A. *Postępowanie o dział spadku* [*The Procedure of the Division of the Estate*]. Warszawa: C.H. Beck, 2006.
Wierciński, J. *Brak świadomości albo swobody przy sporządzaniu testamentu* [*Lack of Awareness or* Free will When Drwaing the Testament]. Warszawa: Lexis Nexis, 2010.
Załucki, M. *Videotestament. Prawo spadkowe wobec nowych technologii* [Videotestament. Succession Law and New Technologies]. Warszawa: C.H. Beck, 2018.

IV. Journals

Kwartalnik Prawa Prywatnego [Private Law Quarterly].
Monitor Prawniczy [The Legal Monitor].
Nowe Prawo [New Law].
Przeglad Notarialny [The Notarial Digest].
Palestra [The Bar]

Państwo i Prawo [The State and the Law].
Prawo Bankowe [Banking Law].
Przeglad Sadowy [The Court Digest].
Rejent [The Notary].
Ruch Prawniczy, Ekonomiczny i Socjologiczny (RPEiS) [The Legal, Economic and Social Society].
Studia Prawnicze [Legal Studies].
Studia Prawa Prywatnego [Studies in Private Law].

Selected Bibliography

Index

The numbers here refer to paragraph numbers.

Index

www.ingramcontent.com/pod-product-compliance
Lightning Source LLC
Chambersburg PA
CBHW071432230926
51846CB00001B/202